Global Perspectives on Subsidiarity

IUS GENTIUM

COMPARATIVE PERSPECTIVES ON LAW AND JUSTICE

VOLUME 37

For further volumes:
http://www.springer.com/series/7888

Michelle Evans • Augusto Zimmermann
Editors

Global Perspectives on Subsidiarity

Springer

Editors
Michelle Evans
Curtin University Law School
Bentley, Perth
Western Australia, Australia

Augusto Zimmermann
Murdoch University School of Law
Murdoch, Perth
Western Australia, Australia

ISSN 1534-6781 ISSN 2214-9902 (electronic)
ISBN 978-94-017-8809-0 ISBN 978-94-017-8810-6 (eBook)
DOI 10.1007/978-94-017-8810-6
Springer Dordrecht Heidelberg New York London

Library of Congress Control Number: 2014938485

Printed on acid-free paper

Springer is part of Springer Science+Business Media (www.springer.com)

The Editors

Michelle Evans (BA, LLB, LLM (Murdoch University), Ph.D. (Curtin University, Chancellor's Commendation)) is a Senior Lecturer and Director of Teaching at the Curtin Law School at Curtin University, and a Barrister & Solicitor of the Supreme Court of Western Australia. She is an award winning teacher whose teaching areas include Constitutional Law, Administrative Law, Property Law and Law, Society and Justice. She is also well known for her research on internet censorship and sex equality. She was recently awarded a Ph.D. (with a Chancellor's Commendation for Excellence) from Curtin University in Western Australia for her thesis titled, 'The Use of the Principle of Subsidiarity in the Reformation of Australia's Federal System of Government'.

Augusto Zimmermann (LLB (PUC-Rio), LLM *cum laude* (PUC-Rio), Ph.D. (Monash University)) is Senior Lecturer and former Associate Dean (Research) and Director of Postgraduate Studies at the School of Law at Murdoch University. He is also a Commissioner with the Law Reform Commission of Western Australia and Adjunct Professor of Law at Universitas Kristen Maranatha in Indonesia. Dr. Zimmermann is the Founder and President of the Western Australian Legal Theory Association (WALTA) and an editor of *The Western Australian Jurist* law journal. He is a prolific writer and his books include *Direito Constitucional Brasileiro* (Lumen Juris, 2014, with Fabio Condeixa), *Western Legal Theory: History, Concepts and Perspectives* (LexisNexis, 2013), *Curso de Direito Constitucional* (4th edition, Lumen Juris, 2006) and *Teoria Geral do Federalismo Democratico* (2nd edition, Lumen Juris, 2006). Dr. Zimmermann has been awarded the 2012 *Vice Chancellor's Award for Excellence in Research*, and also been awarded two consecutive Murdoch School of *Law Dean's Research Awards*, in 2010 and 2011. Dr. Zimmermann has also received the 2013 *Law Lecturer of the Year Award.*

Contents

Contributors

Prof. Nicholas Aroney TC Beirne School of Law, University of Queensland, Brisbane, Queensland, Australia

Prof. Patrick McKinley Brennan School of Law, Villanova University, Villanova, Pennsylvania, United States of America

Prof. Jürgen Bröhmer School of Law, Murdoch University, Murdoch, Perth, Western Australia, Australia

Prof. Jonathan Chaplin Kirby Laing Institute for Christian Ethics, Cambridge, United Kingdom

Dr. Michelle Evans Curtin University Law School, Bentley, Perth, Western Australia, Australia

Prof. Andreas Follesdal Faculty of Law, University of Oslo, Oslo, Norway

Prof. Gabriël A. Moens Curtin Law School, Curtin University, Bentley, Perth, Western Australia, Australia

Rev. Robert A. Sirico Acton Institute for the Study of Religion and Liberty, Grand Rapids, Michigan, United States of America

Dr. John Trone Adjunct Professor, School of Law, Murdoch University, Murdoch, Perth, Western Australia, Australia

Lael Daniel Weinberger Department of History, University of Chicago, Chicago, Illinois, United States of America

Dr. Augusto Zimmermann Murdoch University School of Law, Murdoch, Perth, Western Australia, Australia

Contributor Biographies

Nicholas Aroney is Professor of Constitutional Law at the T.C. Beirne School of Law at The University of Queensland. He is a member of the governing council of the Australian Association of Constitutional Law and was recently awarded an Australian Research Council fellowship to undertake research on comparative federalism. Professor Aroney has initiated and led several international collaborative research projects in constitutional law and legal theory, with particular emphasis on questions relating to the theory and practice of federalism, the design and performance of bicameral parliamentary systems, and freedom of speech. His recent publications include *The Constitution of a Federal Commonwealth: The Making and Meaning of the Australian Constitution* (Cambridge University Press, 2009), *Shari'a in the West* (Oxford University Press, 2010) and *The Future of Australian Federalism* (Cambridge University Press, 2012).

Patrick McKinley Brennan holds the John F. Scarpa Chair in Catholic Legal Studies at Villanova University School of Law. Previously, he was Professor of Law and Vice Dean at Arizona State College of Law. He earned a B.A. in philosophy from Yale College, an M.A. in philosophy from the University of Toronto, and a J.D. from the University of California Berkeley, Boalt Hall, where he was elected to the Order of the Coif. After law school, he clerked for the Honorable John T. Noonan, Jr., on the U.S. Court of Appeals for the Ninth Circuit and later was associated with major law firms in San Francisco and Washington, DC. He has published four books and more than 60 articles and book chapters. He currently has two books under contract, *Christian Legal Thought: Cases and Materials* (with William Brewbaker III) and *The Sovereignty of the Good: An Essay on Law, Authority, and the Church.*

Jürgen Bröhmer is Dean and Professor of Law at Murdoch University School of Law, Western Australia. Before joining Murdoch University he worked at the University of New England, in Armidale, NSW, Australia, having commenced there in 2006 and serving as Head of the Law School from 2007 to 2011 (and as an Adjunct Professor since his departure). He received his law degree from Mannheim University in Germany and his doctorate and post-doctoral habilitation from Saarland University in Saarbrücken, Germany, where he worked at the Europa-Institute of Saarland University from 1992 to 2006 and where he continues to be part of the visiting faculty. His areas of expertise are German and comparative constitutional law, European Union law, public international law and international human rights law. He has authored two and co-authored one monograph in specific areas of public international law (*State Immunity and the Violation of Human Rights*, Kluwer Law International 1997), German constitutional and European Union Law (*Transparency as a Constitutional Principle – Basic Law and European Union*, Mohr Siebeck 2004), edited a number of other books (recent examples: *The Protection of Human Rights at the Beginning of the 21st Century*, Nomos, 2012 and *The German Constitution Turns 60: Basic Law and Commonwealth Constitution – German and Australian Perspectives*, 2011), and published numerous articles and book chapters.

Jonathan Chaplin is the first Director of the Kirby Laing Institute for Christian Ethics, Cambridge, UK (www.klice.co.uk), a position he took up in 2006. He has been a member of the University of Cambridge Divinity Faculty since 2007. He has taught political theory and political theology at Plater College, Oxford and the Institute for Christian Studies (ICS), Toronto. From 2004 to 2006 he held the Dooyeweerd Chair in Social and Political Philosophy at ICS. He served as visiting lecturer at the VU University, Amsterdam from 2007 to 2011. His books include *Herman Dooyeweerd: Christian Philosopher of State and Civil Society* (Notre Dame, 2011), *God and Global Order: The Power of Religion in American Foreign Policy* (Baylor, 2010) (co-editor), and *God and Government* (SPCK, 2009) (co-editor). He is currently working on a book entitled *Faith in Democracy? Towards a Post-secularist Settlement* and co-editing another entitled *God and the EU*. He has authored many articles on Christianity and political thought, most recently 'Law, Religion and Public Reasoning', *Oxford Journal of Law and Religion* (2012). He has also written two reports for the British think-tank Theos, for which he is also consultant researcher: *Talking God: The Legitimacy of Religious Public Reasoning* (2009), and *Multiculturalism: A Christian Retrieval* (2011). He is a Senior Fellow of the Canadian think-tank Cardus, for which he writes regularly. He also writes periodically on religion, politics and secularism for *Guardian* CiF Belief.

Andreas Follesdal is a Professor of Political Philosophy at the Faculty of Law, University of Oslo. He was appointed the Principal Investigator, European Research Council Advanced Grant Multi Rights 2011–2016, on the Legitimacy of Multi-Level Human rights Judiciary; and Director of PluriCourts, a Centre of Excellence for the Study of the Legitimate Roles of the Judiciary in the Global Order. Professor Follesdal holds a Ph.D. (1991) in Philosophy from Harvard University. He publishes in the field of political philosophy, mainly on issues of international political theory, especially international courts and tribunals, globalisation/Europeanisation, human rights, and socially responsible investing.

Gabriël A. Moens is a Professor of Law and Director of Research at Curtin Law School, Curtin University. Prior to his present role he served as Pro Vice Chancellor (Law, Business and Information Technology) and as a long-serving Dean of Law at Murdoch University. He is the co-author of *Lumb, Moens and Trone: The Constitution of the Commonwealth of Australia Annotated* (2012), *Jurisprudence of Liberty* (2011), *Commercial Law of the European Union* (2010) and *International Trade and Business: Law, Policy and Ethics* (2006).

Rev. Robert A. Sirico received his Master of Divinity degree from the Catholic University of America, following undergraduate study at the University of Southern California and the University of London. During his studies and early ministry, he experienced a growing concern over the lack of training religious studies students receive in fundamental economic principles, leaving them poorly equipped to understand and address today's social problems. As a result of these concerns, Fr. Sirico co-founded the Acton Institute with Kris Alan Mauren in 1990. As president of the Acton Institute, Fr. Sirico lectures at colleges, universities, and business organisations throughout the US and abroad. His writings on religious, political, economic, and social matters are published in a variety of journals, including: the *New York Times*, the *Wall Street Journal*, *Forbes*, the *London Financial Times*, the *Washington Times*, the *Detroit News*, and *National Review*. Fr. Sirico is often called upon by members of the broadcast media for statements regarding economics, civil rights, and issues of religious concern, and has provided commentary for CNN, ABC, the BBC, NPR, and CBS' *60 Minutes*, among others. In April of 1999, Fr. Sirico was awarded an honorary doctorate in Christian Ethics from the Franciscan University of Steubenville, and in May of 2001, Universidad Francisco Marroquin awarded him an honorary doctorate in Social Sciences. He is a member of the prestigious Mont Pèlerin Society, the American Academy of Religion, and the Philadelphia Society, and is on the Board of Advisors of the Civic Institute in Prague. Father Sirico also served on the Michigan Civil Rights Commission from 1994 to 1998. His pastoral ministry has included a chaplaincy to AIDS patients at the National Institutes of Health. He is also currently serving as pastor of Sacred Heart of Jesus parish in Grand Rapids, Michigan.

John Trone is an Adjunct Professor of Law at Murdoch University. He is an author of the 6th, 7th and 8th editions of *Lumb, Moens and Trone: The Constitution of the Commonwealth of Australia Annotated* (2001, 2007, 2012), *Federal Constitutions and International Relations* (2001), *Commercial Law of the European Union* (2010) and the 29th edition of *Australian Commercial Law* (2013).

Lael Daniel Weinberger is a Ph.D. student in history at the University of Chicago. He earned a J.D. *summa cum laude* from Oak Brook College of Law and an M.A. in history from Northern Illinois University, where he received a University Fellowship. He clerked for Chief Justice Daniel Eismann on the Idaho Supreme Court. His legal scholarship has focused on issues of law and religion and on legal history. In addition, he recently co-authored (with Robert Renaud) *A Tale of Two Governments,* a book to introduce pastors and church leaders to the basics of church autonomy law.

Chapter 1
The Global Relevance of Subsidiarity: An Overview

Michelle Evans and Augusto Zimmermann

The word subsidiarity derives from subsidiary, which in turn has its roots in the Latin word *subsidium*. In simple words, subsidiarity means the same as assistance or help. As a principle of social philosophy, however, subsidiarity is among the most characteristic directives of the Catholic Church's social doctrine. It has been present since the encyclical *Rerum Novarum* by Pope Leo XIII and it was enunciated by Pope Pius XI in 1931 as a central principle of social theory. In *Quadragesimo Anno* the Sumo Pontiff outlined the principle of subsidiarity as follows:

> Just as it is gravely wrong to withdraw from the individual and commit to the community at large what private enterprise and industry can accomplish, so, too, it is an injustice, a grave evil, and a disturbance of right order for a larger and greater organisation to arrogate to itself functions which can be performed efficiently by smaller and lower bodies. This is a fundamental principle of social philosophy, unshaken and unchangeable. Of its very nature the true aim of all social activity should be to help individual members of the social body, but never to destroy or absorb them.[1]

The principle of subsidiarity states that individuals can only develop freely in society when what they can accomplish by their initiative is not given or taken away from them by a higher authority.[2] In Catholic social theory, the principle is premised upon empowering the citizen, with decision-making 'carried out as close to the citizen as is viable',[3]

[1] Pius XI (1931, p. 25). For a discussion of this quotation see Vischer (2001, pp. 107–108) cited in Widulski (2005, p. 847).

[2] Youth Catechism of the Catholic Church, Question 323.

[3] Hunnings (1998, s 12.0120A) cited in Montgomery (2002, p. 48).

M. Evans (✉)
Curtin University Law School, Kent Street, Bentley, 6102 Perth, Western Australia, Australia
e-mail: michelle.evans@curtin.edu.au

A. Zimmermann
Murdoch University School of Law, South Street, Murdoch, 6150 Perth, Western Australia, Australia
e-mail: a.zimmermann@murdoch.edu.au

M. Evans and A. Zimmermann (eds.), *Global Perspectives on Subsidiarity*, Ius Gentium: Comparative Perspectives on Law and Justice 37, DOI 10.1007/978-94-017-8810-6_1,

or in simpler words, at a 'grassroots level'.[4] This so being, 'intermediate social entities can properly perform the functions that fall to them without being required to hand them over unjustly to other social entities of a higher level, by which they would end up being absorbed and substituted, in the end seeing themselves denied their dignity and essential place'.[5] There is a hierarchy consisting of the individual, the family, the local community, and the Church or the State, whereby centralised power is limited in favour of matters being resolved at the lowest possible level.[6]

One of the most characteristic implications of subsidiarity is political participation. Participation in community is one of the greatest aspirations of the citizen. Democratic governments are characterised by the assignment of powers and functions in accordance with the wishes and aspirations of the people. In this perspective it becomes imperative to encourage individual participation and the cooperation of all citizens in the achievement of the common good. In order for such participation to be put in practice, there is a corresponding need not only for the presence of social pluralism and safeguard of basic human rights, but also for the prevalence of 'appropriate methods for making citizens more responsible in actively "being a part" of the political and social reality of their country'.[7]

On the basis of subsidiarity, societies of a higher order must support lower-order societies, without being these intermediate entities absorbed and substituted by entities of a higher level. When applied to the workings of civil government, subsidiarity aims to empower citizens and enhance democracy[8] by encouraging decision-making closer to the region or problem at hand. Subsidiarity therefore 'sets limits for state intervention'[9] and, when specifically applied to the federal systems of government, the principle focuses on the subordinate performance of the central government so as to rearrange the vertical levels of government in order to give priority to those with the greatest proximity to the citizen.[10] However, at the same time, the principle provides 'justification of central involvement in affairs that cannot adequately be handled at the local level.'[11]

This was the intention behind incorporating the principle of subsidiarity into European Union law. The European Union consists of 28 countries which agreed to form 'an economic trading bloc'.[12] These 'member states' must retain their status as separate and independent countries with their own governments, languages and cultures. Hence, the philosophy of subsidiarity was of utmost importance to the member states wary of centralisation.[13] As it was originally intended in European Union law, subsidiarity provides that if a matter does not fall within the exclusive competence of

[4] Montgomery (2002, p. 48).

[5] Pontifical Council for Justice and Peace (2005, p. 94).

[6] Sirico (1997, pp. 551–552).

[7] Pontifical Council for Justice and Peace (2005, p. 95).

[8] Longo (1999, p. 225).

[9] Catechism of the Catholic Church (2000) para 1883 cited in Widulski (2005, p. 855).

[10] Zimmermann (2000, p. 2).

[11] Halberstam (2009, p. 35).

[12] Moens and Trone (2010, p. 1).

[13] Vause (1995, pp. 64–65).

the Community and can be better resolved by the individual member states, the central authority (Community) should *not* intervene, so that these matters can be resolved at a member state level.[14] The current principle of subsidiarity is referred to on several occasions in the *Treaty on European Union* ('the Treaty'), which came into force on 1 December 2009,[15] specifically in the Resolutions section and in Articles 5(1), 5(3), 5(4)[16] and 12(b). As these sections were originally drafted using general language, and without specific direction as to how the principle should be applied, the application of the principle was subsequently defined in instruments such as the *Protocol on the application of the principles of subsidiarity and proportionality*.

Despite the many facets of subsidiarity described above, the editors' research has revealed that there are no books specifically devoted to the principle of subsidiarity in all its facets. Books on Catholic Social Theory usually contain a chapter, or brief discussion of the principle. The same applies to books on the European Union. This is quite surprising given the potential reach of the principle to inform discussions on democracy, human rights, federalism, and its paramountcy in European Union Law. Hence there is a need to bring together scholarship on the principle of subsidiarity in the one place.

On this note, whilst in this book we, as editors, have endeavored to elucidate many of the more traditional applications of subsidiarity, it was not possible to discuss every possible aspect and application of subsidiarity in the one volume. Instead, we have sought to draw out key themes in subsidiarity in order to help the reader understand its philosophical origins, development and applications. In the conclusion to this book, we provide some observations about how subsidiarity could inform scholarship in other areas that have not been covered in this book, for example, in corporate governance, or employer-employee relations.

Each chapter of this book explores a different aspect or application of the principle of subsidiarity. As the title indicates, this book is inter-disciplinary in nature and explores many different perspectives on the aspects and applications of subsidiarity from authors with diverse national, cultural, political and theological backgrounds. Such diversity of perspectives is something that we consider to be a highly positive outcome of this book, because it can only serve to enhance understanding and scholarship on subsidiarity and to assist in exploring and developing applications of subsidiarity that have previously been neglected.

Before giving an overview of the chapters in this book, we would also like to draw to the attention of our readers the fact that subsidiarity itself is not an entirely neutral concept. It is firstly a Western concept, derived from Western philosophy, and taken up by Western religions such as Catholicism (and, in the case of the related concept of 'sphere sovereignty', Dutch Calvinism). Subsidiarity is secondly,

[14] Moens and Trone (2010, pp. 27–28).

[15] Article 5(3) states: 'Under the principle of subsidiarity, in areas which do not fall within its exclusive competence, the Union shall act only if and in so far as the objectives of the proposed action cannot be sufficiently achieved by the Member States, either at a central level or at a regional and local level, but can rather, by reason of the scale or effects of the proposed action, be better achieved at Union level.'

[16] This article was formerly Article 3(b) of the *Treaty on European Union*.

and primarily, a decentralising principle, which favours decentralised decision making over centralised decision-making. That is not to say that subsidiarity endorses decentralisation at all costs. It does acknowledge, as is evident with subsidiarity in the context of European Union Law, or federalism, that certain decisions and actions are best carried out centrally.

The book is designed so that the reader can choose how they wish to approach it. That is, the reader may choose to read a chapter or chapters that interest them in any order. They may also choose to read the book from cover to cover. Consequently, the reader may find that there are some aspects of the principle of subsidiarity that are repeated in the various chapters in this book.

In Chap. 2, **Nicholas Aroney** situates the principle in the context of its philosophical origins which can be traced back to ancient Greece, in the work of Plato and Aristotle, and ancient Rome and can be seen subsequently in the work of Aquinas, Althusius, and Mill. 'Subsequent echoes' of the principle can be seen in the work of more 'modern' philosophers such as Montesquieu, Locke, Tocqueville, Lincoln and Proudhon. This chapter will explore and elucidate these philosophical origins.

Chapter 3, written by **Patrick McKinley Brennan**, expands upon these origins by examining the meaning and application of subsidiarity in the context of Catholic social thought. In the twentieth century the principle of subsidiarity was most famously enunciated by Pope Pius XI on 15 May 1931 as a central principle of social theory in the Catholic Church. In Part 5 of his Encyclical Letter, *Quadragesimo Anno*, titled 'The Reconstruction of the Social Order', the Pontiff advocated for a social hierarchy starting with the individual, and progressing upwards to the community, to organisations and corporations, and finally the State. The Pontiff advocated action at an individual or lower level, over action at a higher level, wherever possible, thus empowering the individual and ensuring that problems were resolved closest to their source.

The philosophy behind subsidiarity is further elucidated by **Lael Daniel Weinberger** in Chap. 4. Weinberger distinguishes the principle from the concept of 'sphere sovereignty' from the Dutch Calvinist tradition. The concept of 'sphere sovereignty' was developed by Abraham Kuyper in 1880. Kuyper was a Dutch theologian, academic and politician whose view was that God was present in 'every sphere of life' and that consequently, each sphere, for example 'family life, economic life, churchly life, sports' must be sovereign. According to Kuyper, the individual may operate in several spheres at once, for example, as 'a member of a church, a citizen of the state, and a participant in any number of social spheres. In all these aspects of life, the basic convictions of the Christian faith would direct his or her activities.'[17] Thus this chapter explores the relationship between the two concepts in order to shed further light on them both.

The next chapter, Chap. 5, written by **Jonathan Chaplin**, explores the relationship between the principle of subsidiarity and social pluralism. Pluralism is a term in political theory used to describe a political system that has several centres of

[17] Van Til (2008, pp. 619–626).

power and authority, rather than one in which the state is the sole controller of people's actions. Ultimately, pluralism necessarily implies the right for individuals to determine values and beliefs for themselves instead of being forced to follow the will of the government or, indeed, their own social group. For pluralism to function and be successful in defining the common good, it is important to bring about a socio-ethical environment that encourages people to develop their own individual abilities and which promotes self-determination and personal responsibility. This being the case, the principle of subsidiarity is fundamental to achieve social pluralism because it recognises the necessity of a plurality of individuals and social groups that make up the community as a whole, thus letting these individuals and groups to do what can be done by themselves, and leaving up to the state, particularly the central government, only what could not be done otherwise.

In Chap. 6, **Augusto Zimmermann** explores subsidiarity's ability to enhance democracy and individual rights in Brazil. The principle of subsidiarity requires the individual to be able to fully participate in society, including the right to earn a living, and to participate in social and political life. State-based welfare diminishes the individual's autonomy and participation in society through its impersonal nature, and through its failure to address an individual's specific problems and to empower the individual to provide for themselves and their family. The Brazilian Constitution is centralist in nature, containing numerous 'rights' that are of a broad and general policy nature, that are impossible to enforce, and yet that are proclaimed to be policed at a central level. This, in turn has supported the development of a 'welfare culture' in which individuals feel entitled to assistance from the state. This chapter discusses the centralising, statist nature of the Brazilian government, and argues the need for the implementation of subsidiarity to empower individual citizens in Brazil.

In Chap. 7, **The Rev. Robert A. Sirico** analyses how the principle of subsidiarity can be used to reform welfare in a way that respects and empowers individual citizens. Across the Western World, in recent times, there has been a growing reliance of many individuals on social security (welfare) payments. Individuals receive welfare from the government, administered by faceless government departments that often do little to break the welfare dependency, empower the individual or directly assist the individual to resolve their specific difficulties. As a result the individual is disempowered and alienated. Subsidiarity, understood in this sense, is opposed to forms of centralisation, bureaucratisation, and welfare assistance that deprive citizens of their own responsibility toward themselves, their families, and their societies. Rather, subsidiarity supports individual empowerment as much as a proper balance between the public and private spheres, with the resulting recognition of the common good that is inherently promoted through the spontaneous actions and interactions between free and responsible individuals. In such case, the common good can be properly achieved by the defence and promotion of the primary of the individual over the state, and the way this is expressed in society, which remains a substantial element for making decisions applying the principle of subsidiarity.

The book then moves from a philosophical exploration of subsidiarity to a discussion of subsidiarity as a political and constitutional principle. This commences with Chap. 8 by **Jürgen Bröhmer**, which discusses the principle of subsidiarity in the

German *Basic Law*, that is, the German Constitution (*Grundgesetz*). The principle of subsidiarity was introduced by the *Treaty of Maastricht*, due to pressure from Member States such as Germany who were concerned about the expansion of central Union powers. In fact, Germany already had its own version of subsidiarity in article 72(2) of the *Basic Law* for the Federal Republic of Germany, with respect to concurrent legislative powers. This chapter outlines the operation and justiciability of the principle of subsidiarity in German constitutional law and its interpretation by the Federal Constitutional Court of Germany (*Bundesverfassungsgericht*, or *BVerfG*).

Gabriël A. Moens and **John Trone** examine, in Chap. 9, how the principle operates in the European Union as a procedural, political and legal principle. They investigate the role of subsidiarity in providing procedural safeguards in the legislative process, prior to regulations being proposed or enacted. They also examine subsidiarity as a judicial principle, noting that, at a judicial level, the principle has been disregarded by the European Court of Justice. Although the European Court of Justice can annul regulations or directives that infringe the principle, no directives or regulations have been annulled on the basis of it because the European Court of Justice has treated the principle as a political judgment, rather than a legal principle. Hence, although subsidiarity operates as an effective procedural safeguard during the legislative process, it has been unsuccessful as a ground of judicial review.

In Chap. 10, **Michelle Evans** explores, using Australia as a case study, whether subsidiarity can inspire decentralisation in federal systems of government that have become centralised. Subsidiarity in a political sense, discourages centralisation, and advocates that matters should be resolved locally, and closest to the individual, wherever possible. In this sense, it is a characteristic of federalism, the philosophy of which is to protect the autonomy of the States and to discourage centralisation of power. Thus, there is an overall compatibility between the two concepts of federalism and subsidiarity. However, federal systems (with a central government and numerous state governments) can overlook subsidiarity, and countries with federal systems of government such as the United States and Australia have seen state financial and legislative powers be incrementally taken over by central governments. Subsidiarity, as an essential characteristic of federalism, can provide inspiration to reform federal systems of government to decentralise and to restore the balance of State power.

As the world becomes a smaller place, the principle of subsidiarity can no longer be said to apply to governance in one country alone. Hence, in Chap. 11, the final chapter of this book, **Andreas Follesdal** examines the principle of subsidiarity and global governance. The European Union, with its 28 Member States is a good example of the principle's application as a multinational concept. The concept of subsidiarity in a global setting was recognised in the Encyclical Letter of Pope John XXIII entitled *Peace on Earth* and published on 11 April 1963. The Encyclical points out that due to advances in science and technology the world is becoming a much smaller place, with more 'cooperation and association' required between countries. This chapter will explore the future of subsidiarity in a global context.

The authors believe that bringing scholarship on the many facets of subsidiarity together in the one book will help to shed new light on the principle of subsidiarity. In doing so, the book explores and develops applications of subsidiarity that have not previously been discussed. Above all, this book seeks to inspire further scholarship on a somewhat neglected and overlooked principle that the authors believe has the ability to inform and enrich scholarship in so many areas. We hope that this book will appeal to a broad and international readership, and that it will be of interest to academics and students of philosophy, theology, comparative law, European Union law, constitutional law, and politics. More importantly, we hope that it will reinvigorate debate on areas such as the legitimate role of government; the presence of pluralism in society; the safeguard of individual rights and responsibilities; and the appropriateness of methods for making citizens more actively responsible for themselves, for their families, and also for the socio-political reality of their country as a whole. We hope you enjoy the book.

References

Halberstam, Daniel. 2009. Federal powers and the principle of subsidiarity. In *Global perspectives on constitutional law*, ed. Vikram David Amar and Mark V. Tushnet, 34. New York: Oxford University Press.

Hunnings (ed.). 1998. *Encyclopedia of European law*. London: Sweet & Maxwell.

Longo, Michael. 1999. Subsidiarity and local environmental governance: A comparative and reform perspective. *University of Tasmania Law Review* 18: 225.

Moens, Gabriël A., and John Trone. 2010. *Commercial law of the European Union*. Netherlands: Springer.

Montgomery, John Warwick. 2002. Subsidiarity as a jurisprudential and canonical theory. *Law and Justice: The Christian Law Review* 148: 46.

Pius XI. 1931. *Quadragesimo Anno: Reconstructing the social order and perfecting it conformably to the precepts of the Gospel in commemoration of the fortieth anniversary of the encyclical 'Rerum Novarum'*. Melbourne: Australian Catholic Truth Society.

Pontifical Council for Justice and Peace. 2005. *Pontifical council for justice and peace*. London: Burns & Oates.

Sirico, Robert A. 1997. Subsidiarity, society, and entitlements: Understanding and application. *Notre Dame Journal of Law Ethics and Public Policy* 11: 549.

Van Til, Kent A. 2008. Subsidiarity and sphere-sovereignty: A match made in…? *Theological Studies* 69: 610.

Vause, Gary W. 1995. The subsidiarity principle in European Union law – American federalism compared. *Case Western Reserve Journal of International Law* 27: 61.

Vischer, Robert K. 2001. Subsidiarity as a principle of governance: Beyond devolution. *Indiana Law Review* 35: 103.

Widulski, Peter. 2005. Bakke, Grutter, and the principle of subsidiarity. *Hastings Constitutional Law Quarterly* 32: 847.

Zimmermann, Augusto. 2000. The principle of subsidiarity. *Democracy* (Organization of American States) 3(1): 2.

Chapter 2
Subsidiarity in the Writings of Aristotle and Aquinas

Nicholas Aroney

Abstract The philosophical origins of the principle of subsidiarity must be understood historically. This chapter argues that the critical point for the emergence of the principle lay in Thomas Aquinas's theological interpretation of Aristotle's political philosophy and his application of it to the institutional pluralism of medieval Europe. From Aristotle, Aquinas developed the idea that human societies naturally progress from families, through villages to entire city-states, but he recognised that what Aristotle said of city-states could be applied not only to cities but even more emphatically to political communities on the scale of provinces, kingdoms and (perhaps even) empires. Moreover, for Aquinas, the civil order was not the only 'perfect community' in Aristotle's sense: there was also the church in all of its many grades and jurisdictions, alongside the many different religious orders and fraternities of medieval Europe, some of them also organised into their own graded hierarchies. Reflecting on the complexity of the society surrounding him, Aquinas acknowledged the many and various purposes for which various associations and forms of human community exist and are formed, giving rise to a whole host of familial, geographical, professional, mercantile, scholarly and other specialised societies. All of these groups and groupings, from the smallest to the largest, have their place and their proper function, according to Aquinas, and each should to be allowed to make its unique and special contribution as a means to integral human fulfillment, without undue interference from any others, including the state.

Keywords Philosophy • Origins • Subsidiarity • Aristotle • Aquinas • Province • Kingdom • Empire

---

The support of Australian Research Council Discovery Grant DP 120101590 is gratefully acknowledged.

N. Aroney (✉)
TC Beirne School of Law, University of Queensland, W239 Forgan Smith Building,
St Lucia Campus, 4072 Brisbane, Queensland, Australia
e-mail: n.aroney@law.uq.edu.au

M. Evans and A. Zimmermann (eds.), *Global Perspectives on Subsidiarity*, Ius Gentium: Comparative Perspectives on Law and Justice 37, DOI 10.1007/978-94-017-8810-6_2,

2.1 Introduction

Describing the philosophical origins of a concept like subsidiarity is not a simple task. Subsidiarity can mean different things to different people in different contexts. In the law of the European Union it means that the Union will only exercise the competences that it has in common with the Member States in circumstances where—

> the proposed action cannot be sufficiently achieved by the Member States, either at central level or at regional and local level, but can rather, by reason of the scale or effects of the proposed action, be better achieved at Union level (Treaty on European Union, Article 5).

There is some real similarity between this rule and Roman Catholic teaching on the principle of subsidiarity, which was articulated by Pope John Paul II in this way—

> a community of a higher order should not interfere in the internal life of a community of a lower order, depriving the latter of its functions, but rather should support it in case of need and help to coordinate its activity with the activities of the rest of society, always with a view to the common good (*Centesimus Annus*, [48]).[1]

Despite the obvious similarities, though, there are also important differences between these two statements of principle. The first is a legal principle which controls the exercise of power by a supranational body, the European Union. The second is a more general principle which regulates the exercise of the functions of any particular community of a 'higher order' in relation to the functions of a 'lower order'. This fuller conception of subsidiarity rests on a complex social ontology that is much richer,[2] and also more controversial,[3] than the thinner, more 'political' version of subsidiarity that has been made part of the positive law of the European Union. It is with the philosophical origins of this latter, more abstract statement of principle, that this chapter will be chiefly concerned.

A fuller statement of the principle of subsidiarity was articulated by Pope Pius XI:

> Just as it is gravely wrong to withdraw from the individual and commit to the community at large what private enterprise and industry can accomplish, so, too, it is an injustice, a grave evil, and a disturbance of right order for a larger and greater organisation to arrogate to itself functions which can be performed efficiently by smaller and lower bodies. This is a fundamental principle of social philosophy, unshaken and unchangeable. Of its very nature the true aim of all social activity should be to help [*subsidium*] individual members of the social body, but never to destroy or absorb them.
>
> ... The supreme authority of the State ought, therefore, to let subordinate groups handle matters and concerns of lesser importance, which would otherwise dissipate its efforts greatly. Thereby the State will more freely, powerfully, and effectively do all those things that belong to it alone because it alone can do them: directing, watching, urging, restraining, as occasion requires and necessity demands. Therefore, those in power should be sure that

---

[1] John Paul II (1991).

[2] Hittinger (2002).

[3] Despite the evidence that Catholic social philosophy was one of the prime inspirations of the European doctrine, there is resistance to the invocation of Catholic principles: von Borries and Hauschild (1999, pp. 369–70). For a more sympathetic discussion of Catholic ideas in the context of the European principle of subsidiarity, see Barber (2005).

> the more perfectly a graduated order is kept among the various associations, in observance of the principle of 'subsidiary function,' the stronger social authority and effectiveness will be [and] the happier and more prosperous the condition of the State (*Quadragesimo Anno*, [79]–[80]).[4]

In this passage, the idea is basically the same, but several details have been specified. The most abstract statement distinguishes between a 'larger and greater organisation' and 'smaller and lower bodies'. While the main point of the principle is to preserve the integrity of the 'smaller', the statement regards the smaller as also 'subordinate' in the sense, it seems, of being 'lower' within a 'graduated order' which has the characteristics of a hierarchy. Thus, as an illustration of the general principle, it is the '*supreme* authority' of the State that ought to allow '*subordinate* groups' to handle matters of '*lesser* importance', enabling the State more effectively to perform those functions which it only can: functions which include 'directing, watching, urging [and] restraining'. The principle seems to apply to the relationship between any community and its 'members', whether individuals or groups. Certainly, the principle is that the 'smaller and lower' should be allowed to fulfill their functions without 'arrogation', 'destruction' or 'absorption', and to breach the principle is to commit not only an 'injustice', but also a 'grave evil'. But the principle operates within a graduated order in which the larger and higher is superior in authority, and the state is supreme among all.

What are the smaller and lower bodies? In Roman Catholic social thought, they are pre-eminently such institutions as the family, and all manner of private associations, such as sporting clubs and recreational societies, craft guilds and professional bodies, business corporations, employer's groups and trade unions. They may include local communities, such as neighbourhoods and villages, and they can include religious associations, like local churches and other spiritual communities. All of these kinds of association themselves may be organised into graduated orders or hierarchies, such as where a set of political communities is governed at municipal, provincial and national levels, or a church is organised on a parochial, diocesan and metropolitan scale. Being smaller or larger, lower or higher, a part or the whole, is a relative term of comparison. But the prioritisation is more complex than this might suggest, for although the state might be regarded in certain important ways as superior to the other groupings, it also in a sense follows them in time and priority. As Pope Leo XIII put it:

> No human law can abolish the natural and original right of marriage, nor in any way limit the chief and principal purpose of marriage ordained by God's authority from the beginning: 'Increase and multiply.' Hence we have the family, the 'society' of a man's house—a society very small, one must admit, but none the less a true society, and one older than any State. Consequently, it has rights and duties peculiar to itself which are quite independent of the State (*Rerum Novarum*, [12]).[5]

---

[4] Pius XI (1931).

[5] Leo XIII (1891).

What are the philosophical origins of this image of human society that takes this general form and adopts the principle of subsidiarity to determine relationships between smaller and larger social orders?

In *Rerum Novarum*, Leo XIII referred to the 'natural impulse which binds men together in civil society' and which 'leads them to join together in associations which are … lesser and not independent societies, but, nevertheless, real societies' (*Rerum Novarum*, [50]). Drawing on the teaching of Thomas Aquinas, he explained that these 'lesser' and 'larger' societies are in many respects different because their purposes are different. Fundamentally, civil society (the state) is formed for the common good, whereas private societies are formed for private objectives (*Rerum Novarum*, [51]). While the state has a responsibility to intervene to prevent certain associations which are formed for evidently bad purposes (*Rerum Novarum*, [52]), both the public society and the private association have their foundation, he said, in the same principle of human sociality, and so for the state to destroy or forbid the formation of such associations is to contradict 'the very principle of its own existence' (*Rerum Novarum*, [51]).[6]

Plainly, the Pope thought that these principles of relative order and association could be traced to the teaching of Thomas Aquinas. As the Pope's citation of Aquinas suggests, although the use of the term 'subsidiarity' may be relatively recent, the underlying principle is much older. The roots of the idea are embedded in the theology, philosophy, sociology and politics of European civilisation. There are many important writers who have contributed to the intellectual development of the principle of subsidiarity. While vitally important contributions were made by several key figures surrounding the definitive articulation of the principle by Leo XIII in 1891, Pius XI in 1931 and John Paul II in 1991,[7] by common reckoning, the more distant, and yet important roots of the concept lie in the seminal contributions of Aristotle and Thomas Aquinas, among several others.[8]

The role of Aristotle and Aquinas in the development of the theory of subsidiarity is a complex and intriguing one. Neither expressed the principle of subsidiarity in precise terms, although Aquinas went close. Moreover, there is a real sense in which certain important elements of the teaching of Aristotle actually militated against the principle of subsidiarity, and it was certain modifications and adaptions of Aristotle's teaching by Aquinas which were vitally important, intellectually, to the development of the principle. And yet, Aquinas's social thought and the Catholic principle of subsidiarity retain the unmistakable marks of Aristotle's political philosophy.

To explain this, it is necessary to look closely at both Aristotle's and Aquinas's conceptions of human nature, of human sociality, and of the nature and relationship between various forms of social grouping.[9] Care needs to be taken in doing so,

---

[6] See also *Rerum Novarum*, [7]: 'Man precedes the State, and possesses, prior to the formation of any State, the right of providing for the substance of his body.'

[7] Among them: Luigi Taparelli, Matteo Liberatore, Wilhelm Emmanuel von Ketteler and Oswald von Nell-Breuning.

[8] Millon-Delsol (1992), Kelly (1993).

[9] Part III of this chapter substantially draws on Aroney (2007).

however, for although Aquinas was a dedicated and meticulous student of Aristotle, the temporal and cultural gap between the two was substantial, and we must be attentive not to assume that there can be any simple translation from Aristotle's Greek to Aquinas's Latin, let alone to our contemporary usages of terms.

Indeed, the distance between Aquinas and us is also substantial. Several important developments in social and political thinking have since intervened. Among them, there is probably none quite so significant as the Protestant Reformation and the rise of modern liberal democracy. Both of these developments have dramatically shaped the way in which human sociability is today understood. It will not be possible to explore this here, but it needs to be noted that two writers in particular, Johannes Althusius and John Locke (emblematic of reformed and liberal thought respectively) articulated political philosophies which intersect in important ways with the ideas of Aristotle and Aquinas and shed light on how we understand the principle of subsidiarity. This paper does not discuss their specific contributions, but it does refer, in conclusion, to the challenge posed to subsidiarity theory by Thomas Hobbes, another emblematic figure, as a point of contrast that can help to clarify the philosophical presuppositions of the principle of subsidiarity.

2.2 Aristotle

Aristotle's political theory was constructed with the city-state (*polis*) of classical antiquity specifically in mind.[10] The *polis*, he said, is a composition two smaller categories of community, the household (*oikia*) and the village (*kome*) (*Politics*, I.1-2).[11] Every community is established with some good in view. Households and villages are formed to secure the bare necessities of life, whereas the *polis* is fully self-sufficient (*autarkeia*) in securing the necessities of life, and can thus be concerned with securing the 'good life', which is the chief end of humankind. Because it aims at 'the most authoritative and all-encompassing good', the *polis* is 'the supremely authoritative community' (*Politics*, I.2, 1252a1-7). Thus, while families and villages may be prior to it in time, the *polis* is prior to them in nature or essence, just as the whole is prior to the part (*Politics*, I.2, 1253a18-29).[12] The same is true of other smaller or less significant kinds of association—such as clans, tribes, religious guilds and social clubs—these too are formed for limited and partial goods—in

[10] I use the expression 'city-state' conscious of the difficulty of finding a precise English equivalent to the term *polis*.

[11] A Greek household is not quite the same thing as a 'family' in the sense that we understand it today. A household then consisted of all of the property and persons under the authority of the head of the household, an emphasis very different from the close marital, parental and filial bonds with which we associate the family today. See Herlihy (1983).

[12] On the 'whole' and its 'parts', see Aristotle, *Metaphysics*, VII.10–11 and the discussion in Newman (1950, Vol. II, pp. 125–127).

contrast to the *polis*, which is constituted for the common good (*Nicomachean Ethics*, VIII.9, 1160a9-30; *Politics*, III.9, 1280b36-39).

Aristotle denied, however, that the *polis* should simply replace or supplant the smaller associations and communities of which it is composed. Distinguishing his position from that of Plato (*Republic*, V, 449a-466d), Aristotle opposed an 'extreme unification' of the *polis*, and rejected the proposition that 'the highest unity of a state is its highest good' (*Politics*, II.2, 1261b6-15). Rather, a plurality or multitude of persons (*plethos*) is of the very nature of a city-state and a 'lesser degree of unity is preferable to the greater' (*Politics*, II.2, 1260b36-1261b15). The *polis* should not, therefore, altogether displace smaller associations, such as the household, as through the community of wives and property that was suggested by Plato (*Republic*, III, 416d; V, 449a-466d).[13] The city-state, the village and the household are all species of community (*koinonia*),[14] even though the *polis* is uniquely the community of which the lesser communities are but 'parts' (*Politics*, I.2, 1252b15-16, 27–30, 1253a15-18).[15]

Having said in Book I that the city-state is a composition of households and villages, in Book III Aristotle appeared however to set that idea aside, substituting the view that the *polis* is fundamentally comprised of individual citizens (*politai*), formed into a self-sufficing unity (*Politics*, III.1).[16] As part of a political unity, it follows that no citizen should consider that he belongs to himself, for every individual in fact belongs to the city-state (*Politics*, VIII.1). In practical terms, this meant that the head of each household should not be allowed to educate his children as he thinks fit. The entire city-state has a single, all-embracing end, and to achieve this objective the education of children must be made public and uniform (*Politics*, VIII.1-2; *Nicomachean Ethics*, X.9).[17]

For Aristotle, the *polis* exists, both typically and ideally, on the scale of an individual city.[18] He was certainly aware of the existence of discrete villages and sectors within particular cities,[19] as well as of political societies that had expanded to an

[13] See, generally, Dobbs (1985, pp. 29–46).

[14] See Booth (1981, pp. 203–26).

[15] As forms of community, it is therefore anachronistic to interpret the household/city-state distinction in terms of the private/public distinction of modern thought. See the critique of Arendt (1958) in Salkever (1990, pp. 169–74, 179–83).

[16] See Jaffa (1972, pp. 94–96), and compare Plato, *Republic*, II, 369a-c. On the composition of the *polis* in terms of households and villages as well as individuals, see also Newman (1950, Vol. II, pp. 111, 114; Vol. III, pp. 130, 132, 208). There may not altogether be a contradiction as between the individual citizen and the household, since although Aristotle referred to free women as well as free men as citizens, he seems generally to have assumed that the citizen who participates in the rule of the city will typically be an adult, male, head of a household. On this assumption, each citizen represents a household, and thus the city might be viewed quite consistently as both a composition of individual citizens and a composition of households.

[17] See also Aristotle's comments on marriage, reproduction and education in *Politics*, VII.16–17 and the comments in Pangle (1998, pp. 377–97, 381–2). For a contrary interpretation, which emphasises a kind of 'constitutional pluralism' in Aristotle, see Dobbs (1996) and compare Everson (1988, pp. 89–101). See also de Coulanges (1956, p. 219).

[18] That is, including its immediate environs and surrounding countryside.

[19] See the discussion of Cleisthenes' reforms below.

imperial scale, such as Persia under Cyrus and Macedonia under Philip and Alexander (*Politics*, V.10, 1310b37-40). However, the particular empirical examples of *poleis* to which Aristotle made reference were almost always states at the scale of individual cities, such as Athens, Sparta and Carthage (*Politics*, II.9-12). Indeed, Aristotle's ideal *polis* is of such size that, physically, it was possible to survey the city in a single view and, socially, it was possible for each citizen to know every other citizen personally (*Politics*, VII.4-5).[20] It is true that Aristotle expressed the view that if the entire Hellenic race was 'formed into one state it would be able to rule the world' (*Politics*, VII.7, 1327b32-33). However, he was in general highly critical of imperialism: it is quite wrong, he said, for citizens to be trained simply with a view to the expansion and aggrandisement of the state (*Politics*, VII.2, VII.14).[21]

The priority of Aristotle's *polis* as the focal point of human governance and fulfillment was not eclipsed, therefore, by the existence of wider forms of human association, such as inter-state alliances, national peoples and empires.[22] The city-states of ancient Greece are known to have entered into a range of alliances and leagues (*summarchia*, *isopoliteia*, *sumpoliteia*), some of which have been classified as 'confederations' and even (with some anachronism) as 'federal states'.[23] Aristotle appears to have been fully aware of these arrangements; he may even possibly have described the governing institutions of the Lycian League.[24] However, in the two passages of the *Politics* in which Aristotle approached this question, he drew a sharp distinction between the various kinds of treaty-relationships between city-states (*suntheke*, *sumbola*, *summarchia*) and the *polis* itself (*Politics*, II.2, III.9).[25] These inter-state treaties Aristotle characterised as 'agreements (*sunthekai*) about imports, engagements (*sumbola*) to do no wrong against one another, and written articles of alliance (*summarchias*)' (*Politics*, III.9). Such arrangements, he pointed out, involve an incomplete union of states, associated as equals, for the limited purpose of commercial intercourse or mutual defence. In such associations neither contracting party is concerned with the moral welfare or internal virtues and vices of the other. By contrast, the city-state, Aristotle insisted, is a 'true unity', derived from the fact that it is a 'union of unequals', of rulers and the ruled, associated for the purpose of 'the good life', the highest end for humanity (*Politics*, II.2, III.9). But in a mere alliance there is no 'magistracy' that is 'common' to the contracting parties; they each have their own magistracies (*Politics*, III.9, 1280a40-1280b2). There cannot for this

[20] See also *Politics*, II.6, 1265a13-18, criticizing Socrates' ideal city of 5,000 warrior-citizens as being unrealistically large. Aristotle was well aware of 'political communities' which are 'national' in scale, but they are less than ideal: see, eg, *Politics*, III.3, 1276a25-34.

[21] On the gradual expansion of the Athenian city-state into the whole of Attica, however, see Barker (1959, pp. 274, 298).

[22] Lord (1987, p. 134). For the contrary view that Aristotle's political theory was not necessary limited to political communities at the scale of individual cities and their immediate environs, see Everson (1996, xv–xix).

[23] Ehrenberg (1969, pp. 103–31), Larsen (1968, pp. 202–7).

[24] Larsen (1968, xi); Larsen (1945); Newman (1950, Vol. II, p. 232). For the texts, see Müller (1848–1874, Vol. II, pp. 102–77), especially fragments 91 and 145.

[25] See Newman (1950, Vol. III, pp. 203–6).

reason be any real 'government' (*politeuma*) common to city-states united merely by a treaty. Alliances are concerned only with commercial advantage or mutual security—they fall short of the proper concern of the city-state in making its citizens good and just. Political justice is, for Aristotle, justice among those who share life together within the context of the city state (*Nicomachean Ethics*, 1134a24-30). An alliance or league between two or more states cannot, therefore, constitute a truly *political* community—the nature of the two is fundamentally different (*Politics*, II.2, 1261a25-33).[26]

Aristotle applied essentially the same reasoning to ethnic and kinship groups of various kinds. While he considered the possibility that an entire people or nation (*ethnos*) might be unified into a single political community, he denied that an excessively large body of people could be a *polis* because it would not be capable of 'political' or 'constitutional' government (*politeia*) as is proper to a city-state (*Politics*, II.2, 1261a28-9, VII.4, 1326b1-6; cf. *Politics*, III.3, 1276a25-34).[27] Likewise, while the *polis* may be a composition of households, the limited authority exercised by the head of a household was to be sharply distinguished from the authority and power exercised by those who govern a city-state. Paternal command, Aristotle said, does not have the necessary force or compulsive power to establish the sort of well-ordered state in which citizens are trained and habituated throughout their lives to pursue the good life. Only public control, achieved through legislation backed by legal sanctions, has the requisite compulsive power to establish a 'right order' of this kind (*Nicomachean Ethics*, X.9, 1180a14-24; *Politics*, I.1, 1252a7-13).[28] Similarly, Aristotle never entertained the possibility that villages within a city-state might 'legislate' in this way alongside the government of the city-state. The nature and *telos* of a village was too limited for this to be the case.[29]

As such, Aristotle's 'science of politics' (*politike*) was fundamentally concerned with the city-state (*polis*) and its citizens (*politai*).[30] While the city-state was said to be composed of households and villages, the kind of authority exercised at these levels was too limited in scope to be compared with the all-encompassing goals of the city-state as a whole. Similarly, while a city-state might enter into an alliance with

---

[26] Compare de Coulanges (1956, pp. 201–2), referring to the 'profound gulf which always separated two cities' and arguing that for this reason 'the ancients were never able to establish, or even to conceive of, any other social organisation than the city'. See, likewise, Barker (1959, pp. 298–9), who concludes that Aristotle does not discuss 'federation' and thus regarded the city as the 'final form of association'.

[27] See also Newman (1950, Vol. II, pp. 150–51; Vol. III, pp. 346–7); Larsen (1945). On the tension between the Hellenic 'nation' and the Greek 'city-states', see Finley (1954).

[28] Although, see *Politics*, III.6, 1278b31-1279a21.

[29] See *Politics*, III.4, 1276b28-30, where Aristotle states that 'the salvation of the community is the common business of them all [ie, all of the citizens of a particular city-state]'.

[30] The constitution (*politeia*) is, Aristotle notes, the same as the government (*politeuma*): *Politics*, III.6, 1278b10-12; III.7, 1279a25-26. On the relationship between Aristotle's concepts of city-state, community, citizenship, constitution and government, see *Politics*, III.4, 1276b30 and the discussion in Barker (1959, p. 307); Cartledge (2000, pp. 17, 20); Ehrenberg (1969, pp. 38–9, 43, 88); Newman (1950, Vol. II, pp. 156–7). The Aristotelian *politeia*, usually translated 'constitution', 'regime' or 'form of government', should not be confused, of course, with the modern idea of the written constitution as a judicially enforceable, 'higher' law.

other city-states, and while the citizens of a particular city may belong to a larger group of cities which share a common ethnic origin, Aristotle insisted that political governance in the fullest sense of the word is not possible on the basis of a mere treaty between cities; and nor is it possible on the scale of entire ethnic peoples.

Aristotle's conception of the city-state (*polis*) and the citizenry (*politai*) shaped, in turn, his very lengthy and involved analysis of the possible forms of government (*politeuma*) and his evaluation of the ideal political constitution (*politeia*).[31] Space does not permit a detailed exposition of this aspect of Aristotle's thought. But the fundamental assumption underlying Aristotle's treatment of these questions remained a conception of the city-state as essentially a composition of individual citizens, governed by a unified form of government, notwithstanding the important role of households, tribes and villages in the social and economic life of the city. Indeed, when it came to the analysis of the forms of government, the idea that the city-state is fundamentally composed of households and villages was almost entirely displaced.

This is confirmed by what Aristotle said about the constitutional reforms instituted by Cleisthenes.[32] The account in the *Constitution of Athens* suggests that the tribes (*phulai*) and districts (*demes*) of Athens were malleable institutions, restructured in a deliberate attempt to democratise the constitution. Athens, so Aristotle's account goes, had originally been divided into four tribes, each with their tribal-kings (*phulobasileis*), and the magistracies of the entire city were chosen by lot from candidates elected by each of four tribes (*Constitution of Athens*, VIII). Under Cleisthenes, however, the constitution is said to have become more 'democratic' (*Constitution of Athens*, XXII.1).[33] The population was divided up into ten tribes (in substitution for the original four) with the express purpose of redistributing the old, aristocratic familial groups into different tribes and districts, thus breaking down the power of the tribal units and enhancing the power of individual citizens (*Constitution of Athens*, XX–XXII).[34] A uniform system of citizenship was thus introduced, based on artificially reconstituted *demes* and *phulai*, by-passing the Ionic households and tribes of the old constitution.[35]

While certainly cautious about radically democratic regimes of this sort, Aristotle clearly perceived the implications of such a constitution for the tribes, clans and other sub-political groups within the *polis*. In the *Politics*, he said:

> Also useful with a view to a democracy of this sort are the sort of institutions that Cleisthenes used at Athens when he wanted to enhance the democracy … . Other and more numerous tribes and clans are to be created, private rites incorporated into a few common rites, and everything devised so that all are mixed together to the greatest possible extent, and their familiar [associations] broken up (*Politics*, VI.4, 1319b19-26).[36]

---

[31] See Strauss (1977, p. 45).

[32] On the question of authorship, see Rhodes (1981, pp. 58–63).

[33] Compare Herodotus, *The Histories*, V.66.2, 69.2. On the effects of Cleisthenes' democratization and its motives, see Finley (1983, pp. 42–8), Sinclair (1988, pp. 3–4), Lewis (1997, pp. 77–98).

[34] Cleisthenes is said, however, to have left the citizens free to belong to their clans (*genê*) and brotherhoods (*phratrias*) as they had before: *Constitution of Athens,* XXI.6.

[35] Manville (1990, pp. 187–8).

[36] The quotation is from Lord's translation (Chicago, 1984). See also *Politics*, III.2, 1275b34-37.

The malleability of the *demes* and the *phulai* suggests that an individual citizen's membership of 'sub-political' communities, such as households, tribes and villages, was at best peripheral, if not completely irrelevant, to political inquiry as Aristotle understood it. Even though the *phulai* and *demes* of fourth-century Athens seem to have exercised very significant powers of local self-government,[37] Aristotle completely ignored this. As Whitehead put it, neither Aristotle nor the author of the *Constitution of Athens* 'show any interest whatever in the Attic *demes* as an object of study in themselves'. Rather, they are simply and always 'taken for granted'.[38]

Compared to Plato, Aristotle's conception of the ideal *polis* was definitely closer to a 'subsidiarity state'. Aristotle depicted the *polis* as a composition of households and villages, and he rejected Plato's view that there should be a communal ownership of women and property. However, his was not quite a subsidiarity state, for the uniform education of children was a function of the state, not the household. Moreover, much of Aristotle's analysis of the government of the *polis* treated it as being composed ultimately of individual citizens. Each citizen was no doubt a 'head of a household', but as Aristotle's account of the reforms of Cleisthenes suggests, the tribes and districts into which they had been organised could legitimately be reconstituted in order to undermine their power and influence. Finally, for Aristotle, political community ended at the borders of the *polis*. There could be no real politics on a wider scale, only commercial arrangements and military alliances. Ultimately, human beings were political animals, beings whose many attachments and diverse associations were subordinated to the supreme authority of *polis*.

For the principle of subsidiarity to develop fully, human nature would have to be understood in terms more of the pluralistically 'social' than the narrowly 'political'. It was precisely a much more strongly socialised conception of human nature that Aquinas contributed.

2.3 Aquinas

It is well-known that a central motif in Aquinas's thought concerned his attempt to synthesize the deliverances of natural human reason with the propositions of Christian revelation in a manner which admitted the findings of reason as regards those matters falling within the proper scope of each of its sciences, but which preserved the ultimate unity of the truths known by both reason and faith, while insisting that revealed truths exceed those truths that can be known by reason (*ScG*, 1.9.1; 1.3.2, 4; 1.7.3).[39] In large part, this involved for Aquinas a synthesis of the thought of Aristotle (whom Aquinas called simply 'The Philosopher') with the

---

[37] See Gilbert (1895, pp. 200–210), Hignett (1952, pp. 136–8), Glotze (1965, pp. 122–3), Whitehead (1986), ch. 9: Manville (1990, pp. 187–94).

[38] Whitehead (1986, p. 51).

[39] *Summa contra Gentiles* (1259–1265). Unless indicated otherwise, in-text references to Aquinas's works are to the book, section and paragraph numbers.

interpretations of the Bible and developments in philosophy that had been initiated by a whole host of Patristic and Medieval writers, preeminent among them, Augustine of Hippo. This being so, to what extent did Aquinas accept Aristotle's account of the status and function of smaller associations, such as households and villages, within the city-state, and to what extent did Aquinas's theology lead him to develop an account of these and other 'smaller associations' in a way that anticipated the principle of subsidiarity?

Aristotle's account of the *polis* as being composed of households, clans and villages (*Politics*, III.9, 1280b) bears a resemblance to the assumption of modern subsidiarity theory that societies necessarily consist of a graded order of associations and organisations, each of them pursuing legitimate and important ends under the unifying authority of the state. However, Aristotle's view that households, for example, are concerned only with the provision of the mere 'necessities' of life, whereas the *polis* is directed to 'the good life', suggests a relationship of inferiority/superiority that does not quite do justice to the 'goods' which the principle of subsidiarity attributes to the many and various social forms of which the state is composed.

Aquinas was profoundly influenced by Aristotle, but the influence did not prevent him from both disagreeing with Aristotle on certain key points and qualifying Aristotle's teaching in several important ways. Aquinas's Commentaries on Aristotle's *Politics* and *Nicomachean Ethics* are a good illustration. In these works, Aquinas's primary concern was to expound Aristotle's meaning rather than critique it, but in doing so Aquinas frequently injected important qualifications into the exposition. Sometimes Aquinas's qualifications were theologically grounded, as when he insisted that although Aristotle was correct to say that human beings are political animals who find their fulfillment in the *polis*, the proposition must be understood as having to do with 'human affairs' and the order of 'nature'—matters that are addressed in natural philosophy—and are certainly not be understood as concerning those 'ultimate things' that are addressed in sacred theology (*Eth.*, I.9.10-11 [112–113]). In this way, Aquinas simultaneously both affirmed and relativised the goods and goals of the state. For Aristotle, the *polis* presented a comprehensive context in which what is good for human beings is secured. For Aquinas, while the state certainly has this function, it is itself put into a wider theological context, and its goods are understood relative to that framework. This enabled Aquinas to take a view of the 'state' that was relative—not only 'upwards' and 'outwards' as regards its wider context, but also 'downwards' or 'inwards' as regards those forms of human sociality that are 'smaller' than the state.

Aquinas's exposition of Aristotle had an important analytical component as well. At the outset of the Commentary on the *Ethics*, Aquinas made clear that the political societies of which Aristotle wrote were to be conceived as 'wholes' which possess not an 'absolute unity', but rather a 'unity of order' (*Eth.*, I.1.5 [5]).[40] The specific Aristotelian text upon which Aquinas was commenting made no explicit mention of the question of the relationship of the whole to its parts (*Nic. Ethics*, I.1, 1094a1-18), but Aquinas considered it important to emphasise that, while a political community

[40] Grasso (2008, p. 34).

is a composition of households and villages, this does not mean that the state is an absolute unity in which such 'subordinate' units have no independent powers of operation. Indeed, this was a general principle which applied to both church and state. As Aquinas elsewhere explained, 'a single congregation or community [necessarily] includes other [such communities]' (*una congregatio vel communitas includit aliam*) (*Sent.*, IV.24.3.2.3). While the statement was made in the context of a discussion of the church and its orders, Aquinas cast it in the form of the general principle that all communities of human beings naturally form themselves into systems of graded orders (*gradibus unionis*), whether in the church, the state or in other forms of human association. As several students of Aquinas have pointed out, he considered all human communities to consist of parts that in some respects have an operation that is independent and in other respects participate in the operations of the whole (Mueller 1943, 146–9; Phelan and Eschmann 1949, 29–34; Gilby 1958, 251–6; Finnis 1998, 24–5). While this too was broadly consistent with Aristotle's own view (*Politics*, I.2, 1252b, 1253a; II.2, 1261b), Aquinas's emphasis on the idea of a unity of order rather than an absolute unity laid the foundation for several ways in which his political and social thought departed significantly from that of Aristotle.

This can be seen especially in Aquinas's depiction of the human person. Rather than follow Aristotle by always defining human beings simply as a 'political animals', it is important to notice that Aquinas usually preferred to refer to them as 'political and social' or simply 'social' animals, and added in one place that human nature is not only political or civil, but also preeminently 'domestic' (see, e.g., *ST*, I, 96.4; I-II, 61.5, 72.4, 95.4; *De Regno*, I.1.3 [4], I.13.2 [94]; *ScG*, III.85.11; *Eth.*, I.1.4 [4], VII.6.7 [1391], VIII.12.18 [1719–1720]; *Pol.*, I.1.29 [37]).[41] This terminology reflected the fact that Aquinas placed much greater emphasis than Aristotle on the many and varied 'non-political' forms of human association and community that he encountered in his day, such as families, fraternities, religious orders, guilds, universities, and many more besides (Scully 1981; Finnis 1998, ch. 7; Aroney 2007, 177–9). Similarly, although Aquinas generally followed Aristotle in regarding self-sufficiency to be an essential characteristic of the city-state (Greek *polis* or Latin *civitas*) which distinguishes it from a mere household or neighbourhood (*Pol.*, I.1.3 [11], I.1.7-9 [15–17], I.1.23-25 [31–33], I.1.30-32 [38–40]; *ST*, I-II, 90.3 ad 3, II-II, 47.11, 50.1), Aquinas treated self-sufficiency in relative terms: households and neighbourhoods can possess a kind self-sufficiency themselves, and wider political units such as provinces, kingdoms and nations possess degrees of self-sufficiency and completeness which surpass that of an individual city.[42]

The basic principle here, for Aquinas, was that 'a government is the more perfect according as it is more universal, extends to more matters, and attains a more ultimate end' (*ST*, II-II, 50.1). The implications of this principle were stated plainly in *De Regno*, where Aquinas described the self-sufficiency of the various forms and

[41] *Sententia libri Politicorum* (1269–1272).

[42] On cities and provinces, see *De Regno*, I.2.4 [14]; on cities and kingdoms, see *De Regno*, I.14.5 [100]; on nations, see *Quaestiones Disputatae de Veritate* (1256–1259), 5.3 co; and on the universe as a whole, see *ST*, I-II, 91.1, 21.4, 100.5; *ScG*, I.42, 70–71, 78, 85–86, 93, 102, II.39, 42, III.64, 98.

degrees of human society (*De Regno*, I.2.4 [14]). Self-sufficiency (*autarkeia*), according to Aristotle, was the prime distinguishing feature of the *polis*. However, Aquinas strikingly affirmed, in terms very different from Aristotle, that a household enjoys a degree of self-sufficiency, particularly with regard to the giving of birth to offspring and the provision of food, and that a particular street or neighbourhood within a city will be self-sufficient in respect of the particular trade that is practised there. Moreover, while Aquinas further affirmed that a city (*civitas*) is by comparison self-sufficient in respect of all the necessities of life, this was not absolutely but only relatively so, for he went on to assert that a province is even more self-sufficient than a city, particularly in respect of its capacity to defend the community against its enemies. In this way, although Aquinas followed Aristotle in progressing from household to city, as well as in distinguishing the city as a perfect and self-sufficient community, he diverged significantly from Aristotle in identifying a relative self-sufficiency in the household and neighbourhood and an even greater self-sufficiency in the province (Woolf 1913, 274–5; Gierke 1968, 96).

While Aristotle could write simply of the *polis*, Aquinas appears to have been acutely conscious of the fact that he had to address a wide range of both private and public forms of human association and government. As far as public associations were concerned, sometimes he used generic terms, such as 'civic community', 'political society' and so on, and referred to cities, kingdoms and provinces interchangeably—for what he had to say in these cases applied to them all without distinction (Finnis 1998, 219). But at other times, he referred to cities, kingdoms and provinces distinctly, for what he had to say about each one was different. Moreover, while Aquinas's picture was undoubtedly hierarchical (e.g., *ST*, I, 108.1-8, 112.1-4; cf. Beer 1986), it was a hierarchy which included a remarkable diversity of jurisdictions. Although he regarded human beings and angels to be part of the one hierarchy of rational creatures under God, he maintained that there is a real sense in which they live under different hierarchies (Murphy 1997), just as those, he said, 'that cannot be governed in the same way by a prince belong to different principalities' and, therefore, 'under one king there are different cities, which are governed by different laws and administrators' (*ST*, I, 108.1; see also *ST*, I, 22.1 res; *Impugn.*, II.3; *ScG*, II.15.4, III.98.1; *De Malo*, I.1 res).[43] Aquinas also often had occasion to remark about the superior power of the emperor over a proconsul and of a proconsul over a governor and, likewise, the power of the pope over every other spiritual power in the church (*ST*, I-II, 19.5, 96.5; II-II, 69.3, 104.5; *De Regno*, II.3.12 [112]). Yet, elsewhere, he pointed out that 'the subjects of one city or kingdom (*civitate vel regno*) are not bound by the laws of the sovereign of another city or kingdom, since they are not subject to his authority' (*ST*, I-II, 96.5 res).

Aquinas developed a typology of kinds and forms of society which, while distinguishing 'public' societies such as cities, provinces and kingdoms, from 'private' societies such as households, business partnerships, craft guilds and religious

[43] In *Quaestiones de quodlibet*, II, 5.1 res., Aquinas (1256–1259, 1269–1272) likewise described and limited the authority of the head of a household to matters pertaining the management of the home, and that of a king to those matters pertaining to the government of the realm.

associations, nonetheless classified them all as particular kinds of 'society' (*Impugn.*, II.2, co; see also *Impugn.*, II.3, ad 6; *Pol.*, I.1.23 [31]).[44] He understood these various forms of society to possess both a degree of separateness and independence from one another and a degree of integration and interdependence. An individual can be a member of a particular private society which, to a certain extent, governs itself, while at the same time by virtue of that membership he may be a member of a wider public society of which the smaller society is a part and in which governing institutions its representatives participate (*Impugn.*, II.2, ad 2). Aquinas here seems to have had a conception of both an inclusive membership in a set of integrated societies, and a conception of membership of several private or public societies separately and simultaneously, including a conception of dual citizenship of different cities (*Impugn.*, II.2, ad 3). None of this appears in any of Aristotle's extant writings.

This idea of a plurality of communities of a political, ecclesiastical, social, and economic nature, themselves composed of smaller constituent communities, readily suggested the idea of an elective, corporate representation of the smaller community in the governing institutions of the larger. Aquinas appears to have derived this conception from certain texts of the Old and New Testaments in which the idea of the nation of Israel as constructed out of a plurality of tribes, clans and families (*ST*, I-II, 105.1 res., citing *Exodus* 18:21 and *Deuteronomy* 1:13, 15), parallels the idea of the church as a universal community constructed out of a plurality of dioceses and parishes (*Impugn.*, II.3; *Expositio in Lucam*, commenting on *Luke* 10:1), each in a sense self-governing, but also subject to a hierarchy of courts of appeal, themselves constituted by representatives of the constituent communities. Even the pope was presented here as a limited monarch, constrained by the fundamental beliefs, standards and institutions of the Christian faith (*Impugn.*, II.3). Similarly, while in some contexts Aquinas clearly favoured monarchical rule (*ScG*, IV.76.4; *De Regno*, I.3.1-4 [15–19]), he was acutely conscious of the propensity of kings to fall into tyranny, and he suggested several ways in which the authority of a king ought to be tempered, including the formation of compacts (*pacta*) which place constitutional limits on his power, mechanisms by which a tyrannical king can be deposed and systems of 'mixed government' which enable all to have a 'share' in ruling (*Pol.*, II.7.4 [245]; *De Regno*, I.7.1-12 [41–52]; *ST*, I-II, 95.4 and 105.1).[45]

Aquinas's attempt to integrate Aristotle's political thought into a medieval intellectual and cultural context required important adjustments in order to make room for the institutions of the Church at a parochial, diocesan and catholic scale, as well as the cities, kingdoms and provinces of the Holy Roman Empire (compare Nederman 1987; Blythe 1992, 46). Classical antiquity had no conception of church and state as separate institutions, but the seeds of the idea were in Christianity from the very beginning (*Mark* 12:17; *Acts* 5:29). Combined with the Roman law idea of *jurisdictio* and related concepts, medieval jurists developed the idea that church and state, as well as particular institutions within church and state, possessed distinct and limited jurisdictions (Berman 1983, 205–215). Aquinas followed this lead by

[44] On medieval guilds in particular, see Berman (1983, pp. 390–92) and Black (1984).

[45] See, further, Tierney (1997), Blythe (1992), Murphy (1997), Aroney (2007, pp. 198–220).

drawing a definite distinction between spiritual and temporal authority. In those matters which affect the salvation of the soul, he said, spiritual power is to be followed, whereas in those matters which concern the civil welfare, the temporal should be obeyed (*Sent.*, II.44 exposito textus).[46] There is some dispute over the precise lines that Aquinas would draw between the temporal jurisdiction of the state and the spiritual jurisdiction of the church. There are passages which can be interpreted to suggest that the pope's authority extends, at least in some specific contexts, into temporal affairs, and there are others which can be interpreted to suggest that the legitimate concerns of a king include the spiritual well-being of his subjects (*De Regno*, I.16.2 [115]).[47] Wherever the line was to be drawn, however, Aquinas clearly thought that there was such a line, and that church and state had distinct and by implication limited jurisdictions. And, while the nature and functions of each was unique, there was a sense in which they each confronted one another on an equal basis, for Aquinas classified them both as 'public associations' and as 'perfect communities' (*Impugn.*, II.2, ad 9; *ST*, II-II, 31.3 ad 3; 43.8; Finnis 1998, 226, n 31).[48]

2.4 Conclusions

Aquinas said that it is one of the hallmarks of a tyrant that he deliberately undermines all forms of social solidarity among his subjects, preventing them from joining in various compacts and associations (*confederationes*) between individuals and families by which social friendship, familiarity and trust is generated (*De Regno*, I.4.7 [27]). Very nearly the opposite was said by Thomas Hobbes, who cast suspicion on leagues or covenants among subjects as presumptively dangerous, and therefore unlawful (*Leviathan*, II:22). Indeed, for Hobbes, 'the immoderate greatness of a Town' is a threat to the state, just as a 'great number of corporations' are as 'many lesser Commonwealths in the bowels of a greater, like wormes in the entrayles of a naturall man'—implying that they were something to be eradicated (*Leviathan*, II:29).[49] Quite a different perspective was articulated by Leo XIII in *Rerum Novarum*, who observed that both the state and the private association have their foundation in the same principle of human sociality, and so for the state to destroy or forbid the formation of such associations is to contradict 'the very principle of its own existence' ([51]).

A consideration of the Hobbesian account of human nature and sociality helps to shed light on several important presuppositions embedded in the concept of subsidiarity, and gives rise to several questions of detail. The first of these concerns how human sociality is to be understood: how far is it 'natural' and how far is it 'artificial'? In the Hobbesian state of nature there is no natural sociality, only a state

[46] *Scriptum super Sententiis magistri Petri Lombardi* (1256b).

[47] *De Regno ad regem Cypri* (c. 1267).

[48] *Contra impugnantes Dei cultum et Religionem* (1256a), *Summa Theologiae* (1265–1268, 1271–1273).

[49] For a discussion of the role of associations within Hobbes's thought, see Robertson (1966).

of constant war (*Leviathan*, II:xiii). The 'law of nature' is radically thin for Hobbes: it is little more than the rule that we should seek peace, that we should be willing to agree to lay down our natural rights in order to secure peace, and that we should perform our covenants (*Leviathan*, II:xiv, xv). The state is thus an artificial contrivance in the sense that it arises only as a result of this agreement, or social contract. Aristotle's account was vastly different to this. From the outset of the *Politics* we encounter human beings living naturally in households, villages and city-states. There is no social contract; indeed, the Sophist's social contract theory of the state is rejected on the ground that the state is not merely an alliance entered into protect one's rights, but exists to inculcate virtue in the citizens (*Politics* III:9).

Aquinas certainly tended to agree with Aristotle, but there were elements in his thought that pointed to a more limited view of the state. As John Finnis has observed, for Aquinas the purpose of human law is nothing more than 'the temporal tranquility of the state, a purpose which the law attains by coercively prohibiting external acts to the extent that those are evils which can disturb the state's peaceful condition' (*ST* I-II.98.1; Finnis 1998, 224).[50] On this view, it is the particular responsibility of the state to provide the essential conditions under which individuals, families and all manner of associations are able to flourish, namely external peace and justice (Finnis 1998, 225–8).[51] The state provides the essential conditions under which the common good can be secured, but a vital role is reserved to individuals, families and other associations in making 'good choices and actions on the basis of their own deliberation and judgements' (Finnis 1998, 236). As such, a distinction needs to be made between the common good simpliciter (the 'all-inclusive common good') and the specifically *political* dimensions of the common good which Finnis, following Aquinas, calls the 'public good'. According to Finnis, the wider, all-encompassing conception of the common good is more than the state can or should attempt to enact by force of its own authority. All that it is properly responsible to secure is those external conditions which enable individuals, families and associations to pursue and contribute to the all-inclusive common good, as a consequence of which all are enabled to flourish.

As Mark Murphy has pointed out, Finnis's more or less 'instrumental' view of the common good (Finnis 1998, 252) seems especially well suited 'to a conception of government in which government … cannot, even in principle, take over the tasks of lower-level associations' (Murphy 2005, 145). Consistent with this view, as Finnis himself points out (Finnis 1998, 235), Aquinas wrote about three types of practical reasonableness (*prudentia*) associated with the distinguishable goods of the individual, the family and the state:

> the individual good, the good of the family, and the good of the city and kingdom are different ends. Wherefore there must needs be different species of prudence corresponding to these different ends, so that one is 'prudence' simply so called, which is directed to one's own good; another, 'domestic prudence' which is directed to the common good of the home; and a third, 'political prudence,' which is directed to the common good of the city or kingdom (*ST* II-II 47.11).

[50] Finnis (1998).

[51] For a contrary view, see Murphy (2005, p. 148).

Reasoning in this way, Aquinas seems to have anticipated the contemporary principle of subsidiarity in several respects. From Aristotle, he developed the idea that the human societies naturally progress from families, through villages to entire city-states. Reflecting on the complexity of the medieval society surrounding him, he acknowledged the many and various purposes for which various associations and forms of human community exist and are formed, whether they be familial, geographical, professional, mercantile, scholarly, religious, political and so on. Influenced by Aristotle, he considered that the 'state' exists to secure the common good of the society as a whole, except that he recognised that what Aristotle said of the *polis* could be said not only of cities but even more emphatically of provinces, kingdoms and (perhaps even) empires. Moreover, for Aquinas, the civil order was not the only 'perfect community' in Aristotle's sense: there was also the church in all of its many grades and jurisdictions, alongside the many different religious orders and fraternities, some of them also organised into their own graded hierarchies. All of these groups and groupings, from the smallest to the largest, had their place and their proper function, Aquinas thought. Each ought to be allowed to make its contribution as a means to human fulfillment without undue interference from others, including the state. For it would be 'contrary to the proper character of the state's governance', he wrote, for it 'to impede people from acting according to their responsibilities—except in emergencies' (*ScG* III.71; Finnis 1998, 237). Much the same was said, and meant, when Leo XIII stated:

> … the State must not absorb the individual or the family; both should be allowed free and untrammeled action so far as is consistent with the common good and the interest of others (*Rerum Novarum* [35]).

References

Aquinas, T. 1256a. *Contra impugnantes Dei cultum et Religionem*. In *Opera omnia iussu Leonis XIII P. M. edita*, t. 41. Romae: Ad Sanctae Sabinae, 1970. See Proctor, John (trans.). 1902. *An Apology for the Religious Orders*. London: Sands & Co.

Aquinas, T. 1256b. *Scriptum super Sententiis magistri Petri Lombardi = Commentum in quartum librum Sententiarum magistri Petri Lombardi*. In *Opera*, t. 7/2. Parmae: Typis Petri Fiaccadori, 1858. See Molloy, Michael (trans.). 1985. *Civil Authority in Medieval Philosophy: Lombard, Aquinas and Bonaventura*. Lanham: University Press of America.

Aquinas, T. 1256–1259. *Quaestiones Disputatae de Veritate*. In *Opera omnia iussu Leonis XIII P. M. edita*, t. 22. *Quaestiones disputatae de veritate*. Roma: Ad Sanctae Sabinae/Editori di San Tommaso, 1975-1970-1972-1973-1976. See Robert W. Mulligan, S.J. (trans.). 1952. *St. Thomas Aquinas: Truth*. Chicago: Henry Regnery Company, and Maurer, Armand (trans.). 1987. *St. Thomas Aquinas: Faith, Reason and Theology: Questions I-IV of His Commentary on the De Trinitate of Boethius*. Toronto: Pontifical Institute of Mediaeval Studies.

Aquinas, T. 1256–1259, 1269–1272. *Quaestiones quodlibetales*, 9th ed, ed. Spiazzi. Taurino: Marietti, 1956. See Edwards, Sandra (trans.). 1983. *St. Thomas Aquinas: Quodlibetal Questions 1 and 2*. Toronto: Pontifical Institute of Mediaeval Studies.

Aquinas, T. 1259–1265. *Summa contra Gentiles = Liber de Veritate Catholicae Fidei contra Errores Infidelium seu Summa contra Gentiles*. In *Opera Omnia Santi Thomae Aquinatis Doctoris Angelici*, t. 2–3. Taurini-Romae: Marietti, 1961. See Rickaby, Joseph. (trans.). 1905. *Of God and His Creatures: An Annotated Translation (with Some Abridgement) of the Summa contra Gentiles of Saint Thomas Aquinas*. London: Burns and Oates.

Aquinas, T. 1265–1268, 1271–1283. *Summa Theologiae*. In *Opera*, t. 4–12. Romae: Ex Typographia Polyglotta SC de Propaganda Fide, 1888–1906. See *Summa Theologiae*. London: Burns & Oates, 1947–48, and London: Eyre & Spottiswoode, 1964–1976.

Aquinas, T. 1267. *De Regno ad regem Cypri*. In *Opuscula philosophica*, 2nd ed, ed. Spiazzi. Taurini-Romae: Marietti, 1954. See Blythe, James (trans.). 1997. *On the Government of Rulers: De Regimine Principum: Ptolemy of Lucca With Portions Attributed to Thomas Aquinas*. Philadelphia: University of Pennsylvania Press, and Phelan, Gerald, and I.Th. Eschmann (trans.). 1949. *On Kingship, to the King of Cyprus*. Toronto: Pontifical Institute of Mediaeval Studies.

Aquinas, T. 1269–1272. *Sententia libri Politicorum*. In *Opera*, t. 48. Romae: Ad Sanctae Sabinae, 1971. See Lerner, Ralph, and Muhsin Mahdi (eds.). 1963. *Medieval Political Philosophy: A Source Book*. Ithaca: Cornell University Press.

Arendt, H. 1958. *The human condition*. Chicago: University of Chicago Press.

Aroney, N. 2007. Subsidiarity, federalism and the best constitution: Thomas Aquinas on city, province and empire. *Law and Philosophy* 26: 161.

Barber, N.W. 2005. The limited modesty of subsidiarity. *European Law Journal* 11(3): 308.

Barker, E. 1959. *The political thought of Plato and Aristotle*. New York: Dover Publications.

Beer, S. 1986. The rule of the wise and holy: Hierarchy in the thomistic system. *Political Theory* 14(3): 391–422.

Berman, H.J. 1983. *Law and revolution: The formation of the Western legal tradition*. Harvard: Harvard University Press.

Black, A.J. 1984. *Guilds and civil society in European political thought from the twelfth century to the present*. London: Methuen.

Blythe, J. 1992. *Ideal government and the mixed constitution in the Middle Ages*. Princeton: Princeton University Press.

Booth, W.J. 1981. Politics and the household: A commentary on Aristotle's politics book one. *History of Political Thought* 2: 203.

Cartledge, P. 2000. Greek political thought: The historical context. In *The Cambridge history of Roman and Greek political thought*, ed. C. Rowe and M. Schofield. Cambridge: Cambridge University Press.

de Coulanges, N.D.F. 1956. *The ancient city: A study on the religion, laws, and institutions of Greece and Rome*. Garden City, New York: Doubleday.

Dobbs, D. 1985. Aristotle's Anticommunism. *American Journal of Political Science* 29(1): 29.

Dobbs, D. 1996. Family matters: Aristotle's appreciation of women and the plural structure of society. *American Political Science Review* 90(1): 74.

Ehrenberg, V. 1969. *The Greek state*, 2nd ed. London: Methuen.

Everson, S. 1988. Aristotle on the foundations of the state. *Political Studies* 36: 89.

Everson, S. (ed.). 1996. *The politics and the constitution of Athens*. Cambridge: Cambridge University Press.

Finley, M.I. 1954. The ancient Greeks and their nation. *British Journal of Sociology* 5: 253–264.

Finley, M. 1983. *Politics in the ancient world*. Cambridge: Cambridge University Press.

Finnis, J. 1998. *Aquinas: Moral, political, and legal theory*. Oxford: Oxford University Press.

Gilbert, G. 1895. *The Constitutional Antiquities of Sparta and Athens*, Trans. E.J. Brooks and T. Nicklin. New York: Macmillan.

Gilby, Thomas. 1958. *The political thought of Thomas Aquinas*. Chicago: University of Chicago Press.

Glotze, G. 1965. *The Greek city and its institutions*. London: Routledge & Kegan Paul Ltd.

Grasso, K. 2008. The subsidiary state: Society, the state and the principle of subsidiarity in Catholic social thought. In *Christianity and civil society*, ed. J. Heffernan Schindler. Lanham: Lexington Books.

Herlihy, D. 1983. The making of the medieval family: Symmetry, structure, and sentiment. *Journal of Family History* 8(2): 116.

Hignett, C. 1952. *A history of the Athenian constitution to the end of the fifth century B.C.* Oxford: Clarendon Press.

Hittinger, R. 2002. Social pluralism and subsidiarity in Catholic social doctrine. *Annales Theologici* 16: 385.
Jaffa, H. 1972. Aristotle. In *History of political philosophy*, 2nd ed, ed. L. Strauss and J. Cropsey. Chicago: Rand McNally and Co.
John Paul II. 1991. *Centesimus Annus: Encyclical letter on the Hundredth Anniversary of Rerum Novarum*, May 1.
Kelly, J. 1993. The influence of Aquinas' natural law theory on the principle of "corporatism" in the thought of Leo XIII and Pius XI. In *Things old and new: Catholic social teaching revisited*, ed. F.P. McHugh and S.M. Natale, 104. Lanham, Maryland: University Press of America.
Larsen, J.A.O. 1945. Representation and democracy in hellenistic federalism. *Classical Philology* 40(2): 65.
Larsen, J.A.O. 1968. *Greek federal states: Their institutions and history*. Oxford: Clarendon Press.
Leo XIII. 1891. *Rerum Novarum: Encyclical letter on capital and labor*, May 15.
Lewis, D. 1997. Cleisthenes and Attica. In *Selected papers in Greek and near Eastern history*. Cambridge: Cambridge University Press.
Lord, C. 1984. *The politics*. Chicago: University of Chicago Press.
Lord, C. 1987. Aristotle. In *History of political philosophy*, 3rd ed, ed. L. Strauss and J. Cropsey. Chicago: University of Chicago Press.
Manville, P. 1990. *The origins of citizenship in ancient Athens*. Princeton: Princeton University Press.
Millon-Delsol, C. 1992. *L'Etat Subsidiaire*. Paris: Presses universitaires de France.
Mueller, F.H. 1943. The principle of subsidiarity in the Christian tradition. *The American Catholic Sociological Review* 4: 144–157.
Müller, K. 1848–1874. *Fragmenta historicum graecorum: Apollodori Bibliotheca cum fragmentis*, 5 vols. Paris
Murphy, M. 1997. Consent, custom, and the common good in Aquinas's account of political authority. *The Review of Politics* 59(02): 323.
Murphy, M.C. 2005. The common good. *The Review of Metaphysics* 59(1): 133.
Nederman, C.J. 1987. Aristotle as authority: Alternative Aristotelian sources of late mediaeval political theory. *History of European Ideas* 8(1): 31–44.
Newman, W.L. 1950. *Politics of Aristotle*, 3 vols. Oxford: Clarendon Press.
Pangle, T. 1998. Justice among nations in Platonic and Aristotelian political philosophy. *American Journal of Political Science* 42(2): 377.
Phelan, G., and I.Th. Eschmann (trans.). 1949. *On Kingship, to the King of Cyprus*. Toronto: Pontifical Institute of Mediaeval Studies.
Pius XI. 1931. *Quadragesimo Anno: Encyclical letter on reconstruction of social order*, May 15.
Rhodes, P.J. 1981. *A Commentary on the Aristotelian 'Athenaion Politeia'*. Oxford: Clarendon Press.
Robertson, D.B. 1966. Hobbes's theory of associations in the seventeenth-century milieu. In *Voluntary association: A study of groups in free societies*. Richmond: John Knox Press.
Salkever, S. 1990. *Finding the mean*. Princeton: Princeton University Press.
Scully, E. 1981. The place of the state in society according to Thomas Aquinas. *The Thomist* 45(3): 407–429.
Sinclair, R. 1988. *Democracy and participation in Athens*. Cambridge: Cambridge University Press.
Strauss, L. 1977. *The city and man*. Chicago: University of Chicago Press.
Tierney, B. 1997. *The idea of natural rights: Studies on natural rights, natural law and church law 1150–1625*. Atlanta: Scholars Press.
von Borries, R., and Malte Hauschild. 1999. Implementing the subsidiarity principle. *Columbia Journal of European Law* 5: 369.
von Gierke, O. 1968. *Political Theories of the Middle Age*. Trans. F. Maitland. Cambridge: Cambridge University Press.
Whitehead, D. 1986. *The Demes of Attica, 508/7-ca. 250 B.C.: A political and social study*. Princeton: Princeton University Press.
Woolf, C.N.S. 1913. *Bartolus of Sassoferrato: His position in the political thought of his time*. Cambridge: Cambridge University Press.

Chapter 3
Subsidiarity in the Tradition of Catholic Social Doctrine

Patrick McKinley Brennan

Abstract The violent efforts of the eighteenth and nineteenth century revolutionaries to dissolve the social order led the Catholic Church to discern and articulate the principle of subsidiarity. In Catholic social doctrine, social justice is the demand that the common good be realised through societies, institutions, and groups. Derivative of social justice is the principle of subsidiarity or subsidiarity function, which has two aspects. Negatively, it is a principle of non-absorption of lower societies by higher societies, above all by the state. Positively, subsidiarity demands that when aid is given to a particular society, it be for the purpose of encouraging and strengthening that society. Societies are opportunities for activities by which rational agents achieve perfections proper to their nature, specifically by causing good in others through solidarity. The activities of the heterogeneous and pluriform whole that is the commonwealth must be harmonized with regard to the common good. In Catholic social doctrine, subsidiarity is not a principle of devolution or smallness of scale.

Keywords Subsidiarity • Catholic church • Social justice • Social doctrine • Social order • Common good • Pius IX • Leo XIII • Benedict XVI • *Quadragesimo Anno* • *Rerum Novarum*

3.1 Introduction

Although present in germ from the first Christian century, Catholic social thought began to emerge as a unified body of doctrine in the nineteenth century, first in the condemnations issued by Pope Pius IX (r. 1846–1878) and later in the prolific and

P.M. Brennan (✉)
School of Law, Villanova University, 299 North Spring Mill Road,
Villanova, Pennsylvania 19085, United States of America
e-mail: brennan@law.villanova.edu

M. Evans and A. Zimmermann (eds.), *Global Perspectives on Subsidiarity*, Ius Gentium: Comparative Perspectives on Law and Justice 37, DOI 10.1007/978-94-017-8810-6_3,

forward-looking teaching of Pope Leo XIII (r. 1878–1903). Pius IX's *Syllabus of Errors* (1864) established that the Church would not accede to the deracinated and dissolved world imposed with relentless violence by the revolutionaries of 1789. Pius also recognised, however, that wholesale restoration of the *ancien regime* was out of the question. It thus fell to his successor, Leo, and to Leo's successors to recover and apply the enduring principles of a sound social order.

In the social order ripped to bloody shreds by the revolutionaries, the norm had been for the Church to be the soul of the body politic.[1] Church and state, because they were distinct, could constitute a union – the union of throne and altar. The Church served as the conscience of the state; the state served the common goods, both natural and, indirectly, supernatural. This was the logic of Christendom, the ideal of a Christian commonwealth. Separation, where it occurred, was an objectionable aberration. Not always achieved in practice, union remained both the ideal and the normal structure.

The dissolvent experiences of the nineteenth century taught the popes that the Church's place in the world had to be defended, both de facto and de jure. The normal structure had been obliterated, the ideal widely rejected. Faced with "rhetorical adrenaline"[2] and pathological violence on behalf of a laicized state, the question the popes had to answer was this: What was the rightful place of the Church, in all of her pluriform institutional manifestations, in the emergent social order? The Church was fighting for her life, and the transcendent issue faced by the popes was how to differentiate the Church and the rest of the social order without reducing the Church either to a private association like any other or, perhaps worse, to a formless aggregate of members.[3]

The response of the popes, assisted by philosophers and theologians and other experts, proceeded apace, and by 1931 Pope Pius XI (r. 1922–1939) would say that he inherited a body of social "doctrine" handed on from the time of Leo.[4] Pius said this in *Quadragesimo Anno*, the encyclical that gave the principle of subsidiarity – a key component of the socio-political order affirmed by the Church in response to the social dissolution wrought by the revolutionaries – its first, and canonical, formulation in Catholic social doctrine. Down to the present, the popes have continued to develop the entire body of social doctrine, by way of clarification and application, thereby shedding further light on the significance of subsidiarity and its relationship to the other principles comprised by this doctrine, including the common good, social justice, and solidarity. Subsidiarity is not, as it is sometimes said to be, a free-standing principle, but one among several principles of a unified and developing body of doctrine. But what is this body of thought known as Catholic social doctrine, and of what does it consist?

---

[1] See Dickinson's (1927). Berman (1983, pp. 276–288).

[2] Schama (1989, p. 906).

[3] Weber (1981).

[4] Pope Pius XI (1931a). See also Pontifical Council for Justice and Peace (2004).

The Church's social doctrine, Pope John Paul II (r. 1978–2004) explained, "belongs to the field, not of *ideology*, but of *theology* and particularly of moral theology."[5] Catholic social doctrine is, the Pope continued:

> the *accurate formulation* of the results of a careful reflection on the complex realities of human existence, in society and in the international order, in the light of faith and of the Church's tradition. Its main aim is to *interpret* these realities, determining their conformity with or divergence from the lines of the Gospel teaching on man and his vocation, a vocation which is at once earthly and transcendent; its aim is thus to *guide* Christian behavior.[6]

The Church's social doctrine "finds its essential foundation in biblical revelation and the tradition of the Church,"[7] and it also makes use of philosophy, for, as the *Compendium of the Social Doctrine of the Church* (2004) explains, "[b]y means of reason, the Church's social doctrine espouses philosophy in its own internal logic.... It is philosophy.... that shows the reasonableness and acceptability of shining the light of the Gospel on society...."[8] In addition to philosophy, the Church's social doctrine is informed by the human sciences and the social sciences, because while the principles of the social order are natural and therefore unchanging, social realities "change over time with social developments."[9] Social changes call for the fresh application – and indeed sometimes the discovery or re-discovery – of permanently valid principles, always under the authoritative guidance of divine revelation.[10] When he named the principle of subsidiarity in *Quadregesimo Anno* and described it as a "most weighty" ("*gravissimum*") principle, Pius also acknowledged it as "fixed and unshakable" ("*fixum ... immotumque*").[11] The Church proposes subsidiarity, then, not as a "policy" or a mere political preference, but instead as one among the unchangeable ontological principles of the socio-political order.

3.2 A Modern Science of Society and Politics

The *Compendium* introduces subsidiarity by stating that the principle "is among the most constant and characteristic directives of the Church's social doctrine and has been present since the first great social encyclical," a reference to Leo XIII's *Rerum Novarum* (1891), the fortieth anniversary of which Pius XI celebrated in *Quadragesimo Anno*. While *Rerum Novarum* did indeed contain the rudiments of the conceptual structure of subsidiarity,[12] it would take until *Quadragesimo Anno*,

[5] Pope John Paul II (1987, emphasis original).

[6] Id. (emphasis original).

[7] Compendium, supra note 4, at No. 74 (emphasis omitted).

[8] Compendium, supra note 4, at No. 77.

[9] Pope Pius XII quoted in Hittinger (2008). Note 5.

[10] Compendium, supra note 4, at No. 85 (emphasis omitted).

[11] Id. at No. 79.

[12] Pope Leo XIII (1891).

the subtitle of which is "On the Restoration of the Social Order and Perfecting It Conformably to the Precepts of the Gospel," for the term to enter the lexicon of Catholic social doctrine.[13] Or, more precisely, what entered there was the phrase "*servato hoc 'subsidiarii' officii principio*," which means "in observance of the principle of 'subsidiary' function." The Latin work *subsidium*, the focal meaning of which is "help," had been attested since Roman times.[14] Pius's *subsidiarium* was a neologism.[15] The pope does not identify the source of the linguistic *novum* his text sets off in quotation marks, but we know from external evidence that it represents the Latinisation of an earlier Italian neologism by Luigi Taparelli D'Azeglio, the Jesuit whose thought Pius XI recommended by name, quite remarkably, in his encyclical *Divini Ilius*, promulgated in 1929, just 2 years before the promulgation of *Quadragesimo Anno*.[16]

A crucial link in the genealogy of the emergence of the principle of subsidiarity is Taparelli's experience of a "conversion," in 1825, to Thomism, the philosophical theology of St. Thomas Aquinas (1225–1274).[17] By virtue of this conversion, Taparelli became an instigator of a paradigm-shifting intellectual movement. Specifically, Taparelli was in the vanguard of Catholics who re-learned the learning of St. Thomas which had been mostly lost, except in the caricatured form in which it was ridiculed by the protagonists of Enlightenment philosophy, since the early seventeenth century. Taparelli taught as professor in the recently re-founded Jesuit seminary in Rome, where, as providence would have it, Gioacchino Vincenzo Pecci was his student. Half a century later, Pecci, now as Pope Leo XIII, would inaugurate his pontificate by publishing the programmatic encyclical *Aeterni Patris* (1878) calling for the recovery, development, and application of Thomism throughout the Church.

Modern political theory has tended to hold, in one way or another, that "[w]e do not know what man is."[18] Taparelli grasped, in particular, "that the post-Cartesian abandonment of the hylomorphism of Aristotle and Aquinas came at a steep cultural and political price. Unlike the natural sciences, where differences of opinion, Taparelli analogised, have no effect on the actual course of nature, mistaken

---

[13] It is telling that the widely respected *Catholic Encyclopedia* published in 1917 does not so much as contain an entry for subsidiarity (though it does include one for suburbicarian dioceses), but the *New Catholic Encyclopedia* (second edition 2003) does devote an entry, of not quite three pages, to the term.

[14] On the history of the usage of "subsidium" in ancient times, see Lewis and Short, *A Latin Dictionary*, 1781. On its usage during the Middle Ages, see DuCange et al. (1883–1887).

[15] On earlier uses of the neologism, see Leys (1995, pp. 75–78).

[16] Specifically, he recommends Taparelli's textbook *Saggio teoretico di Diritto Naturale* (*A Theoretical Treatise on Natural Right, Based on Fact*) (1840–1843), "a work never sufficiently praised and recommended to university students." No. 50 n.33. *Saggio* has not been translated into English, and very little has been written about Taparelli in English. On the various influences behind *Quadragesimo Anno*, we have the detailed first-hand report of the leading ghostwriter, von Nell-Breuning (1986).

[17] Behr (2003, p. 100). See also Behr (2000).

[18] Manent (1998, p. 124).

metaphysical assumptions have a direct bearing on the direction of individual wills and lead to disorder in society."[19] Taparelli's textbook, *Saggio teoretico di difitto naturale appoggiato sul fatto, Theoretical Treatise on Natural Right Based on Fact*, the study commended by Pius XI, manifested "[h]is thoroughly Thomistic intention ... to merge a deductive theoretical approach with an inductive historico-sociological approach in a dialectical method that would form the basis of a modern science of society and politics."[20] Taparelli believed that he had found in Thomas an empirical method that could discover universal laws of nature in constellations of individual facts, and it was on the basis of those universal laws, one of which is the principle of subsidiarity, that Taparelli insisted that the post-revolutionary socio-political order must be structured.

Taparelli carried on this work of recovery and development not only as a seminary professor but also as a leading contributor to the *La Civilta Cattolica.* That influential journal, co-founded by Taparelli and another Jesuit, represented nothing less than a wholesale movement to realise what the journal's name means, Catholic civilization. Catholic counter-revolutionaries had not been wanting since 1790, of course, but it took the revolutions that convulsed most of Europe in 1848 for a systematic presentation of the Catholic position to emerge, and emerge it did on the pages of *La Civilta Cattolica* starting in 1850, thanks to the endorsement of (including loans from) Pius IX. The contributors to *La Civilta* have been accused of "intransigence."[21] The charge is true if it be understood as confirming the *Civilta*'s confidence in the certainty of its counter-revolutionary position. "[T]he Roman journal believed that respect for the authority of the Word in the Church was itself historically responsible for building confidence in the value of Reason in the first place,"[22] and this very confidence is the context in which to single out "Taparelli's openness to new ideas."[23] The concept neologised as "*subsidiarium*" was just that, a new idea creatively culled from the depths of the Catholic philosophical and theological tradition that had roots in Greek philosophical speculation.

3.3 Subsidiarity Defined

Taparelli's socio-political philosophy is thick with fresh insights and corresponding neologisms, such as "Hypostatic Right," the novel title under which Taparelli gathers the natural and just relations among the countless and varied

[19] Behr, supra note 17, at p. 100.

[20] Behr, supra note 17, pp. 102–03.

[21] Rao (1999, pp. 32–33).

[22] Rao (2011, p. 475).

[23] Rao, Removing, supra note 21, at p. 34. W.E. von Ketteler (1811–1877), Bishop of Mainz, also converged on the social principle that would later be called subsidiarity. Rather than from a neo-scholastic analysis, von Ketteler reached the principle through a combination of Romantic and liberal thought. See Leys, Impacts, supra note 15, at pp. 25–40.

associations that humans tend to form. Both words carry freight. First, "right" is, of course, a jurisprudential commonplace of ancient vintage, and easily given a familiar meaning that would obscure Taparelli's insight. The modern mind must resist, as Taparelli did, the philosophical prejudice according to which only individual rational substances, *but not groups or societies*, are the subject of right and of rights. Subsidiarity is a principle of "group right" and, derivatively, of "group rights," but, as we are about to see, in a far subtler structure than is commonly heard today. Second, then, Taparelli's Italian neologism *ipotattico*, of which the English hypostatic is a transliteration, is a borrowing from the Greek word *hypotaxis*, which refers to the rules of grammar that govern the modalities of coordination among clauses and, specifically, the arrangement of subordinate clauses within the structure of a grammatically complex sentence. The concept of *hypotaxis*, as Thomas Behr has observed, was the starting point for "an excellent extension into the neologism *dritto ipotattico* to convey the rights of social groupings, within their just relationships, organized toward the common good."[24] Behr goes on to explain that "the Greek *hypo taxis* can be rendered directly in Latin as *sub sedeo* [to sit below]. The Latin expression *subsidia* applied, then, not just to mean help but in the first instance to auxiliary troops within the Roman legion, as they 'sat below' ready in reserve to support the battle."[25] Taparelli's critical insight was that all societies, other than the most basic ones such as family or simple partnerships, are always composed of other societies, and there exist social rules governing the relations among such nested and overlapping societies.

Specifically, subjacent societies are to provide "help" *from the bottom up*, each by performing its own proper ("*proprium*") work and by referring the fruits of thereof to the larger and more perfect societies – including the *societas perfecta* that is the state – in the achievement of their respective common goods.[26] We can say, then, that "the point of subsidiarity is a normative structure of plural social forms, not a trickling down of power or aid."[27] It is important to emphasise this point, because subsidiarity is often but erroneously described as a matter of devolution or smallness of scale. In Taparelli's thought, however, and, in turn, in Catholic social doctrine, it is neither. *Pace* much modern political theory, power is not all held at the top in the first place, so the possibility that subsidiarity is a devolution norm turns out to be based on a fallacious premise; smallness, furthermore, is not *per se* good (or bad). The principle of subsidiarity recognises, instead, "that there are plural authorities and agents having their 'proper' (not necessarily, lowest) duties and rights with regard to the common good."[28]

---

[24] Behr, supra note 17, at p. 105.

[25] Behr, supra note 17, at p. 105.

[26] Behr, supra note 17, at pp. 104–05.

[27] Hittinger (2006, p. 23).

[28] Hittinger, Introduction, supra note 27, at p. 23.

It is against this background that we can at last approach Pope Pius XI's articulation of the principle of subsidiary function in *Quadragesimo Anno*:

> 79. As history abundantly proves, it is true that on account of changed conditions many things which were done by small associations in former times cannot be done now save by large associations. Still, that most weighty principle, which cannot be set aside or changed, remains fixed and unshaken in social philosophy: Just as it is gravely wrong to take from individuals what they can accomplish by their own initiative and industry and give it to the community, so also it is an injustice and at the same time a grave evil and disturbance of right order to assign to a greater and higher association what lesser and subordinate organizations can do. For every social activity ought of its very nature to furnish help to the members of the body social, and never destroy and absorb them.
>
> 80. The supreme authority of the State ought, therefore, to let subordinate groups handle matters and concerns of lesser importance, which would otherwise dissipate its efforts greatly. Thereby the State will more freely, powerfully, and effectively do all those things that belong to it alone because it alone can do them: directing, watching, urging, restraining, as occasion requires and necessity demands. Therefore, those in power should be sure that the more perfectly a graduated order is kept among the various associations, in observance of the principle of "subsidiary function," the stronger social authority and effectiveness will be the happier and more prosperous the condition of the State.[29]

As stated in *Quadragesimo Anno*, then, the principle of subsidiarity enjoys both positive and negative aspects. Negatively, it is a principle of non-absorption of lower societies by higher societies, above all by the state. This is the aspect of subsidiarity that is commonly invoked today, but it represents only half the story. Positively, subsidiarity is also the principle that when aid is given to a particular society, including by the state, it be for the purpose of encouraging and strengthening that society; correlatively, flourishing societies contribute to the flourishing of the greater societies of which they are so many irreducible parts.

In sum, "[e]very social activity," Pope Pius XII (r. 1939–1958) explained, "is for its nature subsidiarity; it must serve as a support to the members of the social body and never destroy or absorb them."[30] It bears emphasis that the libertarian misinterpretation of subsidiarity, which reduces the principle to little more than its non-absorption aspect, is falsified by the popes' repeated insistence that the state has a right, and sometimes a duty, to intervene, as Pope John XXIII (r. 1958–1963) made unmistakable in the encyclical *Mater et Magistra* (1961): "in [its] work of directing, stimulating, co-ordinating, supplying and integrating, [the state's] guiding principle must be the 'principle of subsidiary function' formulated by Pius XI in *Quadragesimo Anno*."[31]

The full significance of the principle of subsidiarity comes into focus if we attend to why it took until *Quadragesimo Anno* for the Church definitively to articulate so basic a principle. Until the Revolution of 1789, the Church lived by this as-yet-unnamed principle – and flourished thanks to its countless manifestations – without

---

[29] Pope Pius XI (1931b).

[30] Pope Pius XII, La elevatezza e la nobilita (February 20, 1946), quoted in Hittinger, Introduction, supra note 27, at p. 23 n. 63.

[31] Pope John XXIII (1961). See also Pope John Paul II (1991). See also Calvez and Perrin (1961, pp. 328–337).

being made to feel self-conscious about it. It was perfectly congenial to the Church to manifest her nature as the Mystical Body of Christ in the world through the diverse and irreducible operations of her many social members or organs. The Dominicans did work that was different from the Carthusians' work. (We will have more to say about these two Orders' respective works below). Likewise, no one was tempted to fold Christian Brothers' schools into Benedictines'. Similarly, the Sovereign Military Hospitaller Order of Saint John of Jerusalem of Rhodes and of Malta (Knights of Malta) was not at risk of being suppressed or dissolved into Equestrian Order of the Holy Sepluchre of Jerusalem. All of the just-mentioned associations, along with many more, survive to this day in the life of the Church, and each continues to refer the gift of its unique service to the common good.

Such associations, however, represent exactly what the architects of the modern monolithic nation state wished to eclipse, elide, and eliminate, as circumstances and force would permit. This idea of the all-encompassing Leviathan state that began with Hobbes assumed the following form in the French *Declaration of the Rights of Man* (1789): "The principle of all sovereignty resides essentially in the nation. No body nor individual may exercise any authority which does not proceed directly from the nation."[32] It was this idea that took coercive juridical force, 2 years later, when the French state passed a law de-creating corporations:

> Since the abolition of all kinds of corporations of citizens of the same occupation and profession is one of the fundamental bases of the French Constitution, re-establishment thereof under any pretext or pretence or form whatsoever is forbidden.' (sec. 1) 'Citizens of the same occupation or profession … may not, when they are together, name either president, secretaries, or trustees, keep accounts, pass decrees of resolution, or draft regulations concerning their alleged common interests. (sec. 2)[33]

At a legislative stroke, then, the plurality of society was reduced, as least aspirationally, to the unity of the state through the elimination of the countless and varied societies that previously were nested within political society. The Church knew all along what was wrong about this, but it took time for the Church to articulate, thanks to the insights of Taparelli and others, the principle of "subsidiary function" as the name for the reason to condemn the summary execution of societies.

3.4 Social Functions and Social Justice

Commentators who treat subsidiarity as a matter of devolution or simple smallness of scale overlook the deep ontological springs of the principle. The principle of subsidiarity does not purport to *create* a social ontology. Instead, the principle of subsidiarity *recognises*, and thus honors, the ontological facts about how individuals associate for the performance of unique functions which are so many irreducible contributions to the common good. It *recognises*, specifically, that not just individuals have functions to perform, but so too groups. At the same time as he was articulating

[32] Stewart (1951, p. 114).

[33] Chapelier Law, 14 June 1791. Stewart, supra 32, at p. 165.

and applying the principle of subsidiarity, Pope Pius XI was also developing the complementary doctrine of social "*munera*," and the pope's creative extension of this sacral language into the socio-political realm helps to show the true significance and ontological substrate of the principle of subsidiarity function.

Munera is the plural of the Latin noun *munus*. Serviceably translated as "function," *munus* also denotes gift-giving: the Magi offered *munera* to the Christ child. The key insight is that the performance of social functions constitutes the giving of gifts for the common good. Such functions are *assigned*, explicitly or implicitly, either by nature, as in the state and the family, or by supernature (and nature), as in the Carthusians and the Sovereign Military Order of Malta. The performance of these functions is, moreover, what Pius XI meant by "social justice," another new concept in the development of Catholic social doctrine.[34] As Russell Hittinger explains, "for Pius XI, social justice is nothing other than the manifold organicity of the common good; or, to put it another way, it is the demand that the common good be brought about through organizations, institutions, and groups."[35] In Pius's own words, social justice is realised when "each individual member is given what it needs for the exercise of its proper function … all that is necessary for the exercise of his social *munus*."[36] Subsidiarity, then, is a principle *derivative* of social justice, according to which each member of society is capacitated to perform its social role for the common good.[37]

An example of what Pius XI meant by the performance of a social *munus* may be helpful, and we can do no better than to attend to what that pope said about the aforementioned Carthusians, founded in the south of France in 1084 by St. Bruno of Cologne. The case of the Carthusians, the Church's most contemplatively-focused monastic order, is especially instructive, for the revolutionaries nursed a special hatred of the contemplative orders, for their purportedly passive presence in the social order silently denied the exigency and sufficiency of "liberty, equality, and fraternity," in favour of the social Kingship of Christ and His demand for social worship. So, already in 1790 the self-laicized French state enacted the Decree Suppressing Monastic Vows, which began with this: "The constitutional law of the kingdom shall no longer recognize solemn monastic vows of persons of either sex. Consequently, the regular orders and congregations in which such vows have been made are and shall remain suppressed in France, and no similar ones may be established in the future. All individuals of either sex living in monasteries and religious houses may leave them…."[38]

Following a century of vicissitudes of Catholic resistance and more than ample pushback by the successive Republics, the government raised the stakes still further by enacting the Law of Associations (1901), which provides (in part) as follows: "No religious congregation may be formed without an authorization given by a law

---

[34] Shields (1941, pp. 26–73).

[35] Hittinger (2002, p. 393).

[36] The larger context includes distinguishing "social justice" from the more familiar concept of commutative justice. See Pope Pius XI (1937).

[37] Hittinger, Pluralism, supra note 35, p. 394.

[38] MacLear (1995, p. 77).

which shall determine the conditions of its operation. No congregation may establish any new foundation except by virtue of a decree of the Council of State. The dissolution of a congregation or the closing of any establishment may be declared by a cabinet decree."[39] Few of the required "authorizations" were granted. The Law, which provided for the "liquidation" of religious orders' property, was executed with special ferocity against the Carthusians,[40] as the *New York Times* reported on March 27, 1903.[41] The soldiers came at three o'clock in the morning, while the community was gathered to sing the Divine Office in church, and arrested the monks one at a time. Without the monks' having enjoyed so much as a proper hearing, the community was dispersed, its property liquidated, and its common life of prayer succeeded by men driven into *diaspora*. As Matthew Arnold wrote of the affair and its consequences: No longer "[w]ith penitential cries they kneel/And wrestle; rising then, with bare/And white uplifted faces stand,/Passing the Host from hand to hand."[42]

The dissipation of the Carthusians' irreducibly social *munus*, captured so exquisitely but painfully by Arnold, would have been very much on the mind of Pope Pius XI when, in 1924, he approved the Carthusians' revised statutes in the extraordinary form of an Apostolic Constitution that included a lengthy encomium to their shared way of life, of which the following is indicative:

> According to his great kindness, God, who is ever attentive to the needs and well-being of his Church, chose BRUNO, a man of eminent sanctity, for the work of bringing the contemplative life back to the glory of its original integrity. To that intent Bruno founded the Carthusian Order, imbued it with his own spirit and provided it with those laws which might efficaciously induce its members to advance speedily along the way of inward sanctity and of the most rigorous penance, to the preclusion of every sort of exterior ministry and office: laws which would also impel them to persevere with steadfast hearts in the same austere and hard life.[43]

Pius goes on to make unmistakable that the heart of the matter is the capacity of each group to perform its own particular work, in this case contemplation, and to refer its effects to the common good. Writing a year later, in the encyclical *Rerum Ecclesiae*, Pius explained the reason for his unusual commendation of the Carthusians' unique gift to the work of the Church, and went on to generalise the point with reference to the work of a Trappist Cistercian monastery of contemplatives, some one hundred in number, in what was then called Peking: "It is, therefore, not to be questioned that these hermits, while they guard intact the spirit of their holy Founder and therefore do not engage in an active life, nevertheless they prove themselves of great *assistance in the successful work of the missions*."[44]

---

[39] MacLear, supra note 38, at pp. 294–95.

[40] Brennan (2009, pp. 30–33).

[41] Quoted in Brennan, supra note 40.

[42] Quoted in Brennan, supra note 40.

[43] Pope Pius XI (1924).

[44] Pope Pius XI (1926, emphasis added). Pius certainly did not imply that the Carthusians' or Trappists' only function and gift were the ones he emphasised.

The Carthusians continue to flourish throughout the world to this day, but in the monastery founded by St. Bruno before France as we know it even existed, they live now as tenants of the French government. The Law of Associations of 1901 has not been repealed. The conditions of "passing the Host from hand to hand" remain vulnerable to legislative violence in violation of the non-absorption aspect of the principle of subsidiarity, and this is but one among countless possible examples of why the Church was compelled to resist the revolutionaries' push to dissolve the organs of the Church into the heap of civil society.

3.5 The Common Good Served by Plural Authorities

Taparelli's new idea recognised by Pius XI as a "fixed and unshakable" principle of the social order soon made its way into the leading mid-twentieth century studies of Catholic thought on the socio-political order, and attention to some aspects of those expositions will illuminate facets of subsidiarity sometimes left underdeveloped at the level of magisterial exposition. The distinguished Georgetown political scientist Heinrich Rommen (1897–1967), glossing the relevant language of *Quadragesimo Anno*, explains that "the principle of subsidiarity applies … to the different natural or freely created communities in the social order. Social life is governed by the principles of autonomy, of hierarchy and intervention." With respect to the third principle, intervention, Rommen stresses that "[t]he purpose of this intervention is the reconstruction of the order, the rehabilitation of the function, not the abolition of the part or the substitution of the state for the lower society."[45] Subsidiarity cannot, therefore, be understood as a principle militating in favour of smallness of scale *per se*.[46]

Rather, subsidiarity is an ontological principle of competencies or, to return to Pius XI's complementary insight, *munera*. The principle derives its ontological traction, so to speak, from the fact that subsidiary function is an aspect of the common good, as the distinguished Austrian theologian and social theorist Johannes Messner (1891–1984) explains:

> The principle of subsidiary function … means that the common good does not establish for society any right or authority over what the individual person or the member society can do by his own power. We say that "the common good" establishes no right for society beyond this limit, in order to emphasise the fact that every right to social activity is founded on the common good, the end of society, and that hence the subsidiary principle is inherent in the nature of the common good. Basically, therefore, the common good principle and the subsidiary principle are one. …The common good confers powers and at the same time limits

[45] Rommen (1947, pp. 302, 303).

[46] Johannes Messner is in accord: "The reality of the common good, therefore, is impaired insofar as it is pursued by means of a diminution of the spheres of responsibility and of competence belonging to the members of society.… Here, then, is the fundamental task of social reform today: to reform society with a view to the organization of strong autonomous bodies, both regional and occupational.…" Messner (1965, pp. 210, 214).

> them: it empowers them to do everything necessary for its actual realization, but *only* that. The common good principle and the principle of subsidiary function are two sides of one and the same thing. Thus it was that *Pius XI*, when he coined the term "subsidiary function," called it the "fundamental principle of social philosophy,"... while Leo described the common good principle as "after God, the first and last law in society."

As Pius XI elaborated in the doctrine of social *munera*, the principle of subsidiarity function is a concrete principle, not merely a formal principle. It has content, not just form: it "declares a quite definite distribution of competencies based on the order of being and of ends."[47] Although subsidiarity does not create a social ontology, it discerns and announces the one ordained by the common good.

The functions and competencies of morally upright associations exemplify genuine authority, that is, the right of dominion and command within their respective spheres. It is these genuine authorities, of course, that Leviathan in all of its successive instantiations wished to vaporize, and the principle of subsidiary function responds by observing that the vigor and vitality of such authorities are required by the common good. To that end, Messner notes, such societies are to engage in "[a]s much self-help as possible"[48] to promote and sustain their respective competencies, for (it bears repeating) "the Latin word *subsidiarius*, although it derives from *subsidium*, does not connote help pure and simple in its fundamental military sense, but rather in the sense of 'reserve,' a word used of those forces which were to provide help when the frontline troops failed."[49] Right and authority are preceded by social obligation.

An important but sometimes unwelcome(d) consequence of subsidiarity's being the inverse of which the obverse is the common good follows: the application of the principle of subsidiarity always depends on the particulars of the given situation. Those who look for the certainty of geometry in practical science will be frustrated by the fact, observed by Messner, that "the *range* of its authority widens or contracts according to the energy and will of the individual members of society to undertake responsibility in looking after their rights."[50] Messner is quick to add, though, that (1) the burden of proof that an extension of authority is on the society seeking the extension and (2) any intervention and subvention are to be arranged "to make them superfluous as quickly as possible."[51] Like other forms of justice, social justice – from which, as we have seen, the principle of subsidiarity is derivative – will never take perfect shape in this fallen world. The more the work of a particular state can be accomplished through the competencies and authorities of the many and varied societies that are nested within that state, however, the richer that particular state's socio-political order. States that are frequently obliged to intervene to rescue societies that lack the vigor necessary to fulfill their functions will soon be sapped of their

[47] Id. at p. 210.

[48] Id. at p. 213.

[49] Id. at p. 212.

[50] Id. at p. 214.

[51] Id. at p. 215.

own strength or, in the alternative, become totalitarian as they succumb to the temptation to intervene not to restore but, instead, to colonize.

I have emphasised that the principle of subsidiarity function is a principle of social *pluralism*, and, in fact, Jacques Maritain (1882–1973), perhaps the most influential neo-Thomist of the twentieth century, eschewed the term subsidiarity in favour of "pluralism," "the pluralist principle," and the like. "As opposed to the various totalitarian conceptions of society in vogue today," Maritain wrote in 1935, "the conception here is of a pluralist body politic bringing together in its organic unity a diversity of social groupings and structures, each of them embodying positive liberties."[52] Maritain then went on to quote the sentence of *Quadragesimo Anno* that calls attention to the "injustice" and "grave evil" of withdrawing from groups the functions that they themselves can perform, and concluded as follows: "Civil society is made up not only of individuals, but of particular societies formed by them, and a pluralist body politic would allow to these societies the greatest autonomy possible and would diversify its own internal structure in keeping with what is typically required by their nature."[53] Maritain's preference for "pluralism" rather than subsidiarity highlights an important but often overlooked aspect of the doctrine, but it also invites a misunderstanding. In contemporary political theory, "pluralism" is typically commended either as a way of checking power with other power or, instead, as an acknowledgment of socio-ethical diversity. Maritain, however, understands groups as first of all occasions and opportunities for positive liberties, and these are not all created equal, let alone created for the purpose of producing a "thermodynamics of power"[54]: "The pluralist city multiplies liberties; the measure of these is not uniform, and varies according to a principle of proportionality."[55] The reason for respecting morally upright groups is that they exercise irreducible social functions, some more important than others.[56] A collateral benefit of such plural authorities is that they can, perhaps, thwart totalitarianism, a point to which I return at the end.

3.6 Solidarity, Society, and the Common Good

First, however, we do well to emphasise exactly what the instrumentalist justification of social pluralism – power-checking-power – wholly overlooks: the intrinsic perfections that make society or association worth undertaking for its own sake. As Taparelli saw, the occlusion of the ontology of association is part and parcel of modernity's abandonment of the Aristotelico-Thomistic understanding of man as a

[52] Maritain (1935).

[53] Maritain, Integral, supra 52, at p. 256. See also Maritain (1951, pp. 11, 22, 23, 123, 150).

[54] Hittinger, Coherence, supra note 9, at p. 108.

[55] Maritain, Integral Humanism, supra note 52, at p. 261.

[56] Maritain, Integral Humanism, at pp. 267–68.

naturally social animal. Modern thought would have it that the human person is "social" only by accident or desperation, sometimes memorialised in a fiction called the "social contract." The truth and value of the principle of subsidiarity come into relief if we zero in on the fact that what it protects and preserves is the *intrinsic* and not merely instrumental value of associating. Catholic social doctrine frequently refers to this as "solidarity:"

> Solidarity highlights in a particular way the intrinsic social nature of the human person. … Solidarity must be seen above all in its value as a moral virtue that determines the order of institutions … Solidarity is also an authentic moral virtue … a firm and persevering determination to commit oneself to the common good. … Solidarity rises to the rank of fundamental social virtue since it places itself in the sphere of justice. It is a virtue directed *par excellence* to the common good….[57]

Solidarity is never just one thing, but rather the varied ensemble of firm dispositions that serve the common good by a unity of action for the ends of particular, upright societies.

In defending the value and integrity of the societies "formed in the bosom of the commonwealth," Leo XIII quoted Thomas's *Contra Impugnantes* (1256?), an occasional work usually titled in English "An Apology for the Religious Orders."[58] There, Thomas defended the new mendicant form of religious life against contemporary attack by conservatives who wished the Church to confine contemplatives to monasteries, rather than allow them to travel and teach as participants in the work of these recently founded orders, including the Dominicans to which Thomas himself belonged. Thomas defends the right of individuals to form such community on the ground that to associate is already to "communicate," which, in turn, is to make gifts common, as reflected by the fact that the etymology of "communicate" is *co-* plus *munus*. As Hittinger explains:

> Although *societas* is an analogous term, every society, [Thomas] argues, is constituted by "communications" whereby goods are given and received. In Thomas's works, every analogous use of the word *societas* is mirrored by uses of the word *communicatio*: *communicatio oeconomica, communicatio spiritualis, communicatio civilis*, and so forth. The word *communicatio* simply means making something common, one rational agent participating in the life of another. Society, for Thomas, is not a thing, but an activity.[59]

Thomas's defense of the right to associate – in contravention, it should be noted, of settled norms of social class and vested privilege – rests on the arresting claim that "to prevent free men and women from associating for the purpose of communicating gifts is contrary to the natural law. It is tantamount," Hittinger continues, "to denying to rational agents the perfection proper to their nature, and denying to the commonweal goods it would not enjoy were it not for free associations."[60] It is tantamount, in other words, to denying humans the solidarity by which they, as social

---

[57] Compendium, supra note 4, at Nos. 192, 193 (emphasis and internal quotations omitted).

[58] *Rerum Novarum*, supra note 12, text at nn. 36 and 37.

[59] Hittinger (2003, p. 271).

[60] Hittinger, First grace, supra note 59, at p. 272.

beings, are perfected. The rationale of Thomas's defense of the freedom claimed by the mendicant Dominicans extends not only to Carthusians and all other ecclesial societies but also, in laicized form, to all groups in which good gifts are communicated, from the Boy Scouts, to The Salvation Army, the Benevolent and Protective Order of Elks, labor unions, and so forth.

The meaning of subsidiarity, solidarity, and the common good in Catholic social doctrine turns on what we mean by society. Thomas saw with perfect clarity that a society is neither a mere aggregate of individuals nor a mere partnership, but a *unity of order* that "does not just aim at a common objective, but intends to have it brought about by united action."[61] As Yves Simon observes, "[m]ere partnership does not do anything to put an end to the solitude of the partners,"[62] but in a true society, by contrast, corporate unity is one of the reasons for action. Someone leaving a partnership can export his share; the common good of a society, however, cannot be divided, only shared and participated. Each participant in a society perfects himself and the other members of the society by communicating goods as gifts, and these are in turn help to higher societies.[63] "[W]e are made unto the image of God not only because the individual person possesses the excellence of a rational nature, but also because we must cause good in others."[64] When men and women aim to unite to do this, a society – a reality distinct in dignity – results, and this is what the principle of subsidiarity protects as a matter of social justice and the common good.

> Social justice is the virtue whereby all persons (not just the state) refer the ensemble of their relations to the common good. This is why subsidiarity is not merely an issue of commutation or distribution, but rather manifests itself in the arranging of things in such wise that the operations of a heterogeneous whole are harmonized with regard to the common good.[65]

Social justice and subsidiarity require that the sociality of society be preserved and harmonized, and no argument to benefits external to a particular society itself will prevail, unless there be moral reason to dissolve the society.

In sum, the principle of subsidiarity falsifies the proposition advanced by Rousseau and implemented by the revolutionaries: "It is of necessity that no partial society should exist in the state."[66] Quite the contrary, societies are the perfecting opportunities for naturally social beings to cause good in others, including through the supernatural assistance of grace. Pope John Paul II stressed this in *Centesimus annus* (1991),[67] his encyclical celebrating the hundredth anniversary

---

[61] Hittinger, Coherence, supra note 9, at p. 92.

[62] Simon (1993, p. 64).

[63] For a beautiful phenomenology of association, see Rao, Blindfold, supra note 21, at Ch. 2. Available via http://www.romanforum.org/wp-content/uploads/rem_02.pdf

[64] Hittinger, Coherence, supra note 9, at p. 86.

[65] Hittinger, Coherence, supra note 9, at p. 115.

[66] Jean-Jacques Rousseau, The Social Contract, Bk. II, Ch. 3.

[67] Pope John Paul II, *Centesimus Annus*, supra note 31, at Nos. 48–49.

of *Rerum Novarum*, and Pope Benedict XVI (r. 2004–2012) pursued the demands of subsidiary function in his first encyclical, *Deus Caritas Est* (2005):

> We do not need a State which regulates and controls everything, but a state which, in accordance with the principle of subsidiarity, generously acknowledges and supports initiatives arising from the difference social forces and combines spontaneity with closeness to those in need. The Church is one of those living forces: she is alive with the love enkindled by the Spirit of Christ. This love do not simply offer people material help, but refreshment and care for their souls….[68]

Subsidiarity is a principle to which Pope Benedict returned time and again as he addressed a world that ever threatened to pinion the lone individual against the Leviathan state: "When those responsible for the public good attune themselves to the natural human desire for self-governance based on subsidiarity, they leave space for individual responsibility and initiative, but most importantly, they leave space for *love* (cf. *Rom* 13:8; *Deus Caritas Est,* 28), which always remains 'the most excellent way' (cf. *1 Cor* 12:31)."[69]

3.7 Conclusion

The organic web of Christendom – structured and enlivened by the as-yet-unnamed principle of subsidiary function – was succeeded by nation-states that, acting out their pretensions to absolute sovereignty, eviscerated societies internal to themselves and to the Church, yet lacked, at the same stroke, any principle for coordinating global community. Taparelli addressed the former problem, as we have seen, but also the latter, each thanks to the principle of subsidiary function. With respect to the latter problem, Taparelli saw the inevitable trajectory of the then-emergent global community, and grasped, moreover, why, from the properly universalist perspective of Christianity, such development was in many respects desirable. He also foresaw, however, some of the untenable consequences of a world assembly of nation states shaped and ratified without benefit of the Church exercising her true social role.

The recent popes, including Benedict XVI, have emphasised subsidiarity's place in rightly ordering *global* community.[70] The *Catechism of the Catholic Church* (1991) affirms that place by way of crescendo: "The principle of subsidiarity is opposed to all forms of collectivism. It sets limits for state intervention. It aims at harmonizing the relationships between individuals and societies. It tends toward the establishment of true international order."[71] The outstanding

---

[68] Pope Benedict XVI (2005).

[69] http://www.vatican.va/holy_father/benedict_xvi/speeches/2008/may/documents/hf_ben-xvi_spe_20080503_social-sciences_en.html

[70] Pope Benedict XVI (2009).

[71] Catechism of the Catholic Church (1991).

question is why – or even *whether* – one can reasonably expect a political culture that denies man's intrinsic sociality and, furthermore, treats the Church on the model of the Boy Scouts, that is, as just another group, to structure itself according to the requirements of the common good. The pope who introduced subsidiarity into Catholic social doctrine also taught, as had his predecessors, that the social order cannot but fail if the divine right of the Church and of Christ the King be not recognised.[72] It is no insult to the Boy Scouts to observe that they cannot accomplish the work of the Church – Christ-continued in the world – for the benefit of all of political society, threatened as it is by totalitarianism, individualism, and relativism. Meanwhile, "[a]lthough the world knows it not, the most primordial law of ruling is service, which is always the signature of the divine. Not sovereignty as the moderns understand it, but rather a gift communicated for the good of another."[73]

References

Behr, Thomas. 2000. *Luigi Taparelli and the nineteenth-century neo-scholastic 'revolution' in natural law and catholic social sciences*. PhD dissertation, SUNY Buffalo.

Behr, Thomas C. 2003. Luigi Taparelli D'Azeglio, S.J. (1793–1862) and the development of scholastic natural-law thought as a science of society and politics. *Journal of Markets and Morality* 6: 99–115.

Berman, Harold J. 1983. *Law and revolution: The formation of the Western legal tradition.* Cambridge: Harvard University Press.

Brennan, Patrick McKinley. 2009. Differentiating church and state (without losing the church). *The Georgetown Journal of Law and Public Policy* 7: 29–49.

Calvez, J., and J. Perrin. 1961. *The Church and Social Justice: The Social Teachings of the Popes from Leo XIII to Pius XII.* Trans. J.R. Kirwan. Chicago: Henry Regnery Co.

Catechism of the Catholic Church. 1991. No. 1885. Available via http://www.vatican.va/archive/ENG0015/_INDEX.HTM

Dickinson, John. 1927. Introduction to John of Salisbury. In *The Statesman's Book of John of Salisbury*. Trans. J. Dickinson, xvii–lxxxii. New York: Alfred A. Knopf.

DuCange, et al. 1883–1887. *Glossarium mediae et infimae latinitatis*. Niort: L. Favre.

Hittinger, Russell. 2002. Social pluralism and subsidiarity in Catholic social doctrine. *Annales Theologici* 16: 385–408.

Hittinger, Russell. 2003. *The first grace: Rediscovering the natural law in a post-Christian world.* Wilmington: ISI.

Hittinger, Russell. 2006. Introduction to modern Catholicism. In *The teachings of modern Christianity on law, politics, & human nature*, ed. J. Witte and F. Alexander, 3–38. New York: Columbia University Press.

Hittinger, Russell. 2008. *The coherence of the four basic principles of Catholic social doctrine: An interpretation*. Available via http://www.pass.va/content/dam/scienzesociali/pdf/actapass14.pdf

John Paul II. 1991. Encyclical letter *Centesimus annus*. No 48. Available via http://www.vatican.va/holy_father/john_paul_ii/encyclicals/documents/hf_jp-ii_enc_01051991_centesimus-annus_en.html

[72] Pope Pius XI (1922).

[73] Hittinger, Pluralism, supra note 35, at p. 401.

Leys, Ad. 1995. *Ecclesiological impacts of the principle of subsidiarity*. Kampen: Uitgeverij Kok.
MacLear, J.F. (ed.). 1995. *Church and state in the modern age*. Oxford: New York.
Manent, Pierre. 1998. *The City of Man*. Trans. Marc A. LePain. Princeton: Princeton University Press.
Maritain, J. 1935. Integral humanism. In *Integral humanism, Freedom in the modern world, and a letter on independence,* The collected works of Jacques Maritain, 1996, vol. 11, ed. O. Bird, 256. South Bend: University of Notre Dame Press.
Maritain, J. 1951. *Man and the state*. Chicago: University of Chicago Press.
Messner, Johannes. 1965. *Social Ethics in the Natural Law Tradition*. Trans. J.J. Doherty. St. Louis: Herder.
Pontifical Council for Justice and Peace. 2004. *Compendium of the social doctrine of the Church*. Rome: Libreria Editrice Vaticana. No. 87. Available via http://www.vatican.va/roman_curia/pontifical_councils/justpeace/documents/rc_pc_justpeace_doc_20060526_compendio-dott-soc_en.html
Pope Benedict XVI. 2005. Encyclical letter *Deus caritas est*. No. 28b. Available via http://www.vatican.va/holy_father/benedict_xvi/encyclicals/documents/hf_ben-xvi_enc_20051225_deus-caritas-est_en.html
Pope Benedict XVI. 2009. Encyclical letter *Caritas in veritate* Nos. 57–58. Available via http://www.vatican.va/holy_father/benedict_xvi/encyclicals/documents/hf_ben-xvi_enc_20090629_caritas-in-veritate_en.html
Pope John XXIII. 1961. Encyclical letter *Mater et Magistra* No. 53. Available via http://www.vatican.va/holy_father/john_xxiii/encyclicals/documents/hf_j-xxiii_enc_15051961_mater_en.html
Pope John Paul II. 1987. Encyclcial letter *Solicitudo rei socialis* No. 41. Available via http://www.vatican.va/holy_father/john_paul_ii/encyclicals/documents/hf_jp-ii_enc_30121987_sollicitudo-rei-socialis_en.html
Pope Leo XIII. 1891. Encyclical letter *Rerum Novarum*. Nos. 29, 36. Available via http://www.vatican.va/holy_father/leo_xiii/encyclicals/documents/hf_l-xiii_enc_15051891_rerum-novarum_en.html
Pope Pius XI, 1922. Encyclical letter *Ubi Arcano* Nos. 32–49. Available via http://www.vatican.va/holy_father/pius_xi/encyclicals/documents/hf_p-xi_enc_19221223_ubi-arcano-dei-consilio_en.html
Pope Pius XI. 1924. Apostolic constitution *Umbratilem*. Available via http://www.vatican.va/holy_father/pius_xi/apost_constitutions/documents/hf_p-xi_apc_19240708_umbratilem_lt.html
Pope Pius XI. 1926. Encyclical letter *Rerum Ecclesiae*. Available via http://www.vatican.va/holy_father/pius_xi/encyclicals/documents/hf_p-xi_enc_28021926_rerum-ecclesiae_en.html
Pope Pius XI. 1931a. Encyclical letter *Quadragesimo Anno* Nos. 18–21. Available via http://www.vatican.va/holy_father/pius_xi/encyclicals/documents/hf_p-xi_enc_19310515_quadragesimo-anno_en.html
Pope Pius XI. 1931b. Encyclical letter *Quadragesimo Anno*. Nos. 79–80. Available via http://www.vatican.va/holy_father/pius_xi/encyclicals/documents/hf_p-xi_enc_19310515_quadragesimo-anno_en.html
Pope Pius XI. 1937. Encyclical letter *Divini Redemptoris*. No. 51. Available via http://www.vatican.va/holy_father/pius_xi/encyclicals/documents/hf_p-xi_enc_19031937_divini-redemptoris_en.html
Rao, John. 1999. *Removing the blindfold: Nineteenth-century Catholics & the myth of modern freedom*, Ch. 1. Available via http://www.romanforum.org/wp-content/uploads/rem_01.pdf
Rao, John. 2011. *Black legends and the light of the world*. Forest Lake: Remnant Press.
Rommen, Heinrich. 1947. *The state in Catholic social thought*. St. Louis: Herder.
Schama, Simon. 1989. *Citizens: A chronicle of the French revolution*. New York: Knopf.
Shields, Leo William. 1941. *The history and meaning of the term social justice*. Notre Dame: University of Notre Dame Press.
Simon, Yves. 1993. *Philosophy of democratic government*. Notre Dame: Notre Dame Press.

Stewart, John. 1951. *A documentary history of the French revolution*. New York: Macmillan.
von Nell-Breuning, Oswald. 1986. The drafting of Quadragesimo Anno. In *Readings in moral theology No. 5: Official Catholic social teaching*, ed. C. Curran and R. McCormick, 60–68. New York: Paulist Press.
Weber, Wilhelm. 1981. Society and state as a problem for the church. In *History of the church*, The church in the modern age, vol. 10, ed. H. Jedin, 229–259. New York: Crossroad.

Chapter 4
The Relationship Between Sphere Sovereignty and Subsidiarity

Lael Daniel Weinberger

Abstract Sphere sovereignty is a social theory based on theological principles. Its starting point is the absolute sovereignty of God. From this principle, sphere sovereignty denies that any single human institution can claim absolute sovereignty. As a result, sphere sovereignty principles support an institutionally pluralistic society, where all kinds of power and authority are divided among various "spheres." First propounded by Reformed theologians in the Netherlands, sphere sovereignty initially focused on the limitation of state power so as to preserve the independence of various social "spheres," especially the church, from the state. While sphere sovereignty is rightly opposed to improper consolidation of state power, it does affirm the place of civil government in the social order. The model of society affirmed by sphere sovereignty has certain resonances with the Catholic social teachings on subsidiarity. Some have argued that sphere sovereignty is fundamentally different from its Catholic counterpart. But it is more helpful to see sphere sovereignty and subsidiarity as complimentary, each recognising a distinct aspect of social relationships within healthy and well-functioning society.

Keywords Sphere sovereignty • Calvin • Kuyper • Groen • Dooyeweerd • Dutch reformed tradition • Dutch Calvinism • Pluralism • Catholic social teaching

4.1 Introduction

Sphere sovereignty and subsidiarity are two principles that share much in common. Both are social teachings based on Christian theology. Each belongs to the social pluralist tradition. They were first articulated at about the same time, at the end of

---

L.D. Weinberger (✉)
Department of History, University of Chicago, 1126 E.59th Street,
Chicago, Illinois 60637, United States of America
e-mail: laelweinberger@uchicago.edu

M. Evans and A. Zimmermann (eds.), *Global Perspectives on Subsidiarity*, Ius Gentium: Comparative Perspectives on Law and Justice 37, DOI 10.1007/978-94-017-8810-6_4,

the nineteenth century. They were both responses to the social and political upheaval experienced by Europe in the process of industrialisation. Both attempted to find a middle road between an overly-individualistic liberalism, on the one hand, and an excessively-collectivised socialism, on the other. But sphere sovereignty and subsidiarity also have their differences. They come from different theological traditions (Reformed versus Roman Catholic). They present different visions of the relationship between social spheres (horizontal versus hierarchical).

This chapter will proceed in three sections. Section 4.2 will outline the basic contours of sphere sovereignty as a theological, social, and political theory. Section 4.3 will compare a sphere-sovereignty understanding of the role of the state with subsidiarity's understanding of that role. How does sphere sovereignty fit with subsidiarity? Are the two principles compatible? Complementary? Or in competition? Finally, Sect. 4.4 will use a series of related, concrete court cases on church-state issues to illustrate the ways that sphere sovereignty can promote institutional pluralism when subsidiarity is less conclusive.

4.2 Sphere Sovereignty

4.2.1 A Short History

The intellectual roots of sphere sovereignty can be found in the biblical principles of the sovereignty of God, the diversity within God's creation, the sinfulness of man, and the distinct responsibilities of various human institutions. Caesar is not all-powerful; the family, the church, and the civil government all have God-ordained responsibilities. These themes were developed by a wide array of thinkers throughout church history, from Augustine's distinction between the "city of God" and the "city of man" to the political theories of the sixteenth century Reformation. The Reformed theology in the tradition of John Calvin was especially important in developing a theology that placed limits on state and church alike. Johannes Althusius, a sixteenth century Calvinist theologian, foreshadowed the later development of sphere sovereignty with a political theology that emphasised the importance of diverse jurisdictions in human society.[1]

The central chapter in the development of sphere sovereignty began in mid-nineteenth century Holland with the conservative politician, Guillaume Groen van Prinsterer (1801–1876). In the 1830s, Groen was in government service in charge of the royal archives when he experienced a personal spiritual awakening in an evangelical Pietist revival of the 1830s. Nineteenth century Pietism vacillated between a focus on inner spiritual life and devotion, on the one hand, and an interest in social engagement, on the other. In Groen's case, revitalised faith was no deterrent from an active political career, including long service in parliament. To the contrary, Groen

[1] Woldring (2000); Witte (2008); van der Vyver (2002).

became convinced that active Christian involvement in society was essential. In his lectures and writings, "Groen urge[d] fellow Christians to reread the Scriptures in order to understand the responsibility they have to shape the history of this world to the glory of God."[2]

Groen was a theological conservative but he was not a political reactionary. He hoped to see a new movement of socially-engaged Reformed Christians arise in the Netherlands. At the same time, Groen abhorred radicalism and did not want to foster a movement that would go to extremes. Groens' model was the Reformation; its antithesis was "Revolution." Revolution was the Reformation in reverse, he said.[3] For Groen, "Revolution" included a rejection of God, of authority, and of tradition. In "Reformation," though, Groen believed he could find a healthy middle course between status quo traditionalism on the one hand and anarchical radicalism on the other. Groen believed that society needed basic traditional institutions and infrastructure—most especially the church and the state—and that "Revolutionaries" were misguidedly trying to destroy these and start anew on a blank slate. In his lectures on revolution, Groen critiqued the secular philosophies that, in his view, were responsible for social chaos from the French Revolution on into his own time. He also attempted to articulate a Christian philosophy of social engagement. In this context, Groen used the phrase "sphere sovereignty" (in Dutch, *souvereiniteit in eigen sfeer*) to describe the distinct jurisdictions of the church and the state.

Groen's intellectual and political agenda was picked up by Abraham Kuyper (1837–1920), the central figure in the development of sphere sovereignty. Kuyper studied theology at the University of Leyden, where he showed great scholarly potential. While there, he was influenced by biblical higher criticism and modernist theology. After graduating, Kuyper arrived at his first church as liberal young minister. Rather than converting his congregation to modernism, Kuyper ended up being converted by his conservative, rural congregation to the orthodox Calvinist theology he had spurned as a student. At the time, the prospects for theological conservatism looked dim. By siding with orthodox Calvinism, Kuyper could expect to be relegated to the social and intellectual backwaters. But Kuyper instead began a remarkable career as a defender of theological conservatism.[4]

Kuyper made his first foray into public policy in the 1860s to urge, of all things, the distancing of the church from the state. This might appear to be a counterintuitive move from a politically-active theological conservative. In fact, though, it was entirely logical in light of Kuyper's conception of sphere sovereignty, which we shall examine more closely in the next section. It was also a sensible strategic move. The Dutch Reformed Church was closely tied to the secular, liberal state and Kuyper was convinced that the influence of the state favoured the advancement of modernism. Kuyper urged the orthodox to "liberate the church" from the control of the state. In 1868, Kuyper's activism brought him into direct conflict with the church's

[2] Skillen and McCarthy (1991, p. 54); see also van der Kroef (1948).

[3] Skillen and McCarthy (1991, p. 55); see also Kuyper (1998b, p. 212).

[4] Bratt (1998); van der Kroef (1948); de Bruijn (2000).

General Synod, which was most directly influenced by the state. The controversy reached a national audience and ultimately split the Dutch Reformed Church.[5]

Meanwhile, Kuyper was entering the mainstream political arena. In 1869, Kuyper met with Groen and became involved in the organisation that Groen led, the Christian Orthodox Anti-Revolutionary movement. Kuyper helped transform this loosely-constructed group into a well-organised political party, the Anti-Revolutionary Party (ARP). In 1874, Kuyper was elected to the Second Chamber of the Netherlands' parliament. It was a time of social change and political upheaval. At the time, the dominant Liberal Party was splitting into three factions, the Catholic-Liberal alliance had disintegrated 6 years earlier, and the Conservatives were "bankrupt." As James Bratt[6] noted, "Industrialization was forcing all parties to rethink their notions of individual rights, social well-being, and the government's obligations toward each." A socialist movement came into being and workers' associations and trade unions were formed.[7]

Kuyper skillfully navigated these turbulent waters, bringing the ARP into a position of considerable influence. He was in the Cabinet in the late 1880s and was prime minister from 1901 to 1905. He championed a variety of causes, ranging from the defense of religious education (which the Liberals were attempting to curtail) to the extension of the electoral franchise (towards universal male and female suffrage—accomplished in 1917 and 1919, respectively). After his time as prime minister, he continued to lead the ARP and to serve in government (in both lower and upper houses).

Though he would be in and out of elected office for the next several decades, Kuyper remained active in a variety of other fields. He was an elder at a large Reformed church in Amsterdam and continued to be involved in the struggle between modernists and conservatives in the church. He founded a daily newspaper, *The Standard*, in 1872. He served as its first editor and wrote editorials for it almost every day for the next 50 years. In 1880, Kuyper founded the Free University (Vrije Universiteit) of Amsterdam. It was "free" in the sense that it was entirely independent, controlled by neither state nor church—again reflecting Kuyper's understanding of sphere sovereignty principles. His speech at the dedication of the university was titled "sphere sovereignty" and is a paradigmatic statement of Kuyper's mature thought on the subject. The basic idea of sphere sovereignty, as Kuyper put it in this speech, is that God is absolutely sovereign, while authority among sinful human beings is divided between distinct spheres.

Kuyper was a brilliant thinker but not a systematic theorist. A generation after Kuyper, Herman Dooyeweerd (1894–1977) attempted to thoroughly develop sphere sovereignty in philosophical terms. Dooyeweerd studied law at the Free University, served a short stint in government service, and then returned to join

[5] van der Kroef (1948).

[6] 1998, pp. 11–12.

[7] Jellema (1957); von der Dunk (1978). Across Europe, similar conditions of unrest and upheaval provided the background to Leo XIII's groundbreaking social encyclical, Rerum Novarum. See, e.g., Murphy (1993), Van Til (2008).

the Law Faculty of his alma mater. In his long tenure at the Free University (1926–1965), he proved himself to be an innovative legal philosopher.[8]

Dooyeweerd spent much of his career developing sphere sovereignty as a sophisticated philosophical system. His magnum opus was a massive four volume treatise with the imposing title, *A New Critique of Theoretical Thought*.[9] In *New Critique*, he presented an elaborate ontology of "modal spheres" before going on to apply his version of sphere sovereignty to social and legal theory. Dooyeweerd's philosophical forays received some acclaim in his lifetime—Italian legal theorist Giorgio Del Vecchio went so far as to call Dooyeweerd the most innovative philosopher since Kant.[10] But to contemporary Anglophone legal philosophers, Dooyeweerd's complex system is obscure. Fortunately, the details of his complex ontological system are less important for us than the larger principles of sphere sovereignty in society, to which we now turn.

4.2.2 The Theology of Sphere Sovereignty

The theological heart of sphere sovereignty is the sovereignty of God. While a belief in the power and authority of God is common to all Christian traditions, it was (and is) particularly emphasised in the Reformed tradition (sometimes known as the "Calvinist" tradition). The sovereignty of God is certainly one of the central components of Calvin's theological system (though not the sole dominating principle, as is sometimes thought).[11]

For Kuyper, sphere sovereignty was the outworking of the basic theological principle of divine sovereignty. God is absolutely sovereign, the creator and ruler of all things. Moreover, God *alone* can claim absolute sovereignty. In Kuyper's words, "If you believe in Him as the Deviser and Creator, as Founder and Director of all things, your soul must also proclaim the Triune God as the only absolute Sovereign."[12] If God is absolutely sovereign, then man cannot be sovereign. Any attempt by another person or entity to claim total sovereignty would be usurpation and rebellion against God.

Yet, obviously, God does not usually exercise His sovereignty by direct rule over human affairs. Instead, God usually "delegates his authority to human beings," allowing authority to be exercised through "human office[s]."[13] But this authority is divided. No human or human institution has authority in every area. God has

[8] Skillen (2003); Witte (1993); Caudill (1997).

[9] Dooyeweerd (1969).

[10] Quoted in Witte (1986).

[11] Partee (1987, 2008).

[12] Kuyper (1998a, p. 466).

[13] Kuyper (1998a, p. 466).

ordained specific realms or spheres of authority on the earth. Divine sovereignty thus leads more or less directly to the idea that human sovereignty is exercised in distinct, independent, and limited spheres.

4.2.3 The Social Theory of Sphere Sovereignty

Starting from the idea of divine sovereignty, sphere sovereignty serves to limit human power-spheres. For Kuyper, the idea of sphere sovereignty was to society very much what the idea of "separation of powers" is to political theory. In American political theory, there is perhaps no more familiar structural concept than the idea that governmental powers should be divided among the "different departments" of government. In James Madison's famous formulation, the separation of powers is a precaution against the accumulation and abuse of power in any single part of the government. "If men were angels, no government would be necessary," Madison wrote in the Federalist Papers. "If angels were to govern men, neither external nor internal controls on government would be necessary. In framing a government which is to be administered by men over men, the great difficulty lies in this: you must first enable the government to control the governed; and in the next place oblige it to control itself."[14]

With the concept of sphere sovereignty, Kuyper in effect argued for the separation of powers, not primarily within government, but across the entire society:

> God established institutions of various kinds, and to each of these He awarded a certain measure of power. He thus divided the power that He had available for distribution. He did not give all his power to one single institution but gave to every one of these institutions the power that coincided with its nature and calling.[15]

This follows from Kuyper's reasoning about the sovereignty of God: "[The] perfect Sovereignty of the *sinless* Messiah at the same time directly denies and challenges all absolute Sovereignty among *sinful* men on earth, and does so by dividing life into *separate spheres*, each with its own sovereignty."[16]

The tendency to consolidate power in the state was of primary concern to Kuyper. He believed, as McIlroy put it, that "governmental cliques have a tendency to conduct themselves as though omnipotent."[17] Kuyper argued that non-Christian societies tended to consolidate sovereignty in a single institution and that the state was usually the institution to which power was ascribed. Whether or not they tried to push the exercise of authority to the outermost limits, most states would claim for themselves the sovereign right to rule and command without opposition, until "a

---

[14] Madison, Federalist 51.

[15] Quoted in Van der Vyver (2002, p. 214).

[16] Kuyper (1998a, p. 467) (emphasis in original). See also McIlroy (2003, p. 743).

[17] McIlroy (2003).

free organic life… finally collapses under the iron hand of Caesarism."[18] Sphere sovereignty put up a wall against the tendency of the state to subsume all of life under its authority.

But Kuyper was not only concerned about the expansion of the state. He was also opposed to the dominance of the church over areas of life outside its jurisdiction or competence. If Kuyper's opposition to an overly-close relationship between church and state appears counterintuitive, it is because too often contemporary debates about religion in public life use "church and state" as synonymous with "religion and the state" (or, even worse, "religion and public life"). This linguistic sloppiness would have been anathema to Kuyper. For Kuyper, the limits of the church were not coterminous with the authority of God and of the Christian faith. Every area of life, including every sphere of social life (church, state, family, business, university, to name a few), is under the authority of God (and His authority should be acknowledged as such). All of life is "religious" in the fundamental sense that it is based on the authority of God (or is in rebellion to it)[19] But not all of life is subject to the church, the institution that God ordained for a specific and limited set of roles.[20] The church's authority under God is for a set of distinct purposes. The church should never usurp the role of the state. Thus, for instance, the dominance of the medieval papacy over the civil government was an instance of the church improperly consolidating power. At the same time, of course, the state should not interfere in the affairs of the church. In other words, sphere sovereignty is committed to an institutional separation of church and state.

But Kuyper went even further, arguing that not only was the relationship of church and state an area requiring sharp distinctions, but so too was the area of education. The university that Kuyper helped to found was "free" from the control of church and state alike. Kuyper argued that education needed to be free from any entangling commitment to the agenda of either the church or the state. And Kuyper would often list other social institutions as independent spheres, suggesting that "the family, the business, science, art and so forth are all social spheres," that there was a "corporative sphere of universities, guilds, associations, etc.," and that "[n]either the life of science nor of art, nor of agriculture, nor of industry, nor of commerce, nor of navigation, nor of the family, nor of human relationship may be

[18] Kuyper (1998a, p. 469).

[19] In one of Kuyper's most frequently-quoted statements, he said, "[N]o single piece of our mental world is to be hermetically sealed off from the rest, and there is not a square inch in the whole domain of our human existence over which Christ, who is Sovereign over *all*, does not cry: 'Mine!'" (Kuyper 1998a, p. 488.) Dooyeweerd would later elaborate on this theme. For a recent restatement of a Dooyeweerdian argument against the possibility of religious neutrality, see Clouser (2005).

[20] Wolterstorff (2009, pp. 105–108). A standard Reformed statement listed three essential duties of a true church: (1) The preaching of the gospel, (2) the administration of the sacraments, and (3) the exercise of church discipline. Belgic Confession (1561).

coerced to suit itself to the grace of the government."[21] The lists are varied and the "spheres" named are often varied. So how many spheres are there?

Some of the ambiguities arise because sphere sovereignty has occasionally been expanded beyond its primary sense as a social theory. When Kuyper spoke and wrote about sphere sovereignty, he usually used sphere sovereignty as a way of talking about the social sphere. But Kuyper was fond of analogising social life to nature and describing it in organic terms. Organic metaphors abounded in nineteenth century writings advocating a social pluralist conception of society, including in discussions of Catholic social teaching.[22] In Kuyper's case, it sometimes seemed that he risked getting beyond his analogies and actually equating social spheres with the sphere of nature or the sphere of thought. In his 1880 speech setting out the idea of sphere sovereignty, Kuyper suggested that there was a unique internal logic for the "domain of nature," the "domain of the personal, of the household, of science, of social and ecclesiastical life, each of which obeys its own laws of life…." He also noted that there was a "realm of thought," ruled by the "laws of logic," a "realm of conscience," ruled by God, and a "realm of faith," ruled by the individual.[23] But for Kuyper, sphere sovereignty was *primarily* about human society and the social sphere.

Yet even when it came to human society, Kuyper was not at all systematic in articulating what counted as a distinct "sphere." He often mentioned the church, the state, and the family as separate and distinct spheres. This is hardly surprising, for each has an important place in the biblical narrative and they have together been of central concern to Christian social thought. But Kuyper ventured into more novel territory when he referred to education, business, and science, among other things, as distinct "spheres." Recent commentators—including proponents of sphere sovereignty—have noted that Kuyper is open to criticism for sometimes seeming to place unlike institutions all on the same plane. For instance, it hardly seems that book-discussion clubs could claim to be an independent institution before God in the same way as the family, church, or state.[24]

Dooyeweerd attempted to bring rigor to the delineation of the various spheres. Dooyeweerd distinguished 15 modalities ("ways in which something exists and is experienced") which he argued were irreducible (in the sense that they could not be "explained exclusively in terms of any other modal sense"). These spheres "include the arithmetic, spatial, kinetic, physical, biotic, psychic, analytical, historical, lingual, social, economic, aesthetic, juridical, moral, and fiducial."[25] This classification of the modal spheres was Dooyeweerd's way of acknowledging the diversity built into God's creation and incorporating it into his ontological system. Every concrete reality in God's creation functions simultaneously in all the modal spheres, while each expresses its individuality uniquely and in relation to a particular modal

[21] Kuyper (1931, pp. 90–96).

[22] Chaplin (2005); Grasso (2008, p. 57).

[23] Kuyper (1998a, p. 467).

[24] Wolterstorff (2009, pp. 115–116); Mouw (2000, p. 91); van der Vyver (2002, p. 216).

[25] Baus (2006, p. 211); and see generally Dooyeweerd (1969, volume 3); Cameron (2002).

"guiding" function and "individuality structure." Building on this recognition of diversity, Dooyeweerd moved on to distinguish social spheres in terms of their individuality structures.[26]

Whatever its merits, though, one needs not fully adopt Dooyeweerd's ontological and social philosophy to recognise a core insight: God's creation is full of diversity, and this is a good thing. Dooyeweerd concurred with Kuyper in viewing sphere sovereignty as a limit on the consolidation and abuse of power by any single social institution. But they both also viewed sphere sovereignty as a reflection of the diverse good purposes of God as manifested in human action and in human sociability.[27] Sphere sovereignty, in short, has both a negative aspect, restraining evil in a fallen world, and a positive aspect, empowering human society to fulfill its callings under God.

4.3 Sphere Sovereignty and Subsidiarity: Similarities and Differences

Subsidiarity as a social ontology tells us that society is made up of many levels and layers of human interaction and sociability. Sphere sovereignty does the same thing. But these two theories of social pluralism approach society from different angles.

Subsidiarity emphasises the importance of social pluralism on a vertical axis. The default position is that social needs should be met at the lowest or most local level possible.[28] If the local level of society is not able to adequately address a social need, then it is necessary for the next larger social institution to become involved. As Pius XI put it in *Quadragesimo Anno*:

> Just as it is gravely wrong to take from individuals what they can accomplish by their own initiative and industry and give it to the community, so also it is an injustice and at the same time a grave evil and disturbance of right order to assign to a greater and higher association what lesser and subordinate organizations can do. For every social activity ought of its very nature to furnish help to the members of the body social, and never destroy and absorb them.[29]

The principle of subsidiarity prevents the smaller institutions from being swallowed up by the larger. Yet it also recognises that there are times when it is appropriate for the larger institutions to get involved. The health of the "body social" is the central concern.

Sphere sovereignty emphasises the importance of social pluralism on the horizontal axis. Regardless of whether the activity is taking place on a local level or a national

[26] Skillen (2003, pp. 337–350).

[27] Skillen (2003, p. 334).

[28] McIlroy (2003, p. 739).

[29] Pius XI (1931, p. 79).

level, sphere sovereignty emphasises the distinction between different kinds of social activities and institutions—state and church, for instance. At any level of social activity, there are multiple manifestations of sociability and many kinds of organisations and associations, formed for a variety of ends. The sphere sovereignty vision is for a richly-textured society, as Kuyper explained:

> The cogwheels of all these spheres engage each other, and precisely through that interaction emerges the rich, multifaceted multiformity of human life. Hence also rises the danger that one sphere in life may encroach on its neighbor like a sticky wheel that shears off one cog after another until the whole operation is disrupted.[30]

Some Reformed writers have criticised attempts to bring together subsidiarity with sphere sovereignty. It has been claimed that subsidiarity implies a hierarchical ordering of society, in tension with the sphere sovereignty concept, which places all social institutions as equals before God. But this depends on what is meant when one refers to "greater" and "lesser" institutions. As Kenneth Grasso[31] has noted, ranking communities by their "size and power" is quite different from ranking communities according to their "ontological dignity." Patrick McKinley Brennan has argued in his contribution to this volume that subsidiarity does not imply that either small or large institutions are necessarily good or bad. There has frequently been a lack of clarity as to "which criterion is being employed." So while there is potential for tension between sphere sovereignty and subsidiarity on this point,[32] it is certainly not inevitable.

Nor does subsidiarity necessarily imply the kind of top-down ordering of society that Reformed writers (myself included) would be concerned about. Quite the opposite is true—the social order envisioned by subsidiarity tends to be a bottom-up structure, as Pius XI implied and subsequent Catholic social teaching has made clear.[33] Indeed, the contemporary Catholic position's bottom-up approach seems to mesh quite nicely with similar themes that have historically been sounded by Reformed thinkers (particularly in the Presbyterian tradition) in their political theologies.[34]

It would seem then that sphere sovereignty and subsidiarity have the potential to be compatible and complementary principles for understanding the social order. They each offer a vision for a society that is quite different from that of liberal individualism. Instead, both envision societies in which human sociability leads to the formation of a host of associations and institutions. Both are part of the larger social pluralist tradition by affirming the goodness of this diversity. Both ground their understanding of this goodness not primarily in pragmatic arguments but instead in theological principles about the nature of God and the nature of man.

---

[30] Kuyper (1998a, pp. 467–468).

[31] 2008, p. 54.

[32] See, e.g., van der Vyver (2002, p. 221).

[33] Woldring (2000, p. 186).

[34] Witte (2008); (Kelly 1992).

4.4 Church Autonomy as a Case Study

Church autonomy provides a helpful case study to illuminate the ways that sphere sovereignty can complement the social pluralism promoted by subsidiarity. In American law, the church autonomy doctrine operates to delimit the bounds of judicial competence in deciding cases involving ecclesiastical matters. Based on the religion clauses of the First Amendment, the church autonomy doctrine prohibits "judicial resolution of ecclesiastical disputes that turn on matters of religious doctrine or practice."[35] It has been applied to an array of church-related controversies that have ended up in court. For instance:

1. A church commences disciplinary proceedings on a member who is engaged in a relationship prohibited by biblical doctrine. Following a biblical pattern for dealing with sin in the church outlined in Matthew 18, the pastor informs the other church elders of the conduct so that they could all be involved in admonishing the church member. The member then sues the church, alleging that the pastor has defamed her and violated the duty of confidentiality that he owed to her as a licensed counselor.[36]
2. In a church that allows a board to select its minister, the church's governing body terminated the pastor over a doctrinal dispute. The pastor refused to leave and sued, alleging irregularities in the board's decision.[37]
3. A church leader is accused of sexual assault on a church member. The leader is sued by the injured individual(s).[38]

In the first and second cases, the sphere sovereignty idea of distinct jurisdictions is particularly apropos. Each of these cases centers on the horizontal relationship between distinct spheres. The church and the civil government have different end purposes and thus constitute different spheres of authority. The church has the responsibility for dealing with the standards for its own members. The state does not have a good reason for interfering with the internal standards of a separate sphere.

But it is less clear that these cases implicate subsidiarity's central concern, the vertical relationship between greater and lesser organisations. It might be argued that it is more appropriate for a local church to decide issues pertaining to membership or to the choice of its leaders than for a court to decide the matter as an agent of the state. But suppose that the governing body in the second example was a regional presbytery. It might be the case that the county court is no more or less local than the presbytery. Subsidiarity in its most basic version—as a presumption in favour of localism—would not be able to contribute much to the resolution of this

[35] *Westbrook v. Penley*, 231S.W.3d 389, 396 (Tex. 2007) ('*Westbrook*').

[36] *Westbrook*.

[37] *Solid Rock Baptist Church v. Carlton*, 789 A.2d 149 (N.J. Super. 2002).

[38] The first two cases are based on actual controversies litigated in American courts. The third is a generic composite based on the sexual abuse cases litigated since the 1980s in American courts. See, e.g., Lytton (2007).

case. Certainly, Catholic social teaching provides strong support for the principle of church autonomy.[39] But the point is that subsidiarity on its own (that is, not fully fleshed out in terms of other Catholic teachings) is surprisingly inconclusive about the proper relationship between church and state, one of the most significant manifestations of social and institutional pluralism. This in turn highlights the complementary relationship that is possible between subsidiarity and sphere sovereignty.

The third case brings into focus what might initially appear to be a difficult issue for sphere sovereignty. Some statements of sphere sovereignty's jurisdictional principles seem almost too sharply delineated. Subsidiarity has a considerable degree of flexibility built in. But would a consistent theory of sphere sovereignty prohibit the state from interfering with the "sphere" of the church in the case of serious sexual abuse (for example)? If this were in fact the result, there would be reason to be concerned. But while sphere sovereignty was intended to articulate a degree of independence on the part of different social institutions, it was not intended to make the spheres non-interacting. To the contrary, Kuyper and subsequent exponents of sphere sovereignty emphasised the unique role of the state in exercising its own authority in the jural sphere.

While both Kuyper and Dooyeweerd were wary of the tendency of the state to consolidate power, they both appreciated the fact that the state is a God-ordained institution, not to be dismissed or discounted. As Dooyeweerd explained, the state was ordained by God to hold the sword and to exercise the jural function of administering justice and restraining the operation of sin. As such, "[t]he state is a typically divine institution of 'common grace,' that is, the temporal, preserving… grace of God."[40] They both recognised that the state has a special responsibility to foster fair and just relationships among the various spheres and to prevent abuses within a particular sphere. The government, Kuyper said, has the "threefold right and duty" to, first, enforce the boundary lines of each sphere "whenever different spheres clash"; second, "defend individuals…. against the abuse of power" by others in the same sphere; and third, "coerce all together to bear personal and financial burdens for the maintenance of… the State."[41]

In light of this significant place for the state in the theory of sphere sovereignty, the third example clearly falls outside the legitimate authority of the church. Sexual abuse is morally wrong and is not part of the authority of the church (nor of any other sphere). If a church abuses a member, it has stepped outside its sphere of authority and the state has the right and duty to intervene. No church autonomy protection should be available for the wrongdoer.

The church autonomy cases are important to those who value religious liberty as well as everyone concerned with social pluralism more broadly. While this is not the place to make the pragmatic arguments for why the church plays an important role

[39] See, e.g., Brennan (2009); Garnett (2007).

[40] Dooyeweerd (1996, p. 157).

[41] Kuyper (1931, p. 97).

in society, it can at least be observed that the church has proven itself to be one of the most robust social institutions operating as a moral and cultural check on the state's pretensions to omnicompetence.[42] Catholic social theory has generated extensive discussions of the church and its relationships to the state. But subsidiarity itself is often not incorporated into these discussions. As indicated by this brief and schematic discussion of the church autonomy cases, subsidiarity itself is less than conclusive. Sphere sovereignty, on the other hand, helps to flesh out the relationships between distinct institutions that are (at least arguably) on an equal plane.

4.5 Conclusion

Reformed theology teaches the basic jurisdictions—family, church, and state—are directly ordained by God, without any mediating institutions or authorities. In a sense, they each serve as checks and balances on each other. Moreover, sphere sovereignty also acknowledges the existence of a diversity of other "spheres" of social activity. One may believe (as I do) that there are exegetical and theological reasons to put these on a different plane from the fundamental trio of family, church, and state. But even with this proviso, one can acknowledge with Kuyper that education, science, and business (among others) are all legitimate activities ordained by God. Each is a legitimate "sphere" of human action, of sociality and cooperation, which should be respected by the other spheres.

In short, sphere sovereignty, like subsidiarity, offers a vision of institutional and social pluralism. Sphere sovereignty originates from a different theological tradition than subsidiarity and there are doubtless areas where sphere sovereignty's Reformed theological tradition leads to a different emphasis and distinct theological formulations from that found in the Catholic tradition. Notwithstanding the differences, sphere sovereignty and subsidiarity complement each other by fleshing out two important sides to social pluralism. Subsidiarity focuses on the relationships between larger and smaller, "greater" and "lesser," organisations. Sphere sovereignty focuses on the relationships between organisations with distinct purposes, regardless of their size or position on a chain of command. Both the horizontal and the vertical aspects are important components of any well-functioning, diverse society.

References

Baus, Gregory. 2006. Dooyeweerd's societal sphere sovereignty: A theory of differentiated responsibility. *Griffin's View on International and Comparative Law* 7: 209–217.

Bratt, James D. 1998. Abraham Kuyper: His world and work. In *Abraham Kuyper: A centennial reader*, ed. James D. Bratt, 1–16. Grand Rapids: Eerdmans.

[42] McConnell (2000); Carter (1993).

Brennan, Patrick McKinley. 2009. Differentiating church and state (without losing the church). *Georgetown Journal of Law & Government Policy* 7: 29–49.
Cameron, Alan M. 2002. Introduction. In Herman Dooyeweerd, *Encyclopedia of the Science of Law*. Trans. Robert N. Knudsen, ed. Alan M. Cameron. Lewiston: Edwin Mellen Press.
Carter, Stephen L. 1993. *The culture of disbelief*. New York: Basic Books.
Caudill, David S. 1997. A Calvinist perspective on faith in legal scholarship. *Journal of Legal Education* 47(19): 23–24.
Chaplin, Jonathan. 2005. Toward a social pluralist theory of institutional rights. *Ave Maria Law Review* 3: 147–170.
Clouser, Roy A. 2005. *The myth of religious neutrality: An essay on the hidden role of religious beliefs in theories*. Notre Dame: University of Notre Dame Press.
de Bruijn, Jan. 2000. Calvinism and romanticism: Abraham Kuyper as a Calvinist politician. In *Religion, pluralism, and public life: Abraham Kuyper's legacy for the twenty-first century*, ed. Luis E. Lugo, 45–58. Grand Rapids: Eerdmans.
Dooyeweerd, Herman. 1969. *A New Critique of Theoretical Thought*. Trans. David H. Freeman and William S. Young. Philadelphia: Presbyterian and Reformed.
Dooyeweerd, Herman. 1996. The Christian idea of the state. In *Essays in Legal, Social, and Political Philosophy*. Trans. John Kraay. Lewiston: The Edwin Mellen Press.
Garnett, Richard W. 2007. Church, state, and the practice of love. *Villanova Law Review* 52: 281–302.
Grasso, Kenneth. 2008. The subsidiary state. In Jeanne Heffernan Schindler, *Christianity and civil society: Catholic and neo-Calvinist perspectives*. Lanham: Lexington Books.
Jellema, Dirk. 1957. Abraham Kuyper's attack on liberalism. *The Review of Politics* 19: 472–485.
Kelly, Douglas. 1992. *The emergence of liberty in the modern world*. Phillipsburg: Presbyterian and Reformed.
Kuyper, Abraham. 1931. *Lectures on Calvinism*. Grand Rapids: Eerdmans.
Kuyper, Abraham. 1998a. Sphere sovereignty. In *Abraham Kuyper: A centennial reader*, ed. James D. Bratt, 461–490. Grand Rapids: Eerdmans.
Kuyper, Abraham. 1998b. Maranatha. In *Abraham Kuyper: A centennial reader*, ed. James D. Bratt, 205–228. Grand Rapids: Eerdmans.
Lytton, Timothy D. 2007. Clergy sexual abuse litigation. *Connecticut Law Review* 39: 809–895.
McConnell, Michael W. 2000. Why is religious liberty the "first freedom"? *Cardozo Law Review* 21: 1243–1266.
McIlroy, David H. 2003. Subsidiarity and sphere sovereignty: Christian reflections on the size, shape and scope of government. *Journal of Church and State* 45: 739–763.
Mouw, Richard J. 2000. Some reflections on sphere sovereignty. In *Religion, pluralism, and public life: Abraham Kuyper's legacy for the twenty-first century*, ed. Luis E. Lugo, 87–109. Grand Rapids: Eerdmans.
Murphy, William. 1993. In the beginning: Rerum Novarum (1891). In *Building the free society: Democracy, capitalism, and Catholic social teaching*, ed. George Weigel and Robert Royal, 1–30. Grand Rapids/Washington, DC: Eerdmans Publishing and Ethics and Public Policy Center.
Partee, Charles. 1987. Calvin's central dogma again. *Sixteenth Century Journal* 18: 191–200.
Partee, Charles. 2008. *The theology of John Calvin*. Louisville: Westminster John Knox.
Pius XI. 1931. *Quadragesimo Anno: Encyclical of Pope Pius XI on reconstruction of the social order*. http://www.vatican.va/holy_father/pius_xi/encyclicals/documents/hf_p-xi_enc_19310515_quadragesimo-anno_en.html. Last accessed 18 Dec 2012.
Skillen, James W. 2003. Philosophy of the cosmonomic idea: Herman Dooyeweerd's political and legal thought. *Political Science Reviewer* 32: 318–380.
Skillen, James W., and Rockne M. McCarthy. 1991. *Political order and the plural structure of society*. Atlanta: Scholars Press.
van der Kroef, Justus M. 1948. Abraham Kuyper and the rise of neo-Calvinism in the Netherlands. *Church History* 17: 316–334.
van der Vyver, Johan D. 2002. The jurisprudential legacy of Abraham Kuyper and Leo XIII. *Journal of Markets and Morality* 5: 211–249.

Van Til, Kent A. 2008. Subsidiarity and sphere sovereignty: A match made in...? *Theological Studies* 69: 610–636.

von der Dunk, Hermann. 1978. Conservatism in the Netherlands. *Journal of Contemporary History* 13: 741–763.

Westbrook v. Penley, 231S.W.3d 389 (Tex. 2007).

Witte, John. 1986. Introduction. In Herman Dooyeweerd, *A Christian theory of social institutions*, ed. John Witte. La Jolla: Herman Dooyeweerd Foundation.

Witte, John. 1993. The development of Herman Dooyeweerd's concept of rights. *South African Law Journal* 110: 543–562.

Witte, John. 2008. *The reformation of rights*. Cambridge: Cambridge University Press.

Woldring, Henk E.S. 2000. Multiform responsibility and the revitalization of civil society. In *Religion, pluralism, and public life: Abraham Kuyper's legacy for the twenty-first century*, ed. Luis E. Lugo, 175–188. Grand Rapids: Eerdmans.

Wolterstorff, Nicholas. 2009. Abraham Kuyper on the limited authority of church and state. *Georgetown Journal of Law and Public Policy* 7: 105–117.

Chapter 5
Subsidiarity and Social Pluralism

Jonathan Chaplin

Abstract What has come to be called the 'principle of subsidiarity' is widely taken to be a general norm of decentralisation. The principle is thought to mean that authority should be allocated to the 'lowest level possible' in society; typically, from the state to some intermediate or 'lesser' community. This chapter argues that this is a significant misunderstanding of the principle, resulting from lack of attention to the social ontology underlying its original formulation in Catholic social thought. Such an ontology yields a strong account of social pluralism, namely an affirmation that there is a plurality of human communities necessary for human flourishing, each legitimately claiming a sphere of independent self-governance and properly resisting incorporation by or subordination to other communities, notably the state. Subsidiarity is not a principle of decentralisation, but rather, as Russell Hittinger has put it, a principle of 'non-absorption'. The chapter opens with a brief overview of the emergence of 'social pluralism' in nineteenth- and twentieth-century Europe, of which Catholic social thought was one distinctive strand. The main body of the chapter expounds the meaning and implications of subsidiarity in the light of the larger social ontology it presupposes. The final section tests the contemporary political relevance of subsidiarity by asking how far it is exemplified in the recent 'Big Society' idea propounded by the British Conservative Party.

Keywords Subsidiarity • Pluralism • State • Decentralisation • Catholic social thought • Big Society

---

This chapter draws on material first published in the following: Chaplin (1993, 2010, 2011b). An earlier version was presented at a seminar on theological ethics at the University of Aberdeen in January 2013 and I thank participants for their critical feedback.

J. Chaplin (✉)
Kirby Laing Institute for Christian Ethics, Tyndale House,
36 Selwyn Gardens, CB3 9BA Cambridge, United Kingdom
e-mail: klice@tyndale.cam.ac.uk

M. Evans and A. Zimmermann (eds.), *Global Perspectives on Subsidiarity*, Ius Gentium: Comparative Perspectives on Law and Justice 37, DOI 10.1007/978-94-017-8810-6_5,

5.1 Introduction

What has come to be called the 'principle of subsidiarity' is typically taken to be a general norm of decentralisation. The principle is thought to require that authority should be allocated to the 'lowest possible level' in society; typically, from a political authority to some lower body, political or otherwise, or even to individuals.[1] In the European Union it is invoked to protect the competences of member states against unjustified transfers to EU Institutions.[2] The controlling metaphor in this common usage is spatial and vertical. While this is not an illegitimate usage, I argue that to rely primarily on such a metaphor can lead to significant misunderstandings of the principle as originally formulated in Catholic social thought, resulting from lack of attention to the social ontology underpinning that thought. This ontology is rooted in a strong notion of a differentiated created order for human society. There may, perhaps, be a sound general principle in favour of decentralisation from higher to lower levels of authority, but subsidiarity, in its first formulation, is not it. I will argue that subsidiarity is not first of all a principle of decentralisation but, as Russell Hittinger puts it, a principle of 'non-absorption'. The chapter opens with a brief overview of the emergence of 'social pluralism' in nineteenth- and twentieth-century Europe, of which Catholic social thought was one distinctive strand. The main body of the chapter expounds the meaning and implications of subsidiarity in the light of the larger social ontology it presupposes. The final section tests the contemporary political relevance of subsidiarity by asking how far it is exemplified in the recent 'Big Society' idea propounded by the British Conservative Party.[3]

5.2 Social Pluralism

The term 'social pluralism' refers to a family of social and political theories which strongly affirm that a plurality of human communities is necessary for human flourishing, that each type and instance of such communities legitimately claims a sphere of independent self-governance, and that it must resist incorporation by or subordination to other communities, notably the state. Such plural communities are

---

[1] This is how Denis O'Brien understands it in O'Brien (2007). He also speaks of subsidiarity as 'the primacy of the individual' (p. 236).

[2] The principle is explicitly endorsed in the Lisbon Treaty of 2007 (Treaty of the European Union), art 5(3), but it achieved recognition in EU law well before that. On its meaning within the EU, see Aroney (2011). A valuable earlier analysis of the meaning of the principle in the EU is Centre for Economic Policy Research (1993).

[3] It is important to acknowledge that there are different political readings of subsidiarity, and of Catholic social thought generally. Contributors to Booth, ed., *Catholic Social Teaching and the Market Economy* read Catholic social thought through the lens of economic liberalism. Clifford Longley reads it through the lens of British social democracy (Longley 2009). My reading is partly informed by that found in postwar continental European Christian Democracy.

not creatures or organs of the state. Even if they do not pre-exist the state historically, they do not derive their *raison d'être* or their right to self-government from it.

Catholic social pluralism is one among this family of theories.[4] One of its best known exponents was Jacques Maritain, a leading influence on the Christian Democratic movements in Europe and Latin America. Indeed it is arguable that Catholic pluralism has, through Christian Democracy, been the most politically effective of all strands of social pluralism. Maritain commended a 'pluralistically organized body politic' in which the state would be 'a topmost agency concerned only with the final supervision of the achievements of institutions born out of freedom.'[5] He called for recognition of 'an organic heterogeneity in the very structure of civil society,' which is composed 'not only of individuals, but of particular societies formed by them.' Thus 'a pluralist body politic would allow to these societies the greatest autonomy possible and would diversify its own internal structure in keeping with what is typically required by their nature.'[6]

Catholic pluralism was just one of several strands of pluralistic thought taking shape in the late eighteenth and early nineteenth centuries and reaching their peak in the early twentieth, at which point they were overtaken by the successive crises of depression, fascism and war and then further marginalised when post-war states assumed the far-reaching powers required by reconstruction and welfare-state building. Pluralism re-emerged in the 1980s, however, in response, initially, to the widely-recognised failures of centrally managed economies and bureaucratic welfare systems, and then, in turn, to the failures of those of the newly dominant neo-liberal economic paradigm which displaced them. In the UK Tony Blair's 'Third Way' and David Cameron's 'Big Society' programmes remind us that pluralist aspirations, however poorly grasped, are far from dead.

The flowering of pluralist theories two centuries ago reflects the shared context of its leading contributors, who, surprisingly perhaps, were to be found on many points of the emerging ideological spectrum. All were motivated by an anxiety about two characteristic features of modernity: first, the social and economic atomisation produced by industrialisation and the consequent disintegration of traditional institutions such as estates, communes, guilds and kinship communities; and, second, the political centralisation characteristic of the modern nation-state, which had been dramatically accelerated in the aftermath of the French Revolution. Over against this pincer movement, pluralists of many stripes sought to defend and promote the many associations, communities and institutions standing 'between' state and individual. They were driven by concern both at the isolation of individuals from the supportive bonds of pre-capitalist society, and at the exposure of these unprotected individuals to the encroachments of a dangerously overweening state.[7]

[4] For accounts of Catholic and Protestant traditions of pluralism, see Schindler (2008). See also Michael Fogarty's account of both 'horizontal' and 'vertical' pluralism in the Christian Democratic movement (Fogarty 1957, pp. 41–100).

[5] Maritain (1951, p. 23).

[6] Maritain (1973, pp. 163–164).

[7] Pluralist theories emerged partly in reaction to the persistent marginalisation of intermediate associations in many of the leading social and political theories of the modern age, such as those

These same concerns animated important strands of nineteenth and early twentieth century Christian social thought, which from their inception sought to avoid the distortions of both individualism and statism and to chart a putative 'third way'. This is clearly evident in the document that effectively relaunched modern Catholic social thought, Pope Leo XIII's landmark 1891 encyclical *Rerum Novarum* (*RN*).[8] A remarkably similar diagnosis is seen in, for example, the Dutch neo-Calvinist theologian Abraham Kuyper's influential speech of the same year, 'The Social Question and the Christian Religion'.[9] Forty years later these same anxieties were reiterated in the 1931 encyclical of Pope Pius XI, *Quadragesimo Anno*[10] (*QA*), where the first explicit formulation of the principle of subsidiarity appears – or, as the document actually calls it, 'the principle of the subsidiary function of the state'. The encyclical is often known *only* for that fact, but it also contains a wide-ranging and searching analysis of the condition of inter-war European society as a whole. It echoes a familiar pluralist alarm: 'Things have come to such a pass through the evil of what we have termed 'individualism' that, following upon the overthrow and near extinction of that rich social life which was once highly developed through associations of various kinds, there remain virtually only individuals and the State' (§78). It goes on to warn of the damaging political consequences of this dissolution of the social fabric: 'This is to the great harm of the State itself; for with a structure of social governance lost, and with the taking over of all the burdens which the wrecked associations once bore, the State has been overwhelmed and crushed by almost infinite tasks and duties' (§78). The phrase, 'the loss of a structure of social governance', can stand as the common lament of social pluralists, and its restoration as their shared ambition. They warned of the disastrous fall-out of a deliberate or inadvertent emasculation or suppression of 'intermediate bodies' located between state and individual. Such a development, they held, damages all three components of society: individuals are ungrounded, undirected and unprotected; intermediate bodies are eviscerated and corroded; and states are, as *QA* puts it, 'overburdened and overwhelmed'.

5.3 Subsidiarity: Origins and (Mis)interpretations

Such was the context in response to which modern Catholic social pluralism first received its clear articulation. It can be seen as part of the larger attempt of the European churches to find some credible, albeit belated, response to the unprecedented challenges of the nineteenth century 'social question'. In its own response, Catholic pluralism did not proceed *de novo* but drew extensively on the Thomistic

---

of Hobbes, Locke, Rousseau, Kant, Marx and Bentham. Montesquieu, Hegel, De Tocqueville and (to some extent) J. S. Mill are leading exceptions.

[8] Leo XIII (1954).

[9] For an English translation, see Skillen (1991).

[10] Pius XI (1960).

social metaphysics which Leo XIII had been working to revive since his election in 1878. This metaphysics was to frame the language of official (and much lay) Catholic social thought until Vatican II.[11]

In this metaphysics, human society is envisaged as a divinely ordered hierarchy of diverse, teleologically-oriented communities each 'ordered to' distinctive, non-transferrable ends.[12] Such ends (*tela*), rooted in human nature and governed by natural and divine law, were seen as dynamic inner tendencies guided by reason (and not as naturalistic or biological impulses), each contributing to the realisation of distinctive kinds of human flourishing. Particular associations, communities or institutions were seen as coming into existence over time not as a mere happenstance but in order to realise ends inherent in human nature. Such entities were usually termed 'natural communities' and, in relation to the state, 'lesser communities'.[13] A distinction was quite properly made between communities that existed in every human society (such as the family) and more transitory ones, such as voluntary associations. Leo XIII, for example, designated workers' associations in *RN* as 'natural', even though the ones he had in mind were creatures of the nineteenth century.[14] Such associations, he held, were specifically fitted to channel a potency deeply rooted in human social nature (one that today we might call producer solidarity).

Such natural communities possessed a 'relative autonomy' with respect to the supernatural community of the church. In line with Saint Thomas, Catholic pluralists held that the pursuit of the final, supernatural end of humans transcends all natural ends but also envelopes them and summons them towards it. Humans can only move toward their final end by participating in this plurality of natural communities; the journey travels through them. Accordingly, the 'perfecting' work of grace towards nature embraces the ends of the natural communities, which are thereby honoured as indispensable to a fully human life. They are also brought within the remit of the sanctifying work of the institutional church, the chief medium of grace. This generally meant that the church had to exercise spiritual care of such communities and equip Christians to act faithfully within them. It also led to some pretty sharp turf wars, for example in Catholic trades unions and political parties, over whether priests could exercise any direct or indirect jurisdiction over them. I will not explore that issue here.

This hierarchically ordered, organic conception of society has often been misinterpreted, including by influential Catholic thinkers themselves, as legitimating some form of state corporatism or indeed authoritarianism, but this was always

[11] On Catholic social pluralism, see Hittinger (2008), Grasso (2008). For a comparison between Catholic pluralism and the legal pluralism of Otto Von Gierke, see Chaplin (2005).

[12] The following account draws particularly on Rommen (1945).

[13] 'Communities' in the Catholic thought of this period are classed as either natural or supernatural. Here I focus mainly on the natural ones.

[14] *RN*, §51.

against the deepest intentions of the conception.[15] For in a Thomistic metaphysics the subordination of lesser communities to those above them in the hierarchy never compromises the separate identity of the former or their independent value to human life. As Heinrich Rommen puts it: 'All organizational forms have their intrinsic values and their objective ends, the upper form does not make the lower form superfluous; it must never abolish it, nor may it take over its functions and purposes' (Rommen 1945, 30). And this is not fundamentally for reasons of administrative efficacy but rather because no single community, including the institutional church, could ever remotely channel or satisfy all the differentiated possibilities and capacities placed in human nature by the creator. Only a multiplicity of qualitatively different types of community could secure true human flourishing as designed according to divine wisdom.

What types of community? While Saint Thomas explores church and state in considerable detail, his discussions of 'lesser' natural communities are occasional and dispersed. The nature of the family and the duties and rights of parents come in for extended treatment but few others are treated in any detail (partly because his accounts of social life generally follow the Aristotelian picture of a simple movement from household to polis).[16] Thomists since Leo XIII, however, have extended Saint Thomas's model to many other communities that are characteristic of modern society.[17] In their writings a wide range of natural communities comes in for detailed treatment. In addition to family, marriage, and trade union, the school, the business enterprise, the professional group, the cultural association, the political party and others, have been championed. While this pluralist emphasis is less pronounced in official documents after Vatican II, it is still clearly affirmed. John Paul II restated it in 1991 in *Centesimus Annus*[18]: '[T]he social nature of man is not completely fulfilled in the State, but is realized in various intermediary groups, beginning with the family and including economic, social, political and cultural groups which stem from human nature itself and have their own autonomy, always with a view to the common good' (§13).

This allusion to the 'common good' is a reminder that we have not yet completed our account of Catholic social pluralism. One of the distinctive elements of the Catholic strand of pluralism was its insistence that an emphasis on the plurality and autonomy of many lesser communities must be balanced by a

[15] Oswald Von-Nell Breuning, who was commissioned to write the first draft of *QA*, made this very clear in various places. See, e.g., Von-Nell Breuning (1981).

[16] However, Russell Hittinger has noticed a striking exception to this in Saint Thomas' *Opusculum* entitled *Contra impugnantes* (1256). Written to defend the newly formed mendicant orders, it contains a remarkable account of a natural right to form free associations, appealing to the inherent good of 'communication of gifts' among free persons. This work is cited by Leo XIII in *RN* (§51) precisely to support his defence of a natural right to form 'private societies' such as workingmens' associations. Hittinger (2003).

[17] These include European thinkers such as Heinrich Pesch, Heinrich Rommen, Johannes Messner and Jacques Maritain, and Americans Yves Simon and John Courtenay Murray.

[18] (London: Catholic Truth Society, 1991). http://www.vatican.va/holy_father/john_paul_ii/encyclicals/documents/hf_jp-ii_enc_01051991_centesimus-annus_en.html

consideration of how these relate to the 'common good' of the whole society. The particular ends, and thus goods, of various lesser communities are construed as integral parts of this wider good. The common good is not pitted against those lesser, partial goods as if they were engaged in a zero-sum game; nor is it construed as an aggregation of them; nor is it, as Oliver O'Donovan puts it, seen as a kind of 'millennium dome' overarching them.[19] Rather, the preservation of a proper freedom for many lesser communities to flourish in relative autonomy is itself integral to the common good. Ideally the two blend seamlessly, even though in practice it is recognised that, given persistently and sometimes aggressively contending interests, difficult choices have to be made. The same general point applies equally to the particular goods of individual persons. It is true that in a specific sense the common good is, as Thomists put it, is 'prior to' the particular goods of persons and lesser communities, but only in the sense that those particular goods cannot be attained without the supportive, framing conditions that make up the common good. As Pope John XXIII puts it in *Mater et Magister* (*MM*), the common good is 'the sum total of those conditions of social living, whereby men are enabled more fully and more readily to achieve their own perfection'.[20] The relationship between particular goods and common goods is thus not one of subservience or instrumentality, in either direction, but of co-constitution or mutual facilitation. The obligations of persons to other persons and to society are not to be construed as confining external constraints on free agency but rather as constitutive internal conditions of true personhood. As one commentary puts it, 'the right of society, the common good, is necessarily within the rights of the person which it guarantees. It transcends the person only because it is also indwelling in him'.[21]

Only having set out the larger social ontology underlying Catholic social pluralism can we now make proper sense of the principle of subsidiarity.[22] When the principle is interpreted apart from this ontology it is evacuated of much of normative meaning, with the risk that it is reduced to a flat, rule-of-thumb preference for administrative decentralisation. But viewed in the light of this ontology we will see how this is a travesty of its real point.

Here is the familiar statement of the principle in *QA*: 'it is an injustice and at the same time a grave evil and disturbance of right order to assign to a greater and higher association what lesser and subordinate organizations can do. For every social activity ought of its very nature to furnish help (*subsidium*) to the members of the body social, and never destroy or absorb them' (§79). It is hard to imagine why the pope would have used the strong language of 'grave evil' if subsidiarity were only a rule of administrative decentralisation. I consider the implications for the state in a moment. But notice first how the second part of this statement asserts that

---

[19] O'Donovan (2005, p. 57).

[20] John XXIII (1984).

[21] Calvez and Perrin (1961, p. 118).

[22] For a detailed account of the historical and intellectual roots of the idea of subsidiarity against the background of European social thought, see Leys (1995), Part 1.

subsidiarity is not first of all a political norm but rather a generic social one: it is 'every social activity' that should offer help to members of society. In the widest sense it is *society as a whole*, through every part, that performs a subsidiary function, offers help to, persons and other communities. Later, Pius XII put the point crisply: 'all social activity is of its nature subsidiary'.[23] And it turns out, after all, that this is only another way of saying that the particular goods of persons and lesser communities cannot be realised apart from what is supplied by the common good. Thus Messner asserts that 'the law of subsidiary function and the law of the common good are, in substance, identical'.[24]

The clear implication is that subsidiarity is a call for social functions to be fulfilled, not at *the lowest possible level* but rather at *the right level*; that is, by the community properly fitted to fulfil them, in accordance with what *QA* calls 'right order'. Stated formally, the principle itself does not tell us what the right communities are. It tells us that, once we have identified them, we should assign to them, wherever possible, the functions they are naturally fitted to fulfil.

This conclusion is reinforced by an important textual argument proposed by Russell Hittinger.[25] Hittinger proposes a new term to capture the deeper sense behind the term, 'participated royalty'. At the root of this concept is not so much a metaphysical as a theological notion, that of vocation, gift of service, or office. These English terms are attempts to capture the Latin term *munus* (plural: *munera*) which, Hittinger shows, appears pervasively in official texts from the 1920s. It was Pope Pius XI, author of *QA*, who first began to introduce the language of *munera*, using the term to designate not only the offices (*munera*) of individuals but also those of many communities: families, corporations, churches, even the state and international authorities. These institutions possessed rights (*iura*), but rights arising from and pursuant to the offices (*munera*) they bear. *Munera*, or gifted offices, are the ways in which human beings participate in the kingly quality of ruling (*regalitas*) given to them by God. To exercise a *munus*, then, is to exhibit 'participated royalty'. It is evident from this account that the deeper biblical resonance of the term *munus* has been muted by its being translated flatly as 'role' or 'function'. Hittinger's account helps explain why Pius XI deemed it not just an administrative inconvenience but a 'grave evil' for a higher community to usurp the offices of a lower one, for that wold be to deny them a dignity and authority given them by God. The reading I proposed earlier is thus confirmed by Hittinger: 'subsidiarity cannot be used to settle the debates about the ontology or distribution of *munera*; rather, it is a principle governing the relations of already-distributed functions.... [It] is proposed as a principle of nonabsorption, not a principle that necessarily requires devolution'.[26]

[23] Quoted in Calvez and Perrin (1961, p. 122).

[24] Messner (1949, p. 196).

[25] Hittinger (2008).

[26] Hittinger (2008, p. 16). See also Grasso (2008).

Let us now turn to consider 'the subsidiary function' of *the state*. It is understandable, of course, that this is the application which has attracted most attention, since the first official formulation of the principle was occasioned largely as a response to a perception of encroaching statism. The 'subsidiary function of the state' means that, as supreme guardian of the common good, the state has a duty to offer lesser communities (and persons) such 'help' as is needed for them to realise their distinctive ends and pursue their unique goods, when failure to do so might harm the common good. The state's authority is in principle as wide in scope as the attainment of the common good requires; but no wider. And as it acts to promote the common good, the state must correctly discern, and defer to, its complexly differentiated components. It must honour the freedom of persons and lesser communities even when it may need to take far-reaching initiatives for the good of the whole. The state cannot successfully discharge its mandate at the expense of the intrinsic rights and powers of persons and lesser communities but only by enabling the latter to exercise their own responsibilities more satisfactorily. As the passage in *QA* puts it:

> The supreme authority of the State ought, therefore, to let subordinate groups handle matters and concerns of lesser importance, which would otherwise dissipate its efforts greatly. Thereby the State will more freely, powerfully, and effectively do all those things that belong to it alone because it alone can do them: directing, watching, urging, restraining, as occasion requires and necessity demands. Therefore, those in power should be sure that the more perfectly a graduated order is kept among the various associations, in observance of the principle of subsidiary function, the stronger social authority and effectiveness will be [and] the happier and more prosperous the condition of the State (§80).

A further specific implication of the social ontology underlying subsidiarity can now be highlighted: such an ontology generates a distinctive theory of legal pluralism. The fact that lesser communities originate from the inclinations of human nature, rather than from the state, means that they possess, by 'nature', original rights of self-governance. Catholic pluralists developed out of this claim an account of plural original sources of law parallel to (and indeed influenced by), the nineteenth-century German legal historian Otto von Gierke.[27] As Messner puts it, there is, corresponding to the plurality of communities, a 'plurality of categories of equally original fundamental rights, none of which can be derived from one another'.[28] This claim closely mirrors that of the neo-Calvinist Kuyper, also influenced by Gierke, who spoke of the 'sphere sovereignty', or legal independence, of many human communities from control by others.[29] The later neo-Calvinist legal philosopher Herman Dooyeweerd posited the notion of multiple 'spheres' of genuine law, and repudiated the legal positivist claim that the legal rights and duties of lesser communities were really only 'concessions' from the omnicompetent

[27] See Chaplin (2005).

[28] Messner (1949, p. 177).

[29] Kuyper (1998).

legal sphere of the state.[30] Contemporary natural law philosopher Michael Pakaluk captures the central insight thus:

> [A]ssociations or communities will typically have a certain internal coherence, autonomy, and independence because of various claims and duties, binding upon their members, that arise out of the relationships and activities constitutive of those associations or communities. We can therefore speak of any association as having its own 'law,' formulated and administered by whichever person or persons has authority for that association, and the law of that association is appropriately based upon these claims and duties, and gets its force from them.[31]

Initiatives from the state which impact on the right to self-government of lesser communities, creating a potential risk of distorting their irreducible ends and goods, therefore need a clear and compelling justification. Now it turns out that such a case will sometimes be available, namely wherever it appears that some important component of the common good would be significantly impaired if the state did nothing. So it is crucial to emphasise that no classical liberal doctrine of the 'minimal state' is implied by Catholic pluralism. The state should not be as small as it can be but as big as it needs to be to fulfil its mandate; but no bigger. In fact, over time we see Catholic pluralists advocating a wide range of state initiatives, responding to the expansion of the scope of the common good attendant upon increasing societal complexity and interdependence, and thus the broadening of the remit of the state. Three broad categories can be distinguished. First, there are *enabling* activities, serving to create the necessary legal, economic or infrastructural conditions required for lesser communities to flourish. Second, there are *remedial* activities, intended to remedy some obvious deficiency in the capacity of lesser communities to fulfil their proper responsibilities pursuant to their distinctive *telos*. Writing in the mid-twentieth century, Rommen suggested that these two types of initiative could include actions as wide-ranging as introducing factory legislation, abolishing child labour, curbing monopolies, granting privileges to farmers' cooperatives and imposing tariffs (Rommen 1945, 321–4, 351–2). Third, there could, exceptionally, be *substituting* activities, in which the state, after all, does take over a function naturally belonging to a lesser community, but only where the latter is chronically incapacitated. One commentary terms substitution 'an accidental mode of subsidiarity'.[32] Yet *QA* (§179) also seems to recognise that in certain cases a more permanent assumption of a function by the state might be necessary (even including nationalisation) where that function had become indispensable to the common good; such a claim is also affirmed in *CA* (§48). Today, of course, many such major functions have been either permanently assumed by the state or at least extensively regulated by it – the most spectacular recent example being the banking system. For Rommen, however, the goal of every state intervention should be, wherever possible,

[30] Dooyeweerd (1979), chs. 2, 5. Dooyeweerd was, however, sharply critical of Catholic social thought, reading it as a case of collectivism. See also Chaplin (2011a), ch. 7.

[31] Pakaluk (2002). On early Calvinist formulations of the point, see Carney (1966).

[32] Calvez and Perrin (1961, p. 336).

'a reconstitution of the order of self-initiative' (Rommen 1945, 304). This is, at least, what contemporary governments intend their banking reforms to achieve.

I have argued so far that in Catholic pluralism subsidiarity was never intended simply as a principle of decentralisation but rather as one of 'non-absorption', as Hittinger puts it. Now I want to suggest a consequent correction to the common view of the subsidiary function of the state. One widely-cited commentary asserts that 'subsidiarity only looks one way'[33] – namely, downwards from the state. But if my account of the location of the principle in its larger social ontology is correct, this turns out to be misleading. For if 'all social activity is subsidiary', then, in principle, *all* communities have a potential responsibility towards *all other* communities (and to all persons) to offer them various kinds of 'help' or service. The principle turns out to have not only a vertical but also a horizontal application. The precise form of service each offers to others will reflect their unique *tela*. Each community will, in appropriate and circumscribed ways, offer to wider society the specific resources it alone commands and make them available to others which need them. And, crucially, they will in the first instance do so not by launching some programme of external outreach but simply by being themselves. But then what also seems to follow is that subsidiarity looks *upwards as well as downwards*, insofar as lesser communities offer indispensable kinds of help to the state itself. For example, while schools may be funded by the state under the state's subsidiary function, only schools can offer the specific type of educational formation necessary if citizens are to properly exercise their public duties. They help the state fulfil *its* unique function. In many cases, what one lesser community offers to others (even to the state), will be done spontaneously and without legal compulsion. A key task of the state, however, is to ensure that where such mutual offers of help were failing in ways that damaged the common good, legal facilitation, inducement or compulsion might be required.

We see, then, that the social ontology underlying subsidiarity then turns out to have more interesting implications than is suggested when it is invoked only as a general maxim of decentralisation. When we excavate its deeper intent, it actually seems to imply the need for multiple relationships of solidarity among many kinds of community, and to hold these out as a constitutive element of a flourishing human society organised in line with the imperatives of human social nature. My use of the term 'solidarity' here is deliberate. This is another pervasive term in Catholic social teaching: John Paul II defines it as 'a firm and persevering determination to commit oneself to the common good'.[34] We often find commentators suggesting the need to 'balance' subsidiarity with solidarity, and we can see their point. But on my modified reading, the exercise of a subsidiary function is itself an act of solidarity (though there are other acts of solidarity which are not 'subsidiary' in this sense).

---

[33] Calvez and Perrin (1961, p. 332).

[34] *Sollicitudo rei Socialis (SRS)* (London: Catholic Truth Society, 1998), § 38. http://www.vatican.va/holy_father/john_paul_ii/encyclicals/documents/hf_jp-ii_enc_30121987_sollicitudo-rei-socialis_en.html

It is clear, then, that the claim that 'subsidiarity only looks one way' appears to be a redundant legacy of the hierarchical element in Thomistic metaphysics, an element which, in any case, is no longer to the fore in official Catholic documents. Indeed I suggest we need to go beyond talking even of vertical and horizontal applications. We need to replace the two-dimensional spatial metaphor by means of which subsidiarity has often been handed down to us, with a more complex multi-dimensional picture of mutual interdependencies among numerous, qualitatively different communities of many types, size and location.[35]

Let us now move from ontology to policy. What precisely might subsidiarity mean in contemporary public policy? The next section offers just one, hopefully suggestive, illustration, by asking how far the British Conservative Party's 'Big Society' programme exemplifies the concrete application of the principle. It is not implied that this, admittedly ephemeral, programme is a better instance of subsidiarity in action than others that could be cited (for example, the 'Third Way' offered by 'New Labour' after 1997), but only to show how this seemingly abstract philosophical principle, emerging from an unlikely origin nearly a century ago, can nevertheless yield critical tools for assessing the broad directions of contemporary public policy in an advanced western democracy. I shall outline the programme, assess it against the reading of subsidiarity offered earlier and suggest ways in which it might have better expressed the thrust of that reading.

5.4 A Contemporary Example: Is the 'Big Society' Programme an Example of Subsidiarity?

Initially in opposition[36] and then during its first 2 years in government since 2010, the British Conservative Party under David Cameron's leadership championed the slogan of the 'Big Society' to capture the heart of its social policy agenda.[37] The Big Society vision was projected as a radical shift away from the

---

[35] This might be a way to recapture, in contemporary terms, the truth within the medieval metaphor of society as an 'organism' with many 'parts'. This metaphor is, in turn, indebted to the Pauline image of the 'Body of Christ' with its diverse members each offering their own gifts and deserving of their own honour, as in, e.g., 1 Corinthians p. 12.

[36] David Cameron, 'The Big Society', Scuiet http://www.conservatives.com/News/Speeches/2009/11/David_Cameron_The_Big_Society.aspx

[37] There is a debate over whether the Big Society idea still animates government policy, not least because the substantial reduction in public funding resulting from the government's stringent deficit-reduction programme has starved the voluntary sector – one of the programme's key deliverers – of cash. Yet while the term itself is now little used, the raft of legislative and policy changes since 2010 have already made significant impacts across several areas of policy. For a description and analysis of the programme in the light of Catholic social thought, see Loughlin et al. (2013) (henceforth cited in the text as *VHI Report*). I use the past tense in my account of the programme to indicate that I am referring to the *stated early intentions* of the programme, not to imply that it is entirely dead a time of writing (December 2013). For an assessment of its success and current vitality up to 2012, see *VHI Report*, on which my account draws.

'Big State' model that had supposedly dominated New Labour governments over the previous decade, and as amounting to a major transfer of power from central government to ordinary people, non-governmental organisations and local authorities. The term 'Big Society' was not simply a slogan but had a powerful institutional driver at the heart of government, the Office for Civil Society.[38] Six major pieces of legislation were introduced, some of which are already having far-reaching effects. By 2012 there was, however, a widespread perception of incoherence both in how the programme is understood inside and outside government and in how it is being applied in policy. Notwithstanding this perception, there seems evidence of a partial convergence between the goals, and at least a few of the achievements, of the programme, and certain principles of Catholic social thought. Among the intellectual feeders of the programme were two leading political thinkers influenced by Catholic social thought, so it was reasonable to suppose that the idea might reflect some commitment to subsidiarity (I will only consider this principle).[39] And we do indeed find partial evidence of the operation both of the standard interpretation of subsidiarity as decentralisation and of my proposed reading of it as non-absorption. Analysing the Big Society programme from 2010 to 2012 can help clarify this distinction.

Three components of the Big Society agenda were initially announced: public sector reform; community empowerment; and social (or philanthropic) action. These goals were to be pursued via a threefold strategy of redistribution: of power (decentralisation); of knowledge (transparency); and of money and assets (social finance).[40]

The first component, public sector reform, included (*inter alia*) an expansion of the existing policy of contracting out selected public services to non-governmental organisations (charities, social enterprises, private companies and employee-owned cooperatives), where these might, it was supposed, deliver a more efficient or accountable service. Such services were to include not only routine tasks such as catering and cleaning but also specialist health services, employment support programmes or drug rehabilitation centres. This would amount to a transfer of functions from state to non-state bodies, i.e. third sector civil society organisations or commercial bodies operating in the market. We can see how such a goal could be commendable in principle as an instance of subsidiarity as 'non-absorption', at least

[38] The office's website announced in 2010 that it 'works across government departments to translate the Big Society agenda into practical policies, provides support to voluntary and community organisations and is responsible for delivering a number of key Big Society programmes', namely the Big Society Bank, the National Citizenship Service Scheme, Community Organizers, and Community First. This particular wording is no longer on the office's website (https://www.gov.uk/government/news/office-for-civil-society-appoints-strategic-partners) but the objectives remain in place.

[39] Ian Duncan-Smith, former Conservative party leader and founder of the conservative-leaning think-tank Centre for Social Justice; and the 'Radical Orthodox' theologian Phillip Blond representing a 'Red Toryism' influential in the think tank ResPublica, which he directs. *VHI Report* questions how far Duncan-Smith's thinking was actually informed by Catholic social thought.

[40] *VHI Report*, p. 21.

so long as the services in question would be offloaded to a credible non-government provider. Let us call this *institutional devolution.*

In fact, the goal of public sector reform has pursued this goal, at best, only partially and inconsistently. Consider the health, education and welfare sectors. Part of the government's reforms in health and education can be seen as motivated by the desire for institutional devolution. Its major reorganising of the National Health Service has included at least two significant changes. One has been the transfer of the power to purchase health services from regional authorities (Strategic Health Authorities and Primary Care Trusts) to smaller, local Clinical Commissioning Groups, managed on behalf of consortia of general practitioners themselves. How successful this radical restructuring will prove to be remains to be seen. It is, however, not a case of institutional devolution but only of decentralisation *within* a public service. Similarly, the new powers given to Foundation Trusts (a status all NHS Trusts are set to receive), while billed as creating 'the largest social enterprise sector in the world',[41] in fact amounts to another form of decentralisation *within* a public service.

It should be noted, however, that such decentralisation is also occurring simultaneously with a deepening process of 'marketisation', i.e. the introduction of competitive incentives between purchasers and providers within the system. It remains very unclear what the impact of this apparently countervailing process will be on the quality and equity of health service delivery, and grave fears have been expressed on that score. The process is not, however, adequately described as the straightforward 'privatisation' of the NHS. That would essentially mean transferring large chunks of the existing NHS to the private health care sector, where individuals buy services from profit-making providers (or insure themselves privately for that purpose). That is not currently envisaged: the government remains formally committed to a publicly-funded universal health service 'free at point of use'.

The other significant change in the NHS does qualify as a case of institutional devolution, namely the transfer of health service provision to genuinely non-governmental providers. An early example was Leatherhead Community Hospital in Surrey, now owned by the nurses and therapists who work in it. It is an independently owned producer cooperative supplying services to the public sector, and thus seems to qualify as an exemplary instance of 'non-absorption'.[42] There are many other such examples.

In education, we again see a combination of mere decentralisation with genuine institutional devolution. The government has considerably expanded the number of 'Academies' (set up under the Labour government) and introduced 'Free Schools'. Academies are not subject to local authority control but are still part of the public education sector; they are, then, further examples of decentralisation within a public service. Free Schools, by contrast, are run by parents and teachers outside the public system, while remaining publicly funded (and so are parallels to Leatherhead Community Hospital). Yet a factor which poses a question over the extent to which

[41] Quoted in *VHI Report*, p. 26.

[42] http://csh.dm-test.co.uk/image/csh/72fa7a35-0af0-401d-8b55-23783c1574a8.pdf

these are real cases of subsidiarity as non-absorption is that, while both Academies and Free Schools are exempt from local authority control, they now fall under the direct control of central government.

In the case of welfare reform, we see very different approach. While the government's radical welfare reforms have been presented as flagship cases of the Big Society vision, there is actually little evidence of subsidiarity in either sense being realised. A key policy goal here was getting people off 'welfare dependency' and into work. The central policy was the proposal to introduce a new Universal Credit to replace a battery of existing welfare benefits thought to be reducing the incentive to seek employment. Yet this only envisages changing the 'contractual' relationship between the individual and the state and does not include any provision to utilise third sector organisations in the delivery of welfare. There is no attempt to promote the Big Society goals of either decentralisation or institutional devolution.[43]

The second component of the Big Society programme, 'community empowerment', was to involve a variety of objectives. The most important (under the *Localism Act 2011*) was to transfer a degree of decision-making power from central government to local councils (e.g. over planning, though not, crucially, over finance), or further downwards to local neighbourhoods (who, for example, were empowered to create 'community-led plans'). This amounts to two things: first, again, a process of administrative decentralisation within the sphere of government (from central to local); second, a strengthening of democratic accountability (of local governments to the communities they govern). However, the reluctance to decentralise *financial* powers to local authorities amounted to a failure to equip them adequately with the resources necessary if the transferred powers were actually to be deployed effectively.[44] And, as noted, the parallel policy of removing Academies and Free Schools from control by local authorities amounts to a substantial reduction in their power. The logic of expanding local authority power in some areas but diminishing it in others has not yet been spelled out adequately (to say the least).

The third component of the Big Society programme, social or philanthropic action, was intended to incentivise charitable giving, encourage more volunteering and boost the social enterprise sector. It included initiatives such as the *Giving* White Paper (2011), Big Society Capital (a bank to support social investment), the National Citizenship Service (a youth volunteering scheme), Community Organizers (a training scheme for local activists) and Community First (a fund for community groups in deprived neighbourhoods). These seem to amount to genuine attempts by government to *enable* voluntary action by individuals and local organisations, and as such a valid instance of one of the subsidiary functions of the state. Critics have rightly observed, however, that such initiatives, worthy though they may be, are vastly overshadowed by the severe cuts to voluntary sector public funding under the government's austerity programme and by the constraint on giving at a time of high unemployment and wage restraint.

---

[43] *VHI Report*, p. 41.

[44] Another goal was to 'empower' communities beyond government, but this seems to have added little to what was already envisaged under the first and third components of the programme.

Given the severe financial restraints imposed after 2010 on both local authorities and the voluntary sector, it seems clear that the Big Society programme failed to meet the key objective, implied by subsidiarity, of establishing the 'enabling conditions' required if such bodies were to fulfil their newly devolved responsibilities. More broadly, the partial and limited alignment between the Big Society programme and the requirements of subsidiarity (as interpreted here) reveals the poor grasp of the principle by the policy architects of the programme. Against that benchmark, the programme compares unfavourably with the broad direction of social policy under a number of continental European Christian Democratic governments between the 1950s and at least the 1980s. These were marked by a sustained willingness on the part of government to enlist independent social providers, and families, in securing the objectives of universal welfare and by the provision of funding regimes as generous as those of social democratic governments.[45] They demonstrated a better (albeit still far from perfect) grasp of the essential relationship between protecting against absorption and securing financial viability, and so were better able to bring about a state of affairs in which, as Rommen put it (noted above), there would be 'a reconstitution of the order of self-initiative'.

The purpose of this discussion of the Big Society programme has been neither to offer a complete account of its contents nor to review all its alleged virtues or defects, but only to use it to offer a concrete illustration of the two meanings of subsidiarity distinguished above. In the light of the foregoing account, we can do so in terms of a fivefold typology of policy goals. Each can be seen as intended to significantly shift the balance of power within the state, or between the state and civil society, market or individual. But each does so in importantly different ways. The first, *administrative decentralisation,* only transfers power *within the state itself*; the principal example considered was from *central to local government* (1).[46] This can be distinguished from (2) the *decentralisation of power within a publicly-funded and regulated service* which is not itself part of the government administration, such as the NHS or education system. The third type is *governmental devolution* (3): the transfer of governmental (legislative executive and judicial) authority from a higher body to a lower one (national or federal to state or provincial or Aboriginal; or state/provincial to local). This occurred in the UK in the late 1990s when Scottish, Welsh and Northern Irish legislative bodies were (re)created. But these larger-scale devolutions of power have not so far been cited as examples of the Big Society vision (hardly surprisingly, since they were achievements of the Labour government). Logically, however, they seem of a piece with it. The fourth type is strengthening *democratic accountability* (3) at the level of local government. This is

---

[45] See, e.g., van Kersbergen (1995). Van Kersbergen argues that one distinctive feature of such regimes was that they were 'passive, transfer-oriented systems' (p. 4). That is, instead of using welfare policy to refashion social institutions (such as the family or faith-based welfare providers) according to larger, state-determined objectives, they harnessed the energies of such bodies as they found them, thus, I argue, adhering more closely to the principle of non-absorption.

[46] There are other forms of administrative decentralisation, such as from central government departments to regional offices (sometimes termed "deconcentration") or from one tier of a central department to a lower one. Both could be helpful for effective governance.

in itself a worthy goal, but it also amounts to another a shift of power *within the state*, in this case from local government to people in their capacity as citizens (who are members of the community called state).

For those who interpret subsidiarity as a general principle of decentralisation, all these four types of policy would certainly qualify as such, and each has strong *prima facie* arguments in its favour. It is not my purpose, of course, to disallow this type of usage. But it is important that such objectives, however justifiable in themselves, be clearly distinguished from the fifth type of policy, namely genuine *institutional devolution* (5). Uniquely, this involves transferring tasks from the state, *at any level*, to *non-state bodies* in civil society or the market sector. Unlike the first four types, this is indeed *subsidiarity as non-absorption*. I stress this distinction because, on my reading at least, it is the normative core of subsidiarity as originally formulated in Catholic social thought and is, I submit, the most important in nudging a contemporary society somewhat closer to the 'right order' envisaged in such thought.

5.5 Conclusion

I can best frame my conclusion by briefly responding to another charge levelled by critics of the Big Society idea, namely that it was essentially a (covert) strategy to 'shrink the state'. The first thing to say here is that, on the basis of Catholic social pluralism, there is no justification for seeking a big state *per se*. The *size of the state* is not the deepest question of public policy (though it is far from irrelevant to good governance). Thus if the net result of the government's Big Society programme turns out to be to reduce the proportion of national income spent by government, or to increase non-state employment relative to public sector employment, it would not thereby be deemed illegitimate (so long as key components of the common good were not thereby damaged). Where there is no compelling need to expand the scope of state intervention in order to promote the common good in a particular sector of society, it should not be done. Equally, it could never be a credible political goal to make the state *as small as possible*. While subsidiarity supports a *limited* state (a state limited by law and by other social authorities) it emphatically does not imply a *minimal* state. The concrete implications of the point made earlier can now be more clearly seen: the state should be *as big as it needs to be* in order to properly discharge its core task of securing the basic conditions of the common good. The key objective is not, first of all, to get the *quantity* of government right but to correctly identify the *characteristic purpose* of government and then to allow it to deploy its necessary power to realise that purpose, a purpose which includes creating enabling conditions for other institutions to pursue theirs.

Equally, we must now add that society – the realm of individuals, civil society associations, and the market sector – should also be *as big as it needs to be* in order that its diverse components can properly discharge their own core tasks. Now it is possible that society could be *too small*, crowded out by an ever-expanding state which gobbled up resources and stifled social initiative. Or, society (or parts of it) could be *too big*, such as when large and resource-rich institutions (businesses, trades unions, professions, for example) or powerful social networks (financial markets, the media) are able to ride roughshod over weaker institutions (small businesses, voluntary bodies, arts associations, independent newspapers) or vulnerable individuals (non-unionised employees, the unemployed, members of ethnic minorities, single parents). When society – or part of it – is too big, the state must act to redress the imbalance of power or resources in order to protect the common good. If the state is too small to bring this about, it must seek where possible to make itself bigger by expanding its legislative power, its administrative muscle, its revenue base; or sometimes all three.

The pluralistic social ontology underling the Catholic principle of subsidiarity obviously does not itself resolve any detailed policy debates regarding when and how any particular state should expand, contract or be restructured. I have tried to show how it may, nonetheless, offer an instructive framework against which such policy debates might be more illuminatingly conducted.

References

Aroney, Nicholas. 2011. European lessons for Australia's federal balance. *Federal Law Review* 39(2): 213–234. Available at Social Science Research Network: http://papers.ssrn.com/sol3/papers.cfm?abstract_id=1912215

Calvez, H., and J. Perrin. 1961. *The church and social justice*. Chicago: Henry Regnery.

Carney, Frederick. 1966. Associational thought in early Calvinism. In *Voluntary associations*, ed. D.B. Robertson, 39–53. Richmond: John Knox.

Centre for Economic Policy Research. 1993. *Making sense of subsidiarity: How much centralization for Europe?* Monitoring European integration 4. London: CEPR.

Chaplin, Jonathan. 1993. Subsidiarity and sphere sovereignty: Catholic and reformed conceptions of the role of the state. In *Things old and new: Catholic social teaching revisited*, ed. F.P. McHugh and S.M. Natale, 175–202. Lanham: University Press of America.

Chaplin, Jonathan. 2005. Toward a social pluralist theory of institutional rights. *Ave Maria Law Review* 3(1): 147–170.

Chaplin, Jonathan. 2010. The concept of "civil society" and Christian social pluralism. In *The Kuyper Center review, vol. 1: Politics, religion and sphere sovereignty*, ed. Gordon Graham, 14–33. Grand Rapids: Eerdmans.

Chaplin, Jonathan. 2011a. *Herman Dooyeweerd: Christian philosopher of state and civil society*. Notre Dame: University of Notre Dame.

Chaplin, Jonathan. 2011b. Why a "just society" must also be a "big society". *Cardus Policy in Public*, June 8. http://www.cardus.ca/policy/article/2812/

Dooyeweerd, Herman. 1979. *Roots of Western culture*. Toronto: Wedge.

Fogarty, Michael. 1957. *Christian democracy in Western Europe 1820–1953*. Notre Dame: University of Notre Dame.

Grasso, Kenneth L. 2008. The subsidiary state. In *Christianity and civil society: Catholic and neo-Calvinist perspectives*, ed. Jeanne Heffernan Schindler, 31–65. Lanham: Lexington.

Hittinger, Russell. 2003. Reasons for civil society. In *The first grace: Rediscovering the natural law in a post-Christian world*, ed. Russell Hittinger, 270–275. Wilmington: ISI Books.

Hittinger, Russell. 2008. Social pluralism and subsidiarity in Catholic social doctrine. In *Christianity and civil society: Catholic and neo-Calvinist perspectives*, ed. Jeanne Heffernan Schindler, 11–30. Lanham: Lexington.

John XXIII. 1984. Mater et Magister (§65). In *Proclaiming justice and peace: Documents from John XXIII to John Paul II*, ed. Michael Walsh and Brian Davies, 1–44. London: CAFOD/Collins. http://www.vatican.va/holy_father/john_xxiii/encyclicals/documents/hf_j-xxiii_enc_15051961_mater_en.html

Kuyper, Abraham. 1998. Sphere sovereignty. In *Abraham Kuyper: A centennial reader*, ed. James Bratt, 461–490. Grand Rapids: Eerdmans.

Leo XIII. 1954. On the rights and duties of capital and labor (*Rerum novarum*). In *The church speaks to the modern world: The social teachings of Leo XIII*, ed. Etienne Gilson, 200–244. Garden City: Image Books. http://www.vatican.va/holy_father/leo_xiii/encyclicals/documents/hf_l-xiii_enc_15051891_rerum-novarum_en.html

Leys, Ad. 1995. *Ecclesiological impacts of the principle of subsidiarity*. Kampen: Kok.

Longley, Clifford. 2009. Government and the common good. In *God and government*, ed. Nick Spencer and Jonathan Chaplin, 159–179. London: SPCK.

Loughlin, John, Peter Allott, and Richard Crellin. 2013. *The UK government's 'big society' programme and Catholic social teaching*. Cambridge: Von Hügel Institute.

Maritain, Jacques. 1951. *Man and the state*. Chicago: University of Chicago.

Maritain, Jacques. 1973. *Integral humanism*. Notre Dame: University of Notre Dame.

Messner, Johannes. 1949. *Social ethics*. St. Louis/London: B. Herder.

O'Brien, Denis. 2007. Subsidiarity and solidarity. In *Catholic social teaching and the market economy*, ed. Philip Booth, 233. London: Institute of Economic Affairs.

O'Donovan, Oliver. 2005. *The ways of judgment*. Grand Rapids: Eerdmans.

Pakaluk, Michael. 2002. Natural law and civil society. In *Alternative conceptions of civil society*, ed. Simone Chambers and Will Kymlicka, 133. Princeton: Princeton University Press.

Pius XI. 1960. *The social order (Quadragesimo Anno)*. London: Catholic Truth Society. http://www.vatican.va/holy_father/pius_xi/encyclicals/documents/hf_p-xi_enc_19310515_quadragesimo-anno_en.html

Rommen, Heinrich. 1945. *The state in Catholic thought*. New York: Herder.

Schindler, Jeanne Heffernan. 2008. *Christianity and civil society: Catholic and neo-Calvinist perspectives*. Lanham: Lexington.

Skillen, James W. (ed.). 1991. *Abraham Kuyper: The problem of poverty*. Grand Rapids/Washington, DC: Baker Book House/Center for Public Justice.

van Kersbergen, Kees. 1995. *Social capitalism: A study of Christian democracy and the welfare state*. London: Routledge.

Von-Nell Breuning, Oswald. 1981. 50 jaar "Quadragesimo Anno". *Christen Democratische Verkenningen* 12: 599–606.

Chapter 6
Subsidiarity, Democracy and Individual Liberty in Brazil

Augusto Zimmermann

Abstract Subsidiarity holds that nothing should be done by a larger and more distant level of power which can be done as well by a smaller and closer level of power. In other words, anything that can be performed by a more decentralized entity should not be done by a more centralized one. As such, subsidiarity can be seen as a bulwark of limited government and individual liberty, conflicting with the desire for bureaucratic centralization which is characteristic of the welfare state. First, this chapter contains a general discussion of subsidiarity and its ability to enhance democracy and individual liberty. This discussion is followed by a critical analysis of how individual autonomy and dignity are undermined by the welfare state. Finally, the chapter discusses the centralising, statist nature of the Brazilian government, thus highlighting subsidiarity's potential to enhance democracy and individual liberty in Brazil.

Keywords Brazil • Brazilian Constitution • Welfare state • Centralisation • Human rights • Democracy • Statism • Centralisation • Individual liberty

In a liberal democracy efforts are made to limit the power of the state. Citizens are told that they have basic human rights and that not only the state but also other citizens themselves have to respect these basic rights. In this context, subsidiarity sets the limits of governmental action, by allowing the citizen and social groups to freely interact among themselves, to do what they can do by themselves, thus leaving to the state only what cannot be done otherwise. In a country like Brazil, however, subsidiarity does not fit very well with the more "providential" nature of the Brazilian state, which has been historically highly interventionist and,

A. Zimmermann (✉)
Murdoch University School of Law, South Street, Murdoch, 6150 Perth, Western Australia, Australia
e-mail: a.zimmermann@murdoch.edu.au

M. Evans and A. Zimmermann (eds.), *Global Perspectives on Subsidiarity*, Ius Gentium: Comparative Perspectives on Law and Justice 37, DOI 10.1007/978-94-017-8810-6_6,

accordingly, failing to recognise the role played by the individual and social groups, and not just the state, in the realisation of the common good.

This chapter explores the principle of subsidiarity's potential to enhance democracy and individual liberty in Brazil. The first part of this chapter contains a general discussion of subsidiarity and its ability to enhance democracy and individual liberty. Secondly, this chapter will comment on how individual autonomy and dignity are undermined by the welfare state. It will then apply this discussion in a Brazilian context to highlight the lack of subsidiarity in Brazilian society, and how the failure to implement subsidiarity has been detrimental to democracy and human rights. It will conclude with a discussion of the centralising, statist nature of the Brazilian Constitution, thus highlighting the need for reform in order to transfer responsibilities from the state, back to the individual.

6.1 Subsidiarity

Subsidiarity means the same as "assistance" or "help", implying, among other things, that the state has an obligation to help or assist citizens and social groups to flourish, not to swamp or absorb them. Despite similarities to be found with Calvinist teaching and its concept of 'sphere sovereignty',[1] the principle of subsidiarity is regarded as a cornerstone of the social doctrine of the Catholic Church. First introduced in the encyclical *Rerum Novarum* (1891), it has also been mentioned in subsequent encyclicals, such as *Quadragesimo Anno* (1931) and *Mater et Magistra* (1961).

More recently, in the encyclical *Centesimus Annus* (1991) Pope John Paul II stated that human nature 'is not completely fulfilled in the State, but is realised in various intermediary groups, beginning with the family, including economic, social, political and cultural groups which stem from human nature itself and have their own autonomy'.[2] The encyclical goes on to explain that the 'malfunctions and defects' of the 'welfare state' are the direct result an 'inadequate understanding of the tasks proper to the state'.[3] John Paul II concluded:

> [T]he principle of subsidiarity must be respect[ed] [so that] a community of a higher order should not interfere in the internal life of a community of a lower order, depriving the latter of its functions, but rather should support it in case of need and help to coordinate its activity with the activities of the rest of society, always with a view to the common good. … In fact, it would appear that needs are best understood and satisfied by people who are closest to them and who act as neighbours to those in need.[4]

---

[1] See Chap. 4 of this book.

[2] John Paul II, *Centesimus Annus*, Para 13.

[3] Ibid., Para 48.

[4] Ibid., Para 48.

6.2 Subsidiarity, Democracy and Individual Liberty

Subsidiarity requires that citizens must have basic rights to fully participate in society, including the right to earn a living and the right to participate in social and political life. In this context, subsidiarity aims to empower the citizen through encouraging decision-making closer to the region or problem at hand. As such, subsidiarity can be linked to a basic right also to belong to social and political institutions, including marriage and family, nationality, religious affiliation, cultural life and education.

In this sense, subsidiarity implies acknowledging the right of citizens to participate in various social and political relationships, such as the right to freedom of religion, for example. Such principle conveys a self-conscious re-orientation of public policies toward the realisation of the common good. This can be achieved, for instance, by leaving to the citizens, to citizens' families, and to their communities, what they can do by themselves, and leaving in the hands of the state only what is not possible to be done otherwise.

Subsidiarity enhances democracy because it prevents concentration of power, which is so often inimical to political participation.[5] By approximating the citizen to the centres of deliberation, subsidiarity consists in leaving up to the central power only what cannot be done otherwise, and by lesser circles of power.[6] Of course, that is not to say that there is no role for a more distant level of government. For example, certain powers might need to be vested in a national government, such as where there are overriding national interest concerns (such as defence), where national uniformity is required for reasons of equity (such as social security benefits), or where there are significant potential inter-jurisdictional spill-overs if a lower level of government is given responsibility.

When we speak of subsidiarity as applied to constitutional design, we should not just think about decentralising power. Indeed, we should think about strengthening a model of governance that is not just a blanket call to strengthen the local power, but rather a call for a more effective and clear balance between national and local responsibilities. Because subsidiarity is focused on the subordinate performance of the state, it rearranges governmental functions so that the tiers of power with greatest proximity to the citizen are prioritized. Implicit in the idea is the understanding that the local power can perform most activities and community services just as efficiently as a more distant, central one, if not more so. That so being, subsidiarity provides

> … that functions should, where practical, be vested in the lowest level of government to ensure that their exercise is as close to the people as possible and reflects community preferences and local conditions … The principle of subsidiarity places the onus on those who seek to place a function with a higher level of government to make the case for it.[7]

[5] Walker (2001, p. 37).

[6] See Zimmermann (2000, p. 7).

[7] Twomey (2008, p. 59).

There are enormous difficulties associated with attempting to govern countries the size of Brazil, with a single, centralised government. Additionally, there are numerous other advantages apparent in adopting subsidiarity with the goal of improving institutional arrangements that tend to produce more stable and efficient democratic governance, as well as higher rates of economic growth and greater accountability in government. If one looks at quantifying the benefit of implementing public policies based on this principle, it is possible to suggest that subsidiarity could provide a number of advantages such as the plurality to be achieved through increased democratic participation and access to the political system, as well as regional autonomy and political diversity.[8] An awareness of these benefits means recognising that policies based on subsidiarity would make governments more adaptable to the preferences of the citizen, more open to experiment and rational evaluation, more resistant to shock and misadventure, and, ultimately, much more stable.

Subsidiarity helps promote a decentralized participatory structure of government. Such decentralisation of power might work as a buttress of individual liberty and a counterweight to elitism. It may foster the qualities of personal responsibility and self-government, so that through greater ease of monitoring the bureaucratic apparatuses of the state become less of a burden on the citizen. By preventing further concentration of political power, subsidiarity achieves a better protection of our individual rights as well as a closer supervision of government. Thomas Jefferson no doubt had this in mind when he uttered these words about the government of the United States:

> It is not by the consolidation or concentration of powers, but by their distribution that good government is effected. Were not this great country already divided into States, that division must be made that each might do for itself what concerns itself directly and what it can so much better do than a distant authority. Every state again is divided into counties, each to take care of what lies within its local bounds; each county again into townships or wards, to manage minuter details; and every ward into farms, to be governed each by its individual proprietor. Were we directed from Washington when to sow and when to reap, we should soon want bread. It is by this partition of cares descending in gradation from general to particular that the mass of human affairs may be best managed for the good and prosperity of all.[9]

The enhancement of democracy arises from the citizens being given multiple points of access to the government, and through greater choice and diversity provided. The distribution of powers supported by subsidiarity implies in the creation of policies enabling the national strength of a large nation to be combined to the enhanced participatory qualities of small democratic units.[10] The enhancement of democratic

[8] Heywood (2002, p. 10).

[9] Jefferson (1829, p. 66).

[10] Montesquieu expressed the same idea in *The Spirit of the Laws* (1789): "If a republic be small, it is destroyed by a foreign force; if it be large, it is ruined by an internal imperfection … It is, therefore, very probable that mankind would have been, at length, obliged to live constantly under the government of a single person, had they not contrived a kind of constitution that has all the internal advantages of a republican, together with the external force of a monarchical, government. I mean a confederate republic. This form of government is a convention by which several petty states agree to become members of a larger one, which they intend to establish. It is a kind of assemblage

participation through multiple tiers of government is a considerable advantage for democracy.[11] As the late jurist Hans Kelsen pointed out:

> Democracy … may be centralized as well as decentralized in a static sense; but decentralization allows a closer approach to the idea of democracy than centralization. This idea is the principle of self-determination. Democracy demands the utmost conformity between the general will as expressed in the legal order and the will of the individuals subject to the order; this is why the legal order is created by the very individual who are bound by it according to the principle of majority. Conformity to the order with the will of the majority is the aim of democratic organization. But the central norms of the order, valid of the whole territory, may easily come into contradiction with the majority will of a group living on a partial territory. The fact that the majority of the total community belongs to a certain political party, nationality, race, language, or religion, does not exclude the possibility that within certain partial territories the majority of individuals belong to another party, nationality, race, language, or religion. The majority of the entire nation may be socialistic or Catholic, the majority of one or more provinces may be liberal or Protestant. In order to diminish the possible contradiction between the contents of the legal order and the will of the individuals subject to it, in order to approximate as far as possible the ideal of democracy, it may be necessary, under certain circumstances, that certain norms of the legal order be valid only for certain partial territories and be created only by majority of votes of the individuals living in these territories. Under the condition that the population of the State has no uniform social structure, territorial division of the State territory into more or less autonomous provinces … may be a democratic postulate.[12]

As can be seen, greater flexibility in public choice allows the needs of citizens in different localities to be met through the customisation of policies at the sub-national level. For countries with large territories such as Brazil, the benefits of subsidiarity are obvious. The needs and issues of somebody living in Porto Alegre will never be the same as those of someone living in Rio de Janeiro, and it is simply unrealistic to expect a bureaucrat in Brasília to be responsive to these differing local concerns. Therefore, a federal system based on subsidiarity serves to strengthen participatory democracy by bringing about a government that is much closer to the citizen, and which allows local people to have a greater say in the decisions that directly affect them.

Related to this is the assumption that subsidiarity protects individual liberty. It does so by preventing excessive accumulation and concentration of power in the state, in particular at the central level. Sir Harry Gibbs, a former Chief Justice of the High Court of Australia, once remarked that the most effective way to curb political power is to divide it.[13] This idea that decentralisation secures the protection of individual rights was fully supported by the longest-serving Prime Minister in Australia's history, Sir Robert Menzies, who stated that 'in the division of power, in the demarcation of powers between a Central Government and the State Government there

---

of societies, that constitute a new one, capable of increasing by means of further associations, till they arrive at such a degree of power as to be able to provide for the security of the whole body". – Charles-Louis de Secondat (1900, p. 126).

[11] Galligan and Walsh (1992, p. 195).

[12] Kelsen (1945, p. 313).

[13] Gibbs (1991, p. 326).

resides one of the true protections of individual freedom'.[14] A similar point is also made by James Madison, in *Federalist No. 51*:

> In a single republic, all the power surrendered by the people is submitted to the administration of a single government; and the usurpations are guarded against by a division of the government into distinct and separate departments. In the compound republic of America, the power surrendered by the people is first divided between two distinct governments, and then the portion allotted to each subdivided among distinct and separate departments. Hence a double security arises to the rights of the people. The different governments will control each other, at the same time that each will be controlled by itself.[15]

6.3 Subsidiarity and the Welfare State

Subsidiarity recognises that there are aspects of human life that the state may not legitimately control. Subsidiarity therefore advocates the opposite of totalitarian dictatorship, meaning the absolute control by the state of our individual lives. The embodiment of totalitarianism is not legal authority but naked power, which is created by a progressive degeneration of social relations that occurs when ambition usurps the rule of law, which is also the rule of reason.[16] In sum, totalitarian dictatorship amounts to a repudiation of the demands of democratic society for individual rights and the rule of law.

The transition from democracy to totalitarian dictatorship is a process of both individual and social disintegration by which the latter has its roots in the former. When passion and desire are exalted above reason and responsibility, when all desires become acceptable and no objective standard is left for choosing among them, then a master-passion emerges and appetitive desires are 'liberated' from all personal restraint. The final result is a complete 'anarchy in the human soul and society'.[17]

And as just as an oppressive government desires to take full possession of the citizen, so it happens with the citizen who knows nothing about personal restraint and to whom 'freedom' has become unsustainable. Such a person will be voluntarily willing to submit him-or-herself to the arbitrary will of the state so as to escape the tyranny of their own individual passions. Freedom now having become a mere license is transformed into an intolerable burden for the individual, so that the individual seeks to escape from it by accepting his or her complete submission to the political ruler.[18]

When life is subject to no order or personal restraint, freedom becomes a mere licence to do as one pleases. Such distinction was commonly made by the American

---

[14] Menzies (1967, p. 24).

[15] Madison (1961, p. 323).

[16] Hallowell (2007, p. 100).

[17] Ibid.

[18] Ibid., pp. 99–100.

Founding Fathers as well as classical liberal theorists such as John Locke. By "liberty" they meant those freedoms which people ought to possess. "License", by contrast, refers to those freedoms which people ought not to have, and thus those freedoms which are lawfully constrained.[19] Ultimately, wrote John H. Hallowell, 'freedom conceived as license leads to anarchy, and anarchy manifests itself in political tyranny'.[20] Indeed, as Plato put it five centuries before Christ, the citizens will become so insensitive 'that they resent the slightest application of control as intolerable tyranny, and in their resolve to have no master they end by disregarding even the law, written or unwritten'.[21]

Christianity informs that all human beings are born of a sinful nature. One finds here an excellent justification for the separation of governmental powers. That is, power must be checked because everyone is a sinner and nobody can be trusted with too much power. The Christian ideal of civil government has therefore much more to do with avoiding the concentration of powers, than with providing any unchecked power or a 'right' for the government to impose its own understanding of the common good, whatever it might be. Instead, Christianity refers mainly to the primary responsibility of the individual, and not of the state, in protecting the weak, the poor, the widows, and the orphans. Accordingly, we must be held personally accountable for our own actions and omissions, and we should never leave to the state what we as individuals can do not only for ourselves but also for our families, for our fellow citizens, and for our community as a whole.

Perhaps one of the hardest things today is to convince others that they ought to govern themselves. With the rise of the modern welfare state and subsequent decline of Christian values and traditions, significant moral restraints on social behaviour have been removed. As a result, in a country like England, for example, it appears that the highest levels of criminality have occurred precisely at a time of unheard-of prosperity, public healthcare and government welfare. Referring to this interesting phenomenon, Peter Hitchens comments:

> The highest levels of crime in memory have occurred at a time of unheard-of prosperity, health, social welfare provision, good housing and material contentment. This destroys the idea that increased welfare leads to a reduction in crime. On the contrary, it raises the possibility that well-meaning state intervention to improve the lot of the poor can actually lead to increased crime… It is the decay and destruction of moral values and self-restraint… that have led to the misery of the modern poor.[22]

The poor are those who are hurt the most by welfare policies and their situation would be improved without intervention by the 'welfare state' for several reasons. First of all, government welfare undermines private charity, because all the dollars collected in taxes from citizens become unavailable for private charity. When all

[19] Barnett (1998, p. 2).

[20] Hallowell (2007, p. 102).

[21] Plato (1945, p. 289).

[22] Hitchens (2003, p. 23).

these assets are taken from the people by their government, it leaves very little or nothing for them to donate to private charity. According to John Gray, the regime of high taxation inseparable from government welfare diminishes the sphere of free services in which the individual engages in spontaneous relations, thereby 'corroding the culture of civility that sustain liberal civilization'.[23] Furthermore, by making it impossible for people to support charitable activities and associations out of their shrunken incomes, the state then acquires greater financial power to invest and to choose which it supports.[24] This, writes Gray, leads to a greater centralization of power in the hands of the state:

> If the state confiscates high incomes and imposes penal rates of taxation on saving and investment, the state must take over the saving and investment activities that private individuals are no longer able to undertake. If, because of the confiscation of higher incomes, there are important social and cultural activities that can no longer be sustained privately, such as provision for high culture and the arts, then once again the state must assume responsibility for such activities through a program of subsidy. Inevitably, the state comes to exercise ever-increasing degree of control over them. The consequence of redistributionist policy, accordingly, is the curtailment of private initiative in many spheres of social life, the destruction of the man of independent means, and the weakening of civil society.[25]

As can be seen, the principal consequence of government welfare is to expand the centralising power of the state, which is made acceptable only by measures of redistribution.[26] Such redistribution, according to Bertrand de Jouvenel, 'is in effect far less a redistribution of free income from the richer to the poorer … than a redistribution of power from the individual to the State'.[27] The final result, he says, '[is] a transfer of power from individual to officials, who tend to constitute a new ruling class as against that which is being destroyed. And there is a faint but quite perceptible trend toward immunity for this new class from some part of the fiscal measures directed at the former'.[28]

In this sense, it seems that the greatest gainer from public expenditure induced by welfare policies 'is not the lower-income class as against the higher, but the State as against the citizen'.[29] In other words, the ultimate beneficiaries of public expenditure for 'social welfare' are not the poor, as the intended recipients, but rather the bureaucrats who are employed to administer these services. The socio-welfare bureaucracies were legislated in the name of the poor, but much of the money spent in such 'welfare' has been consumed by the bureaucracy itself. These agencies are oriented to more powerful groups, which

[23] Gray (1990, p. xiii).

[24] Ibid., p. xii.

[25] Ibid., p. xiv.

[26] de Jouvenel (1990, p. 76).

[27] Ibid., p. 72.

[28] Ibid., p. 77.

[29] Ibid., p. 73.

provide them with the sort of political support they need for their own survival and expansion.[30] Indeed, in our modern welfare states, Tom G. Palmer explains:

> Each one thinks himself or herself lucky when he or she gets a benefit, but don't stop to think of the cost of the benefits to everyone else; when everyone acts that way, the costs become enormous. The poor suffer the worst, because a trickle of benefits may seem like a boom to them, when their very poverty is both perpetuated by the welfare state and deepened by the hidden transfers from the powerless to the powerful caused by protectionism, licensing, and other restrictions on labor market freedom, and all the other privileges and special deals the powerful, the educated, the articulated, and the empowered create for themselves at the expense of the weak, the uneducated, the voiceless, and the disempowered.[31]

Though government aid can do some good for some people who may need only a temporary boost to get back on their feet, it has created a huge and expensive bureaucracy that is sustained by a permanent underclass of chronically poor individuals and their families. Such poverty is ultimately related to social pathologies that cannot be properly addressed by the state, such as alcohol addiction, drug abuse, fatherless homes, and crime. Hence, what the recipient of 'welfare' more often needs is a strong message of work, sobriety, and personal responsibility from the surrounding culture. Therefore, to a great extent, Dr Nancy Pearcey suggests:

> Government aid can actually make things worse. By handing out welfare checks impersonally to all who qualify, without addressing the underlying behavioural problems, the government in essence 'rewards' antisocial and dysfunctional patterns. And any behaviour the government rewards will generally tend to increase. As one perceptive nineteenth century critic noted, government assistance is a 'might solvent to sunder the ties of kinship, to quench the affections of family, to suppress in the poor themselves the instinct of self-reliance and self-respect – to convert them into paupers.[32]

---

[30] Palmer (2012a, p. 45).

[31] Palmer (2012b, p. 8). Moreover, as Palmer also points out, "immigrants are systematically demonized as "here to get our welfare benefits". Rather than welcoming people to come and produce wealth, subjects of welfare states act to protect "their welfare benefits" by excluding would-be immigrants and demonizing them that then as locusts and looters. Meanwhile, political elites loudly proclaim that they are helping poor people abroad by using money taken from taxpayers to fund a parasitic international "aid industry", dumping huge quantities of the agricultural surpluses that have been generated by welfare state politics (to subsidize farmers by guaranteeing floor prices for their products), and handing over loot to autocratic governments: in short, by internationalizing the welfare state". – Ibid., p. 8.

[32] Pearcey (2004, p. 61). A similar point is made by Wilhelm von Humboldt in *The Limits of State Action* (1792): "The evil results of a too extensive solicitude on the part of the State, are still more strikingly shown in the suppression of all active energy, and the necessary deterioration of the moral character. This scarcely needs further argument. The man who is often led, easily becomes disposed willingly to sacrifice what remains of his capacity for spontaneous action. He fancies himself released from an anxiety which he sees transferred to other hands, and seems to himself to do enough when he looks to their leadership and follows it. Thus, his notions of merit and guilt become unsettled. The idea of the first no longer inspires him; and the painful consciousness of the last assails him less frequently and forcibly, since he can more easily ascribe his shortcomings to this particular position, and leave them to the responsibility of those who have made it what it is. If we add to this, that he may not, possibly, regard the designs of the State as perfectly pure in their objects or execution – that he may suspect that his own advantage only, but along with it some other additional purpose is intended, then, not only the force and energy, but also the purity of his moral nature

Above all, the assistance or help afforded by the state cannot address the more pressing moral and spiritual needs that lie at the heart of dysfunctional behaviour. These needs go much beyond what any government can do. This is something that the citizens, individually or with the help or assistance of their families, churches and charity groups should be doing, and not the state. And yet, in today's society, said H.B. Acton, 'families are so scattered and friendships are so dispersed, that … fewer people think they ought to help one another in these ways … and people in distress no longer expect to obtain much help this way'.[33] According to Acton, 'no doubt this unconcern has been encouraged by the establishment of public [i.e., government] relief organisations'.[34]

True compassion means suffering with the poor and acting on the consciousness of those who are suffering and those who are assisting. And yet, the 'welfare state' has not fulfilled the literal meaning of Christian compassion – 'suffering with others'. On the contrary, government aid undermines personal responsibility, which, in the long term, tends to perpetuate, not to eliminate, socio-economic problems. It certainly does not assist people to change specific lifestyles that might have contributed to the problem.[35] Arguably, redistributionist policies cannot fight poverty effectively simply because it does not affect the attitudes that often undergird poverty. Rather, such policies undermine personal responsibility by transferring authority for crucial life-decisions from the individuals who make them to the State. By further minimising responsibility, government aid pushes the community 'toward a spiritual and moral crisis, with the familiar

suffers. He now conceives himself not only completely free from any duty which the State has not expressly imposed upon him, but exonerated at the same time from every personal effort to improve his own condition; and, even fears such an effort, as if it were likely to open out new opportunities, of which the State might take advantage. And as for the laws actually enjoined, he tries as much as possible to escape their operation, considering every such evasion as a positive gain. If we reflect that, among a large part of the nation, its laws and political institutions have the effect of limiting the sphere of morality, it is a melancholy spectacle to see the most sacred duties, and mere trivial and arbitrary enactments, often proclaimed from the same authoritative source, and to see the infraction of both met with the same measure of punishment. Further, the pernicious influence of such a positive policy is no less evident in the behaviour of the citizens to each other. As each individual abandons himself to the solicitous aid of the State, so, and still more, he abandons to it the fate of his fellow-citizens. This weakens sympathy and renders mutual assistance inactive: or, at least, the reciprocal interchange of services and benefits will be most likely to flourish at its liveliest, where the feeling is most acute that such assistance is the only thing to rely upon; and experience teaches us that oppressed classes of the community which are, as it were, overlooked by the government, are always bound together by the closest ties. But whether the citizen becomes indifferent to this fellows, so will the husband be to his wife, and the father of a family towards the members of this household". Wilhelm von Humboldt, *The Limits of State Action* [1792], Chapter III, available at http://ebooks.adelaide.edu.au/h/humboldt/wilhelm_von/sphere/chapter3.html

[33] Acton (1993, pp. 81–82).

[34] Ibid.

[35] Indeed, surveys carried out in the homeless shelters ran by Doe Fund in the 1990s, has showed that four out of five of their residents were chronic drug users, whose problem was not unaffordable housing but self-destructive behaviour – enabled by a culture that downplayed individual responsibility, self-control, and deferral of gratification necessary for success and self-sufficiency. – Magnet (1993, p. 2).

symptoms of broken or never-formed families, teen drug abuse and pregnancy, crime, civic disengagement, and disenchantment with public life'.[36]

Subsidiarity informs that we should strive to help or assist our fellow human beings to flourish. In so doing, we must shift power away from the bureaucrats to the real people in the community, who can deal much better with these problems.[37] It is not for anyone to excuse or neglect his or her own responsibilities by transferring them to others, in particular to the state.[38] The goal here is first to look within the family and if the family cannot help, maybe an individual or group within the neighbourhood can; if not, then organisations outside the neighbourhood but within the community should be called on. If it is really necessary to turn to government, then we should look first to municipal, then to state, and only then to federal offices. At each governmental level, the preference should be levels of power which are closer to the individual, before proceeding to the higher or more distant levels of government.[39]

6.4 Subsidiarity in the Brazilian Context

Subsidiarity opposes statism and it recognises the primacy of the individual and social groups that makes up civil society; letting them do what they can do by themselves and leaving up to the state only what cannot be done otherwise. And yet, if statism is defined as an ideology providing a preferential role for the state in society, placing the state as the principal agent of socio-economic transformation, then it is patently clear that statism is highly pervasive in Brazil.[40] It unites people from all social classes and political inclinations. Indeed, Brazilians seem to expect just about everything from their government. From jobs, stable prices, credit, subsidies for carnival masquerades, there is hardly anything for which the government is not expected to provide.

It is not so much that the ruling elite comprises only of bureaucrats, but rather that the Brazilian state is the base to which all individuals and social groups adhere either through alliance or dependence. Since the state in Brazil is the ultimate provider of all meaningful resources, 'the citizenry expects to live at government expense and under full protection'.[41] As a result, Brazilian-style statism has been fully supported by old-fashioned socialists, neo-mercantilist businesspeople, conservatives who oppose social change, the nationalistic military, privileged bureaucrats, intellectuals who seek after state subvention, and all sorts of 'compassionate' individuals who think the state is the only entity with power to eradicate poverty and promote 'social justice'.

In today's Brazil, many are those who still expect all sorts of favours from their government. These favours can come in the form of such things as t-shirts, bags of

[36] Olasky (2000, p. 11).

[37] Olasky, above n.27, p. 13.

[38] Santamaria (2006, p. 6).

[39] Olasky, above n.27, p. 19.

[40] See: Paim (1994).

[41] Heitor de Paula (2006).

basic foodstuff, bags of cement, beer, telephone lines, musical instruments, and paint for buildings.[42] A survey of city councillors in Rio de Janeiro has found that 40 % of those politicians owned multi-service centres for the purposes of providing voters with free yoga classes, massages, gyms, dental care, and so forth.[43] Ultimately, the electoral process in Brazil may be described as a great bargaining process that might even include the purchase of votes.[44] Indeed, a survey carried out by *Transparency International* has revealed that no less than 6 % of all Brazilian voters in 2000 had received pay-offs in exchange for votes during that year's municipal elections.[45]

Another example is the distribution of money to families in the form of a supposed anti-poverty program called *Bolsa Família* (family fund), which provides cash to around 8.7 million families, roughly a fifth of the country's population. Of course, such 'generosity' offers no solution to eliminating the causes of poverty but it makes millions of individuals and their families entirely depending on the state to survive, thus making them approach the government as a paternal provider for themselves. And yet, such 'generosity' in public spending is one of the major reasons why public debt, taxes and interest rates are so high in the country. Real interest rates in Brazil are among the highest in the world, with its government grabbing approximately 40 % of GDP in the form of taxes and contributions.[46] Moreover, it is quite evident that such paternalism has provoked widespread corruption, which can be demonstrated, among many other things, by a 2006 finding that federal resources destined for food relief victims have been used to build houses for employees of local government.[47]

6.5 Understanding the Lack of Subsidiarity in Brazil

To understand the lack of subsidiarity in Brazil, one needs to consider the reality of a government that has historically been above society.[48] The problem is primarily a by-product of an old 'spoils-system' inherited from Portugal, a country where the monarch granted to his staff, and preferred subjects, all sorts of graces and favours at the expense of fairness and the rule of law. In Portugal's Catholic medieval hierarchy, the class of entrepreneurs (traders) was ranked lowest on the social scale. 'As in Communist China and Marxist Russia', wrote C.R. Boxer, 'the merchant was regarded as a parasitic and profiteering middle-man, resolved to enrich himself at the expanse of his fellow-men'.[49] As a result, not only the Portuguese Crown had an enormous variety of commercial monopolies – ranging from the importation of

[42] Kuschnir (2005, p. 3).

[43] Ibid., p. 2.

[44] Ibid., p. 9.

[45] Speck and Abramo (2002).

[46] *The Economist* (2006).

[47] Fitzpatrick (2006).

[48] DaMatta (1987, p. 296).

[49] Boxer (1969, p. 319).

sugar to the control of the soap industry –, but regional and district monopolies were granted to favoured individuals and courtiers.[50] According to Boxer:

> It would take too long to enumerate ... all the overseas sources of wealth which were exploited by the Crown at one time or another, whether in the form of a (theoretically) rigorous monopoly, or a percentage of the profits, or in the way of Customs duties and export and import dues... Even such trivia as river ferry-crossings and the dues from washermen, Limeburners and fishermen were often rented out by the Crown or by its representatives. Perhaps more than any other country, it was a long-established practice in Portugal for the Crown (and its successor republic) to farm out the smallest public offices which might be expected to produce any revenue; and the same procedure was followed in Portuguese India, Ceylon, Africa and Brazil.[51]

Another factor that decisively contributed to the lack of subsidiarity was slavery. The abhorrent institution lasted longer in Brazil than in any other nation in the Western hemisphere, only being abolished in 1888. In his 1879 visit to the country, United States historian Herbert H. Smith associated slavery with a 'culture of indolence, pride, and selfishness' that, in his opinion, made the majority of Brazilians aspire to live 'as parasites on others or on the government'.[52] Overall, slavery left as its principal heritage a mass trained to be utterly dependent on the government and others.[53] According to the late Brazilian historian José Honório Rodrigues:

> It was not recognized that... poverty could be overcome by work and saving. Work was scorned; it was reserved exclusively for slaves. No attention was paid to saving, with the result that the capital required for possession and enjoyment of the riches so greatly vaunted in speeches was never accumulated.[54]

Centuries of slavery had the dramatic effect of debasing the value of labour and perverting any sense of personal liberty and responsibility.[55] Slavery left deep prejudices against active life and 'disinclination to serious endeavor in the areas of commerce and industry'.[56] It brought about a whole society with marked contempt for any work other than that of a public employment. The state became, in the words of anti-slavery leader Joaquim Nabuco, 'the refuge of the descendants of the rich and noble families who squandered the fortunes acquired through slavery'.[57] He identified the following link between slavery and statism in the country:

> Among the classes which slavery artificially generates, the largest is that of the public employees. The close relationship between slavery and the epidemic of bureaucratism is not more open to doubt than the relationship between it and the superstition of the All-Providing State. Under that system, the government is counted on for everything. Being the only active organization, the state covets and absorbs all disposable capital by means of taxation and loans, distributing among its clients by means of public employment, absorbing the

[50] Ibid., p. 321.

[51] Ibid., p. 322.

[52] Smith (1967, p. 134).

[53] Harris (1972, p. 216).

[54] Rodrigues (1967, p. 40).

[55] See: Carvalho, *The Struggle for Democracy in Brazil*, p. 135.

[56] Rodrigues, above n 48, p. 41.

[57] Nabuco (1977, p. 127).

> savings of the poor through inflation and rendering precarious the fortunes of the well-to-do. Any twenty or thirty Brazilians to be met wherever our most cultivated society gathers can provide the example. All of them either once were, or now are, or will one day be public employees; and if not they themselves, then their sons.[58]

Complaints over statism have been commonplace throughout the country's history. In 1870, for example, liberal politician A.C. Tavares Bastos wrote that there existed in Brazil a certain 'fear of companies', which he then associated with an 'anachronistic tradition of despotism that denies the modern spirit of liberty'.[59] As early as 1853, entrepreneurs like the Viscount of Mauá complained that 'everything is expected from the government and that individual initiative does not exist'.[60] He explained that any economic activity depended on 'official sensibilities' continuing to exist, and that people were deeply inclined to consider the state as the 'tutor' (paternal protector) of society.[61] As a result, the most successful businesspeople were the 'clients' of the landed gentry who controlled the state machinery. Such businesspeople expected to receive 'unbearable tutelage of the government'.[62] They saw this as an easier means of acquiring wealth than through work and production.

This problematic reality has not changed so much over the years. Brazil's most successful businesspeople are still the neo-mercantilists who practice some sort of cartel capitalism with the state. Under the pretext of protecting so-called 'national interest', they request manifold privileges such as preferential interest rates and special loans from state banks and other public agencies, which they often do not even have to repay. As a result, 'aspiring entrepreneurs are unable to seek relief, because economic decision-making is based on political concerns rather than rational dictates of the rule of law'.[63] Ultimately, cartel capitalism is developed once the state exercises its power for the enrichment of private interests. It involves, in countries like Brazil, a form of embezzlement of private wealth disguised as protection of so-called 'national interest'.

The deleterious effects of statism were perhaps more aggravated in the 1960s, with the ascension to power of army officers. At the end of their long authoritarian regime, in March 1985, those officers left behind more than 600 state-owned companies. By 1983, such companies accounted for more than three-quarters of the assets and half of the sales, profits, and employment of the 200 largest corporations in Brazil. In 1985, the year those army officers relinquished power, government expenditure represented 37.6 % of GDP, by far the highest of all countries in Latin America.[64] The enormous bureaucratic sector charged with managing this huge and notoriously inefficient state machinery resembled, in many respects, the *nomenklatura* of the former communist regimes in Eastern Europe. For example, some public employees worked only 9 months per year and yet they received a salary that was

---

[58] Ibid.

[59] Bastos (1870, p. 264).

[60] Graham (1968, p. 223).

[61] Ibid., p. 216.

[62] Silveira da Motta (1869, p. 21).

[63] Prillaman (2000, p. 9).

[64] Hagopian (2004, p. 102).

the equivalent of 16 working months. In an attempt to finance their manifold privileges the country became one of most heavily taxed in the world.[65]

Although Brazil has been a formal democracy since 1985, it is possible to argue that the state bureaucracy inherited from the past has retained most of its power and prestige. According to the *2013 Index of Economic Freedom* by *Heritage Foundation* in partnership with *The Wall Street Journal*, public spending still remains over one-third of GDP, whereas the current overall tax burden amounts to 32.5 % of GDP.[66] However, many Brazilians still believe that the archaic model of national-statism is a valid option for their country. This is so even though *Transparency International* has found that further privatisation would 'significantly reduce the amount of resources and positions subjected to political bargain'.[67] Naturally, a good reason for concern about the continuing 'omnipresence' of the Brazilian state has to do with bureaucratisation of social relations and widespread corruption. There is indeed a visible link between statism and corruption, in part because a 'big government' always provides a fertile breeding ground for more abuses of power, particularly in countries such as Brazil, with a government which is well-known for its corruption.

In conclusion, regardless of its would-be democratic constitution, the collective fancy in Brazil remains as one that is deeply dominated by the idea of 'omnipotence' of the Brazilian state. The Brazilian government is still widely regarded as being the ultimate provider of society and individuals. Thus, despite the military period coming to an end in 1985, statism has subsisted in a society invariably 'colonized' by the bureaucratisation of all social relations. Arguably, societies with such extensive governmental presence and state property holdings are considerably more susceptible to the problems of corruption and political tyranny. As Randy E. Barnett has asserted, in more generic terms, whenever the state authorities 'enjoy a vast range of privileges denied to their ordinary citizens, and are subject to few of the economic constraints of private institutions, their citizens are forever vulnerable to governmental tyranny.'[68]

6.6 Democracy, Individual Liberty and the Brazilian Constitution

Brazil has had eight constitutions since the country separated from Portugal in 1822.[69] Most of these constitutions were, in theory, based on liberal-democratic models of constitutionalism by virtue of establishing a bill of rights and a threefold

[65] Fitzpatrick (2005).

[66] 'Brazil', *2013 Index of Economic Freedom*, The Heritage Foundation and The Wall Street Journal, at http://www.heritage.org/index/country/brazil

[67] 'Report on Brazil'. Paper presented by the Brazilian branch of *Transparency International* to the *Global Forum II on Fighting Corruption*, Hague, May 2001, p. 9.

[68] Barnett (1998, p. 220).

[69] Whether Brazil has had seven or eight constitutions is still an unresolved issue among Brazilian constitutional lawyers. In 1969, a military junta which replaced President Costa e Silva, an army officer, when he suffered a stroke, issued an amendment that rewrote and re-numbered the whole

separation of state powers. In following this long, rights-based tradition, which began with the Imperial Constitution of 1823, the current *Constituição da República Federativa do Brasil* (Constitution of the Federal Republic of Brazil) lists a vast number of human rights, and describes remedies to ensure that these rights will be protected. However, all have suffered from extra-legal factors of a socio-political nature that have undermined the normal implementation of democratic constitutionalism.[70]

In fact, what the current, constitution states in Brazil can differ remarkably from what is in reality the case. Focusing on this, one might note for instance that the protection of women's rights enshrined in Brazil's Constitution has been lauded by international agencies such as the Inter-American Commission on Human Rights.[71] And yet, despite this formal protection, the reality is that Brazil has one of the world's highest levels of rape, attempted rape, and indecent assault against women. Such violent crimes are often underreported, with the perpetrators very likely to go unpunished.[72]

Offering another example, public security is explicitly regarded by the Brazilian Constitution as a 'fundamental right' of the individual citizen. And yet, criminals quite often have very little or nothing to fear by way of punishment, since only a very small minority of crimes, even first-degree murder and rape, are ever successfully prosecuted.[73] One reason for the soaring crime rates in Brazil is that the police are notoriously unqualified, poorly paid, corrupt and violent. It may be said that police officers would not be so corrupt and violent were they properly payed, trained and equipped.[74] The lack of an effective police system, together with the distrust in the court system, explains why some communities have set up their own system of 'counter-violence'.[75]

In relation to the lack of confidence in the judiciary, one might observe that Brazilians believe that their magistrates punish criminals inadequately. Instead, lenient sentences against dangerous criminals and certain categories of people, particularly the rich, politicians, and judges themselves, are applied. It is believed that these people are never suitably punished for breaking the law.[76] Moreover, the judiciary has historically been plagued by corruption, nepotism, inefficiency, and politicisation.[77] As a means of attenuating these problems, institutional reforms were suggested. Some of these reforms have been implemented by Amendment

---

text of the 1967 Constitution. Because this amendment resulted in an entirely new document, many have therefore concluded that it ended up creating a new constitution for Brazil.

[70] See Zimmermann (2010).

[71] Organization of American States (OAS) (2000).

[72] 'State of the World's Cities: Trends in Latin America & the Carribean – 2004', UN-Habitat, at: http://www.unhabitat.org/mediacentre/documents/sowc/RegionalLAC.pdf

[73] Unger (2004, p. 30).

[74] Hite and Morlino (2004, p. 59).

[75] By 'counter-violence' I mean things such as lynchings and vigilante justice.

[76] Prillaman, above n. 64, p. 95.

[77] See: Zimmermann (2008, pp. 196–198).

n.45 of November 2004. This amendment produced significative changes in the court system, providing, among other things, a better system of binding precedent.

Because the 1988 Constitution is recognised as being a particularly lengthy and convoluted document, with no regard whatsoever for the principle of subsidiarity, one important suggestion is that appeals to the country's Supreme Court (*Supremo Tribunal Federal – STF*) be restricted to issues really important to the nation's political organization. Such issues are those that the 1988 Constitution explicitly considers 'fundamental' to its democratic framework, namely: a federative form of State; a direct, secret, universal and periodic vote; the separation of government powers and individual rights and guarantees. Article 60, paragraph 4, protects these as 'stone clauses', prohibiting any proposal of constitutional amendment that is aimed at abolishing them.

Not restricting criticism to judges, a change of mentality is also required of Brazil's political players. The transition from a military regime to the existing model of constitutional democracy did not eliminate certain patterns of centralist and authoritarian behaviour that still provoke a great deal of corruption, arbitrariness, and bureaucratic red tape. These values benefit only a minority of privileged politicians and bureaucrats at the expense of society as a whole. Practical measures for reducing the problem could include the redefinition of the country's federal system, the reduction of public jobs held by political appointees, the restriction of spending schemes for politicians who obtain more funding when the government needs their votes in the legislature, and further privatisation of government-owned companies. Further research on the benefits of such measures is strongly recommended.

The principle of subsidiarity, once applied to federal models of government, focuses on the subordinate performance of centralist functions and rearranges the vertical levels of government so as to give priority to those with the greatest proximity to the citizen. It is thus a matter of great interest to the Brazilian state, which is a federation, to draw on such a principle for the decentralisation and further democratisation of its bewildering legal-political institutions. Predictably, the Brazilian federation has always been heavily influenced by the nation's ongoing tradition of centralised government. Arguably, the application of subsidiarity would lead to a more realistic appreciation being made of the country's natural pluralities, together with the need for redistributing governmental functions in order to empirically analyse what could be adequately transferred to the lower level of government, the one which is the closest to the individual, or simply be kept within the sphere of central government.[78]

Perhaps it is opportune to make a few more comments about the Brazilian Constitution. Promulgated on 5 October 1988, such constitution is a 'minutely detailed charter' designed to deal with 'almost every aspect of life in Brazil'.[79] It is a lengthy and convoluted document without regard for subsidiarity, and full of trivial details and unaffordable promises to be undertaken at a central governmental

---

[78] Zimmermann (2005, pp. 199–215).

[79] Page (1995, p. 22).

level.[80] For example, Article 3 informs that that the government must eradicate poverty and reduce all social and regional inequalities. Unfortunately, the mere enunciation of such objectives will bring no solution to the real problem. The result, instead, is an abysmal distance between law and social reality. Indeed, in countries like Brazil, Keith S. Rosenn points out:

> Constitutions typically contain a substantial number of aspirational or utopian provisions that are either impossible or extremely difficult to enforce. Some of these provisions contain social rights that seem far more appropriate in a political platform or a sermon than in a constitution.[81]

The Brazilian Constitution is called a "programmatic" document. A constitution is called programmatic if it lays down policy-making. The idea comes from the 1976 Constitution of Portugal, which demanded, in its original document, the country's 'gradual transition to socialism'.[82] Programmatic constitutions amount to a gross distortion of the traditional understanding of constitutionalism. They represent, in the words of Giovanni Sartori, 'a deviation and an overload of constitutional capacities that results, in turn, in their failure to function well'.[83] In the case of the Brazilian Constitution, its drafters have brought about a substantial amount of unsustainable promises, confounding real rights with mere expectations of rights.[84] Thus a great quantity of 'constitutional rights' seems to exist on paper only, and never in reality.[85] According to Joseph A. Page, the whole process of drafting the Brazilian Constitution, in 1987–1988, was surrounded by a 'surreal aura' in which representatives at the Constituent Assembly 'seemed to assume that constitutional fiat in and of itself could somehow transform the country, and that constitutional guarantees that all citizens would have equal access to basic rights would somehow concretize these aspirations'.[86]

The Brazilian Constitution grants all citizens the rights to education, health, work, and leisure.[87] It also assures protection of motherhood and childhood, as well as public assistance for the needy and disadvantaged. As for the protection of labour rights, the list includes protection against arbitrary dismissal, social security, minimal wage, the right to strike, paid weekly leave, maternity leave, and prohibition of difference in wages between men and women.[88] The constitutional text even contains the right to 'ecologically balanced environment',[89] thus creating the duty

---

[80] As example of trivial detail, Article 242 declares that a certain public school in Rio de Janeiro must be owned by the federal government.

[81] Rosenn (1990, p. 36).

[82] Prado (1994, p. 35).

[83] Sartori (1997, p. 200).

[84] Prado, above n.83, p. 62.

[85] See: Zimmermann (2007).

[86] Page, above n.80, p. 22.

[87] Braz. Const., Art.6.

[88] Braz. Const., Art.7, and Braz. Const., Art.9.

[89] Braz. Const., Art.225.

of the state to provide for the treatment of the nation's eco-system, preserving its eco-diversity against practices that can endanger species or subject animals to cruel treatment.[90] Finally, the state is required to guarantee the exercise of cultural rights as well as access to sources of national culture. The government is constitutionally obliged to support and foster the appreciation and diffusion of cultural expression, particularly expressions of popular, Indian and Afro-Brazilian cultures, or of any significative group participating within society.[91]

In the rather unlikely situation that the Brazilian Constitution might have 'forgotten' to mention any 'fundamental right', Article 5 then adds that all these rights explicitly mentioned therein do not preclude others that may be derived from the ideal of a democratic state under the rule of law (*Estado Democrático de Direito*) or from international treaties and conventions entered into by the Brazilian government. Finally, there is even a *cláusula pétrea* ('stone clause') in Article 60, which forbids any amendment aimed at abolishing: (1) federalism; (2) the direct, secret, universal and periodic vote; (3) the separation of governmental powers; and (4) individual rights and remedies.

As can be seen, the Brazilian Constitution is heavily committed to the ideal of human rights. Unfortunately, however, in describing the real situation it is not so difficult to observe the vivid contrast between rights on paper and how such rights might work in practice. The great paradox is that, despite its rights-based democratic constitution, even the most basic rights of many Brazilians are not necessarily respected. Clearly, law may deem a right 'fundamental', but it does not follow that such right will actually be guaranteed. Rather, it may simply be abused or just ignored by authorities and even other citizens. As a matter of fact, it would seem that some 'rights' described in the Brazilian Constitution are 'honoured' more in their breach than in their effective application.

The problem is related not only to the content of positive laws, even though some laws are indeed too unrealistic to bear any practical or positive results, but it more fundamentally resides in the lack of subsidiarity that is found in the rather exaggerated expectations that Brazilians seem to have about what their government can do, coupled with a widespread sense of lawlessness and lack of accountability that pervades all sectors of society. Such lack of subsidiarity reveals itself most glaringly in the empirical manifestation of a society that is deeply colonised by the government, whereby so many citizens have abdicated from their own personal responsibilities by transferring such responsibilities to a highly inefficient, notoriously corrupt government.

6.7 Conclusion

This chapter has explored instances whereby Brazil has not developed a culture of personal responsibility that underpins the principle of subsidiarity. Instead, the lack of subsidiarity is the result of centuries of a highly inefficient centralist government

[90] Braz. Const., Art.225.

[91] Braz. Const., Art.215.

conducting the country's affairs, wasting its own resources, and protecting private and corporate interests. The latter reap immense, often illegal, benefits from a notoriously corrupt government, which overtaxes the citizens and conducts its abnormally ineffective action in areas such as public security, healthcare, and education; areas where there is a moral and legal obligation for the state to exercise its power much more effectively.

In this sense, subsidiarity could be developed in Brazil as a principle of constitutional reform aiming at the gradual transference of responsibilities from the state to the individual, as well as from the state to the individual's family, intermediate groups and local community, thus involving a throughout re-definition of the role of the Brazilian state in society. Ultimately, subsidiarity must be applied as a principle of authentic help or assistance, which sets the limits of the state action and it seeks to achieve the realisation of a democratic society of more responsible (and compassionate) individuals.

References

Acton, H.B. 1993. *The morals of markets and related essays*, ed. D. Gordon and J. Shearmur. Indianapolis: Liberty Fund.

Barnett, Randy E. 1998. *The structure of liberty: Justice and the rule of law*. Oxford: Oxford University Press.

Bastos, Aureliano Candido Tavares. 1870. *A Província: Estudo sobre a Descentralização no Brasil*. Rio de Janeiro: Garnier.

Boxer, C.R. 1969. *The Portuguese seaborne empire (1415–1835)*. London: Hutchinson.

Charles-Louis de Secondat, Baron de. Montesquieu. 1900. *The spirit of laws*. New York: Prometheus Books.

DaMatta, Roberto. 1987. The quest for citizenship in a relational universe. In *State and society in Brazil: Continuity and change*, ed. J.D. Wirth, E.O. Nunes, and T.E. Bogenschild. London: Westview.

de Jouvenel, Bertrand. 1990. *The ethics of redistribution* [1952]. Indianapolis: Liberty Fund.

de Q Walker, Geoffrey. 2001. *Ten advantages of a federal constitution*. Sydney: Centre for Independent Studies.

Fitzpatrick, John. 2005. Growing old (dis)gracefully in Brazil. *Brazil Political Comment*, São Paulo, August 11, 2005, at: http://www.brazilpoliticalcomment.com.br/content/view/38/29

Fitzpatrick, John. 2006. Lula – Brazil's Big Spender. *Brazil Political Comment*, São Paulo, June 7, 2006, at: http://www.brazilpoliticalcomment.com.br/content/view/131/1/lang.en/

Galligan, Brian, and Cliff Walsh. 1992. Australian federalism: Yes or no? In *Australian federation*, ed. Greg Craven. Melbourne: University Press.

Gibbs, Harry. 1991. Courage in constitutional interpretation and its consequences: One example. *University of New South Wales Law Journal* 14: 325.

Graham, Richard. 1968. *Britain and the onset of modernization in Brazil: 1815–1914*. Cambridge: Cambridge University Press.

Gray, John. 1990. Introduction. In *Bertrand de Jouvenel, The ethics of redistribution* [1952]. Indianapolis: Liberty Fund.

Hagopian, Frances. 2004. Authoritarian legacies and market reforms in Latin America. In *Authoritarian legacies and democracy in Latin America and Southern Europe*, ed. Paola Hite and Katherine Cesarini. Notre Dame: University of Notre Dame Press.

Hallowell, John H. 2007. *The moral foundation of democracy*. Indianapolis: Liberty Fund.

Harris, Marvin. 1972. Portugal's contribution to the underdevelopment of Africa and Brazil. In *Protest and resistance in Angola and Brazil*, ed. R.H. Chilcote. Berkeley: University of California Press.

Heitor de Paula. 2006. *The concept of democracy in Latin America*. Hispanic American Center for Economic Research – HACER, Arlington, July 2006, at: http://www.hacer.org/current/Brazil109.php

Heywood, Andrew. 2002. *Politics*, 2nd ed. New York: Palgrave Macmillan.

Hitchens, Peter. 2003. *The abolition of liberty: The decline of order and justice in England*. London: Atlantic Books.

Hite, Katherine, and Leonardo Morlino. 2004. Problematizing the links between authoritarian legacies and 'good' democracy. In *Authoritarian legacies and democracy in Latin America and Southern Europe*, ed. K. Hite and P. Cesarini. Notre Dame: University of Notre Dame Press.

Jefferson, Thomas. 1829. *The papers of Thomas Jefferson*, vol. 1. Charlottesville: F. Carr & Co.

Kelsen, Hans. 1945. *General theory of law and state*. New York: Russell & Russell.

Kuschnir, Karina. 2005. *Political clientelism in contemporary democracies: The case of Brazil in comparative and interdisciplinary perspective*. Paper presented as workshop report by the Centre for Brazilian Studies, Oxford University, Oxford, 18 February 2005.

Madison, James. 1961. *The federalist no. 51* [6 February 1788]. New York: Mentor Books.

Magnet, Myron. 1993. *The dream and the nightmare: The sixties' legacy to the underclass*. San Francisco: Encounter Books.

Menzies, Robert. 1967. *Central power in the Australian commonwealth*. London: Cassell.

Nabuco, Joaquim. 1977. *Abolitionism: The Brazilian antislavery struggle* [1883] Chicago: University of Illinois Press.

Olasky, Marvin. 2000. *Compassionate conservatism*. New York: Free Press.

Organization of American States (OAS). 2000. *Report on the situation of human rights in Brazil – Inter-American Commission on Human Rights*. http://www.cidh.oas.org/countryrep/brazil-eng/index%20-%20brazil.htm

Page, Joseph A. 1995. *The Brazilians*. Reading: Addison-Wesley.

Paim, Antônio. 1994. *A Querela do Estatismo*. Rio de Janeiro: Tempo Brasileiro.

Palmer, Tom G. 2012a. Bismarck's legacy. In *After the welfare state*, ed. Tom G. Palmer. Ottawa: Jameson Books.

Palmer, Tom G. 2012b. The tragedy of welfare state. In *After the welfare state*, ed. Tom G. Palmer. Ottawa: Jameson Books.

Pearcey, Nancy R. 2004. *Total truth: Liberating Christianity from its cultural captivity*. Wheaton: Crossway.

Plato. 1945. *Republic*. London: Oxford University Press.

Prado, Ney. 1994. *Razões das Virtudes e Vícios da Constituição de 1988*. São Paulo: Editora Inconfidentes.

Prillaman, William. 2000. *The judiciary and democratic decay in Latin America: Declining confidence in the rule of law*. London: Praeger.

Rodrigues, José Honório. 1967. *The Brazilians: Their character and aspirations*. Austin: University of Texas Press.

Rosenn, Keith S. 1990. The success of constitutionalism in the United States and its failure in Latin America: An explanation. *University of Miami, Inter-American Law Review* 22: 1.

Santamaria, Joseph. 2006, November. The primacy of the family and the subsidiary role of the state. *The Australian Family* 27(3): 4.

Sartori, Giovanni. 1997. *Comparative constitutional engineering: An enquiry into structures, incentives and outcomes*. New York: New York University Press.

Silveira da Motta, José Ignácio. 1869. *Degeneração do Sistema Representativo*. Rio de Janeiro: Typographia Americana.

Smith, Herbert H. 1967. Slavery is a curse for both Negroes and Whites. In *History of Latin American civilization*, vol. 2, ed. Hanke Lewis. Irvine: University of California Press.

Speck, Bruno, and Claudio Abreu Abramo. 2002. Second survey on vote buying in Brazilian elections. *Ibope, Transparência Brasil and Unacon*, December 10, 2002, at http://ww1.transparency.org/surveys/dnld/vote-buying2002.br.pdf

The Economist. 2006. Brazil: Lula's Leap. Hispanic American Center for Economic Research – HACER, Arlington, March 7, 2006, at: http://www.hacer.org/current/Brazil099.php

Twomey, Anne. 2008. Reforming Australia's federal system. *Federal Law Review* 36: 57.

Unger, Brooke. 2004. Not-so-swift justice: How to reform Brazil's justice. *The Economist*, March 25.
Zimmermann, Augusto. 2000. The principle of subsidiarity: A policy for the democratic reform of the Brazilian Federal State. *Democracy (General Secretariat of the Organization of American States)* 6: 2.
Zimmermann, Augusto. 2005. *Teoria geral do federalismo democrático*, 2nd ed. Rio de Janeiro: Lumen Juris.
Zimmermann, Augusto. 2007. Constitutional rights in Brazil: A legal fiction? *Murdoch University Law Review* 14(2): 28–55.
Zimmermann, Augusto. 2008. How Brazilian judges undermine the rule of law: A critical appraisal. *International Trade and Business Law Review* 11: 179.
Zimmermann, Augusto. 2010. Constitutions without constitutionalism: The failure of constitutionalism in Brazil. In *The rule of law in comparative perspective*, ed. Mortimer Sellers and Tadeusz Tomaszewski, 101–141. New York: Springer.

Chapter 7
Subsidiarity and the Reform of the Welfare of the Nation State

Rev. Robert A. Sirico

Abstract The principle of subsidiarity holds that matters of social management ought to be handled by the smallest and least centralised authority whenever possible because those closest to a problem are more likely to understand and be well situated relationally to deal with the issue effectively. This idea is a central guiding principle in the corpus of papal social encyclicals, and yet it is strangely neglected in much writing on Catholic social thought. As we face the mounting pathologies of the modern welfare state and seek meaningful reforms rooted in love of neighbour, the principle of subsidiarity (an idea with deep roots in Christian thought in and beyond the Catholic Church) can and should function as a guidepost for a new direction in the provision of social welfare and charity. Subsidiarity must take its place alongside the principle of solidarity at the center of serious reflection on social ethics and social structure, since it offers crucial guidance for our understanding of the role of the state, the family, the individual, the church, educational institutions, and the enterprising economy.

Keywords Subsidiarity • Charity • Welfare • Civil society • Government • The Church • Moral hazard • Dependency • Human dignity

7.1 Introduction

> "The principle of subsidiarity is opposed to all forms of collectivism. It sets limits for state intervention." – *Catechism of the Catholic Church*, par. 1885.
>
> "Christian charity is first of all the simple response to immediate needs and specific situations." – Pope Benedict XVI, *Deus Caritas Est*

Rev. R.A. Sirico (✉)
Acton Institute for the Study of Religion and Liberty, 98E Fulton Street,
Grand Rapids, Michigan 49503, United States of America
e-mail: rsirico@acton.org

M. Evans and A. Zimmermann (eds.), *Global Perspectives on Subsidiarity*, Ius Gentium: Comparative Perspectives on Law and Justice 37, DOI 10.1007/978-94-017-8810-6_7,

The purpose of Catholic social teaching is not to provide a top-down blueprint for the structure of society. It offers no specific sets of regulations and law that are deemed universally valid for all times and places. Rather, it offers broad principles rooted in morals and faith that provide guidance in thinking about important issues of public policy. These principles are best thought of as contingent in their application, developing in their scope, and flexible in their instantiation in real-world situations. Nonetheless, certain principles emerged from within Catholic social teaching that permit us to have a firm evaluative lens through which to examine institutions of public life.

Primary among these principles is the idea of subsidiarity, the principle that matters of social management ought to be handled by smallest and least centralised authority because those closest to the problem at hand are the most competent to understand and deal with the issue. The principle of subsidiarity was first integrated into Church teaching with Leo XIII's encyclical *Rerum Novarum* of 1891,[1] but the principle derives primarily from the natural law tradition. It places limits on the rightful duties of the state and imposes obligations on the lower order institutions such as the community, parish, family, and individual, and it obliges those lower orders to fulfill certain moral and practical functions essential to the functioning of a well-ordered and free society.

The idea is a foundational principle of Catholic social teaching, as emphasised by Pope Benedict XVI in *Caritas in Veritate*. The principle of subsidiarity is

> …an expression of inalienable human freedom. Subsidiarity is first and foremost a form of assistance to the human person via the autonomy of intermediate bodies. Such assistance is offered when individuals or groups are unable to accomplish something on their own, and it is always designed to achieve their emancipation, because it fosters freedom and participation through assumption of responsibility. Subsidiarity respects personal dignity by recognizing in the person a subject who is always capable of giving something to others. By considering reciprocity as the heart of what it is to be a human being, subsidiarity is the most effective antidote against any form of all-encompassing welfare state. It is able to take account both of the manifold articulation of plans – and therefore of the plurality of subjects – as well as the coordination of those plans. Hence the principle of subsidiarity is particularly well-suited to managing globalization and directing it towards authentic human development.[2]

We can immediately see that there is a paradox at work here. Subsidiarity is not the same as decentralisation and a focus on the small. It is an urge for those who are

[1] Par. 14: "The contention, then, that the civil government should at its option intrude into and exercise intimate control over the family and the household is a great and pernicious error. True, if a family finds itself in exceeding distress, utterly deprived of the counsel of friends, and without any prospect of extricating itself, it is right that extreme necessity be met by public aid, since each family is a part of the commonwealth. In like manner, if within the precincts of the household there occur grave disturbance of mutual rights, public authority should intervene to force each party to yield to the other its proper due; for this is not to deprive citizens of their rights, but justly and properly to safeguard and strengthen them. But the rulers of the commonwealth must go no further; here, nature bids them stop. Paternal authority can be neither abolished nor absorbed by the State; for it has the same source as human life itself."

[2] *Caritas in Veritate* (2009) par. 57.

closest to the social problem to maintain the status of the being the primary locus of control, not in order to reduce attention but rather to broaden it effectively, even unto the entire globe.

Nor is subsidiarity some new notion that needs to be reinvented; rather it lies at the core of the concept of the free and virtuous social order. It is a crucial, if still largely tacit, part of our common understanding of the components of a free and virtuous society: power and authority reside among the many units that are most capable of carrying out their functions properly within the context of human rights, dignity and freedom.

The principle has found its political expression in the American concept of federalism, and, in Europe, the concept has become a critical part of the debate on the relations between nations and the central authority of the European Community. In these political contexts, the principle has been invoked by the partisans of limited government over centralised management of people, states, and nations.

As a philosophical notion, it provides an intellectual framework for the rightly-considered social order rooted in the Christian faith and human liberty. It does not and cannot give fixed answers to the burning questions of the day, such as: how much should the state tax, to what extent should religion and public policy be separate, how generous should the social assistance state be, or whether it should even exist? These questions still remain within the realm of prudence and circumstance.

As Franz H. Mueller reminds us "the Church calls upon her members to make their own prudential decisions within the framework of what is generally demanded by faith and morals. She marks the boundaries and puts up signposts, but she does not ordinarily prescribe the route to be taken to the goal in question."[3] In the area of policy and the moral obligations of individuals in public life, subsidiarity highlights many such boundaries and signposts, and provides an overall framework for evaluating how consistent social structures are with Catholic teaching.

7.2 What Is Subsidiarity?

The thesis of the subsidiarity principle is at once simple and deeply meaningful. The concept posits a hierarchy of social action and responsibility that begins with the claim of primacy for the smallest units in society, including community associations, families, and individuals. These groups have the first responsibility for caring for their own needs and for those with whom they come in contact. On the occasion when they fail to function as they should, higher social structures, beginning with the closest level of government, are permitted to temporarily assume responsibility for those same functions, but only for the duration that the higher orders can perform the job more effectively than can the lower ones. If higher-order intervention takes places in absence of systemic failure, lower orders are forcibly divested of

[3] Mueller (1984, p. 73).

what they do best, the common good of all suffers, and the principle of subsidiarity has been violated.

The word subsidiarity is derived from the Latin *subsidium*, meaning to help or to aid. This root implies that fundamental to the principle is that a permanent state of usurpation of one function by another order (for example, the government, and not the family, rearing children) is to be ruled out. Higher orders can intervene in the affairs of the lower ones only as auxiliary aids and never as permanent substitutes, and only then under certain, well-defined circumstances. Moreover, the authority between spheres of influence and power within society are internally legitimate and not merely derivative. The state, for example, is better suited to the provision of national defense than to the provision of income security; neither is the authority for it to provide such national security necessarily derived from other institutions.

In *Rerum novarum*, for example, Pope Leo XIII argued that "man is older than the state," and the family is anterior in idea and fact to civil society. Intervention is only warranted if a family "finds itself in great difficulty, utterly friendless, and without prospect of help," or if "there occur grave disturbances of mutual rights" within the family.[4]

Even so, the family exercises authority which is suitable to its structure and place in society, and that authority is neither delegated to nor approved by higher authorities. The principle does not imply that society is bound to provide certain social services in all possible contingencies, but rather illuminates the division of competencies among social institutions.

Societies which adhere to the principle of subsidiarity create and maintain a bottom-up social structure, with the departure point being families and community relations. Paradoxically, this harmony, though giving primacy to lower orders, tends toward the establishment of true international order. As Richard Neuhaus argued, the principle means that "the state is subsidiary to the society in service, as it is also derived from the society in its moral legitimacy."[5]

Indeed, the principle speaks to moral issues first. It suggests that people closest to the problem at hand are the ones with the strongest moral claim on finding a solution. To empower higher authorities as anything but second best solutions or even last resorts endangers the rights and liberties of those who are most affected. The subsidiarity principle also embodies the practical point that those closest to the problem have the strongest interest in seeing to it that the problem is solved most competently. The application of this practical side goes beyond social structure to speak to issues even of business management. Michael Novak has argued, "the more a corporation embodies the principle of subsidiarity in its organisation, the closer to its work force it becomes."[6] The same is true other institutional structures like the family.

A society respecting the principle of subsidiarity contrasts with a top-down model of society in which the central government presumes to have the primary

[4] *Rerum Novarum*, par. 14.

[5] Neuhaus (1992, p. 243).

[6] Novak (1982, p. 178).

role in ordering people's lives. The latter only delegates power when lower orders will carry out functions in accordance with the government's overall plan. "Just as it is wrong to withdraw from the individual and commit to a group what private enterprise and industry can accomplish," writes Pius XI in the *Quadragesimo Anno* – this century's most famous statement of the subsidiarity principle – "so too it is an injustice, a grave evil and a disturbance of right order for a larger and higher association to arrogate to itself functions which can be performed efficiently by smaller and lower societies. This is a fundamental principle of social philosophy, unshaken and unchangeable."[7]

Experience teaches us that the top-down model operates at the expense of practicality, creativity, knowledge and liberty. As Pope Pius XII said, "the conception which assigns to the State unlimited authority is not only pernicious to the internal life of the nation, to its prosperity, and to the orderly increase of its well-being; it also damages relations between peoples, because it breaks the unity of international society, it rips out the foundations of the value of the rights of the people."[8]

"Excessive intervention by the state," adds the *Catechism* in this same tradition, "can threaten personal freedom and initiative."[9] The purpose of the subsidiarity principle, in contrast, is to establish a way of thinking about social life that has a high regard for the freedom of individuals, families, and communities. To understand the idea of subsidiarity is to acknowledge its existence and recognise its importance, and not dismiss it as contrary to some other postulate of Christian ethics. Rather, it speaks to the right ordering of society itself and its capacity for self management as a normal principle of the social order.

Pope Benedict XVI states the proposition very clearly in *Deus Caritas Est*:

> There is no ordering of the State so just that it can eliminate the need for a service of love. Whoever wants to eliminate love is preparing to eliminate man as such. There will always be suffering which cries out for consolation and help. There will always be loneliness. There will always be situations of material need where help in the form of concrete love of neighbor is indispensable. The State which would provide everything, absorbing everything into itself, would ultimately become a mere bureaucracy incapable of guaranteeing the very thing which the suffering person – every person – needs: namely, loving personal concern. We do not need a State which regulates and controls everything, but a State which, in accordance with the principle of subsidiarity, generously acknowledges and supports initiatives arising from the different social forces and combines spontaneity with closeness to those in need.[10]

J. Brian Benestad makes the point that, "taking a look at the principle of subsidiarity is a good way to begin the study of Catholic social teaching."[11] But this is evidently a step many religious social thinkers are unwilling to take. A brief look at the vast literature on ethics and Church social teaching shows little interest

[7] *Quadragesimo Anno*, 1931, par. 79–80.

[8] Cited in Franz Mueller, p. 121.

[9] *Catechism of the Catholic Church*, par. 1883.

[10] Deus Caritas Est, par. 28(b)

[11] Benestad (1990, p. 30).

on the part of intellectuals in consistently applying the principle. The tendency is rather to postulate the centrality of some worthwhile goal – for example, universal charity – and to pursue it without regard to the proper ordering of society in bringing about this goal.

Both conservatives and liberals can be faulted in this regard. For example, a collection entitled *One Hundred Years of Catholic Social Thought* contains discussions of all aspects of social policy and social justice with a decided bias towards government solutions, but nary a word about subsidiarity or the moral imperative of limiting centralised power in economic or political life.[12] It is as if the concept simply was not relevant to the discussion, whereas it should be featured in any overview of Catholic social thought.

Charles Curran's once a standard text, *Direction in Catholic Social Ethics*, mentions the issue of subsidiarity. At the same time, he offers a number of peculiar interpretations and applications of it. First, subsidiarity is disparaged as "a deductive, abstract approach" that prevented German Catholic liberals from understanding the merits of child labour laws.[13] Second, it is seen as underscoring, but not "absolutising," the right to procreate; yet it turns out that "in practice this means that larger communities including the state may have to intervene in population control if this is deemed necessary."[14] Third, subsidiarity teaches us to "avoid overcentralisation" when we get around to socialising all medicine and health care; yet there is no hint provided as to how this would be possible.[15] And fourth, subsidiarity is approved of as a model for bottom-up political action on the model pioneered by socialist activist Saul Alinsky.[16] In none of these cases does the author take the concept as a serious effort to delimit state power and thus fails to apply it with attention to its definition or authentic meaning.

Surprisingly, Rodger Charles, S.J. and Drostan MacLaran, in their 1982 treatise *The Social Teaching of Vatican II*, published by Ignatius Press, provides only one isolated mention of subsidiarity.[17] And the subject arises not at all in the section evaluating the relative merits of capitalism versus communism. The books cites "some of the positive aspects of the Soviet economic system," speculating that "it might be just as easy, or perhaps even easier, for the Church to live with it than with a free enterprise structure which encourages permissiveness, anarchy or gross social injustice…"[18]

It is my contention that a proper application of the subsidiarity principle would have at least tempered these judgments on the application of Catholic social teaching to totalitarian regimes, thus avoiding the embarrassment of such faulty analysis.

---

[12] Coleman (1991).

[13] Curran (1985, p. 85).

[14] Curran, p. 231.

[15] Curran, p. 274.

[16] Curran, p. 167.

[17] Rodger Charles and MacLaran (1982, p. 209).

[18] Charles et al., p. 294.

The trouble with ignoring the crucial concept of the social structure of subsidiarity is that the tendency to universalise can quickly lead to absurdity and error. For example, it is right and proper that all children be cared for and immoral and unjust that even one be neglected. Can we conclude from this that there would be no Christian objection to empowering a global government authority to take away the rights and privileges of the family to bring about such a goal? Or are there guide-posts to be obeyed in assigning the implementation of normative postulates regarding rights and duties? Merely asking the question highlights the dangers of overlooking the issue of subsidiarity and its application to social, legal, and economic structures.

Why is it that so many Catholic intellectuals are inclined to overlook the concept of subsidiarity and its clear implications? The answer may lie in the tendency to conflate the universality of the faith and the universality of social organisation. There exists a tendency to import such absolutist categories such as ethics and morals – and their applications to such ideas as rights and obligations – into the application of the Church's social teaching. Thus, there may be a universal right to minimum material subsistence; but the universalist frame of mind is tempted to conclude that there must be a universal agency empowered to guarantee this right, just as there is a universal Church to administer other rights of the faithful, such as the sacraments. But this is a profound categorical error. Questions of how and under what institutional arrangements these rights and obligations should be discharged and enforced are really distinct questions. The overwhelming bulk of Catholic social teaching concentrates on what constitutes a human right to the exclusion of how it should best be guaranteed and secured.

I am not proposing that subsidiarity should be considered the only or even the first principle of social ethics. Indeed, John Paul II also elevates the idea of "solidarity" in *Centesimus Annus*. This is the proposition that the social dimension of public life must never be overlooked and that social institutions should foster social cooperation within and among groups. As one example, we find that the state must place "certain limits on the autonomy of the parties who determine working conditions" and the provision of "support for the unemployed worker."[19] What the Pope proposes is that there be an interactive relationship between state, society, and economy. Economic and political systems cannot by themselves assure a healthy society; neither can society be expected to be healthy absent a coordinative relationship with the economy and the state. Yet the notion of solidarity can only make sense and be realised in the context of subsidiarity. The primary role the state plays in assuring solidarity is to provide a "juridical framework" for society and economy, and not take over their proper functions. Expansive state intervention can harm this cooperative relationship as much as businessmen who pay no mind to the rule of law or the needs of society.

By merely getting the debate going – and not dismissing the subsidiarity principle as a mere contingent recommendation – we can lift the debate on social teaching to a higher plane. We can go beyond what we agree on – notions such as the moral

---

[19] *Centesimus Annus*, par. 15.

obligation to be charitable – to a much more fruitful and practical area. We can begin to discuss concrete realities of social and political life, and move beyond abstractions that have very little bearing on the really contentious areas of modern political debate.

7.3 Objections to Subsidiarity

There have emerged a number of objections to the traditional application of the principle as I have explained it and applied it. Some thinkers have said the traditional application is wrongheaded: the principle of subsidiarity is as much a call for government to correct social and market failure as it is a caution to the dangers of centralised government power. But this is a difficult proposition to justify. The clear meaning of the subsidiarity principle is to *limit* the powers and responsibilities assumed by the higher orders of society. In nearly every occasion in which the principle has been invoked in the last 100 years of official Catholic social teaching, it is in the context of limiting the uses of power. It is also true, of course, that the lower orders are by no means relieved of their responsibilities.

Some say that modern society is too complex to be ordered in this fashion; economic and social complexity requires overarching social management. But this turns a valid point on its head. It is indeed true that society is vastly more complex and diverse than it once was. Rather than making the case for more state intervention, this fact merely underscores the inability of the state to undertake competent normative and overall intervention at all. This insight is carefully worked out in the writings of F.A. Hayek, and in particular, his insight regarding the use of knowledge in society. In Hayek's understanding, the information necessary for the well-functioning of society is necessarily dispersed among individuals and the various organic units of society. It is not practicable for all the knowledge necessary for society to work to be accumulated in central units of society, much less in the minds of single individuals presuming to plan society.[20] The common objection to this understanding of subsidiarity relies on the fact that we live in a multicultural society in which common values can no longer be taken for granted. This fact makes a free and decentralised social order unpractical. Subsidiarity only works, some would argue, when society as whole is united by common values and shared religious understanding; insofar as these conditions are not realised, centralised authority must take a more expanded role.

Here again, we witness an effort to transform a major strength of the subsidiarity principle into an objection to it. The more diverse a society is in terms of its demographic, religious, and normative makeup, the more its functions must be devolved to the lower orders where problems can be understood and dealt with on their own terms. A centralised authority lacks the information necessary to proscribe solutions for a diverse society; it must of necessity treat citizens and community as

[20] Hayek (1972).

relatively homogeneous. Let's ask this question, for example: if a single society is composed of communities of very different religious persuasions, is a central religious authority emanating from the state more or less viable than it would be in a society composed of members of a single faith? The answer should be obvious: diversity in religion requires freedom of religious practice, and the conflicts that arise between groups should be solved at the lowest possible level (that is, if we value freedom versus forced conformity). So it is with other aspects of a nation's life, whether familial or economic. The more heterogeneous the society's makeup, the more the subsidiarity principle needs to be recognised and practiced.

7.4 Subsidiarity and Evangelisation

The subsidiarity principle deeply informs religious concerns. If we can agree that values and morals make up the indispensable bulwark of sustaining a viable social order, and that the religious traditions of the West are the essential framework in which to understand and fully express those values and morals, we need some transmission mechanism to impart religious values to those in society who do not accept them due to unfortunate circumstances (for example, alienation, rejection, dependency). That mechanism is evangelisation: bringing the *evangel* of Christ to people and cultures and inspiring them towards belief and the practice of the faith in their lives. The subsidiarity principle helps in this regard because the people most capable of evangelising non-believers are the believers closest to them.

The loss of the evangelical function of the lower orders has been one of the most costly aspects of the modern tendency toward centralisation. The codification of services in public institutions tends to crowd out similar services provided community groups. It is through personal contact with the poor, weak, and disadvantaged, that the Church can present a more authentic and credible witness for Christ in their lives. Part of what has been perceived as a decline in the vibrancy of the witness of the Church in recent years is due to a loss of a sense of her mission and identity. This is due to losing (or surrendering) to secularised governmental agencies the crucial function of caring for families in need.

The loss of values and morals, occasioned by the transfer of rightful authority to higher and less capable orders, is the primary cultural, political, and moral characteristic of our times. To regain those values and morals requires a greater cultural appreciation of the virtue of subsidiarity and a greater institutional recognition of the central place it must have in the right ordering of the economic and political culture.

This is most clearly seen in the field of education, a major issue in contemporary political controversies. As education has become more public and centralised, it has tended to proceed without the benefit of the moral lessons of subsidiarity and the more intimate involvement of families. As a result, the quality of schools has declined, and the traditional evangelical role of education has been pushed to the margins, replaced by other goals such as socialisation, politicisation and acculturation according to the designs of secular-state authorities. A good contrast to this dominant structure is the Catholic parochial school, which has had a better record in every area that secular authorities deem important – including the education of people from all socio-economic groups – while also maintaining the crucial responsibilities of meeting the spiritual needs of students.[21]

Once the education of children was entirely a function of the local community and the states, but is now, to an alarming extent, a social task undertaken by the federal government. This approach, in contrast to a social policy based on the subsidiarity principle, must be to give parents and local communities a greater degree of control over their children's education. And given the unparalleled success of the Catholic Church in providing education in the United States, Catholic schools must necessarily play a large role – whether institutionally or by providing tested models – in the future of an education system based on the idea of subsidiarity.

The subsidiarity principle also informs our view of the government's relation to family policy, making the centralisation of the last 30 years indefensible. Far from having corrected for grave problems in society's lower orders, the higher orders have intervened and usurped the prerogatives of the family and community to the detriment of the common good. In the case of economic need and other forms of social deprivation, if these problems had been addressed at the local level, the needs of families would have been met apart from the materialist assumption at the root of the modern welfare state.

"The family," says the *Catechism*, "is the original cell of social life"[22] and the essential bulwark of a free and well-ordered society. The family serves as the crucial means of acculturation and the key to transmitting values from generation to generation and it is the family that enables us to make good use of freedom. Yet contemporary public policy has served to both interfere with and assume the functions of the family, with disastrous consequences.

7.5 Subsidiarity and Charity

The primary non-military source of state expansionism this century has been in the area of welfare provision. Every Western industrialised democracy has erected massive social assistance states that are hugely expensive, largely unpopular among the paying groups, yet tightly guarded by the recipients and administrators of the system. The principle of subsidiarity speaks directly to both the morality and the practicality of such systems, and renders a generally negative verdict.

Of course, every society includes a large and ever-changing group of people who are not in a position to be completely independent, whether physically, economically,

---

[21] Bryk et al. (1993).

[22] *Catechism of the Catholic Church*, par. 2207.

mentally, or spiritually. They require the help of others. Children, the elderly, the sick and infirm, those who suffer mental and spiritual debilitations, and those who are victims of unfortunate circumstances in family and professional life – they all require social aid. Many of these people are also poor, even if that is more often a symptom rather than a cause of their problem. The philosopher John Rawls is usually cited in defense of social structures designed to help those in need. Rawls asks us to put ourselves behind a "veil of ignorance"[23] and imagine that we could be any person in society, whether a well-paid and secure corporate executive or an unskilled person without a home who is unsure where his next meal will come from. It is an interesting mental exercise that suggests everyone would choose, behind the veil, to seek the kind of society where no matter where anyone ended up in the socioeconomic and generational system, he or she could be assured of basic rights, to life, to liberty, and to the pursuit of happiness.

Society does indeed need structures to insure that this is the case, and surely a social safety net is essential. The American response to this challenge has varied from the colonial times to the present. For several generations, Americans have thought about charity and welfare as proscribing a response from the federal welfare state – a vast apparatus consisting of more than a 100 programs, involving millions of workers in tax-funded bureaucracies, and designed mainly to enhance the *economic* standing of the recipients. And though Americans are a very charitable people, the sheer size and scope of the federal effort has led many to believe that the social safety net is sufficiently secure; thanks to government intervention, some believe that the care of those in need requires very little private attention.

At the same time, there is wide public recognition of the omnipresent and multifarious failures of the welfare state, failures which have caused political movements from the right and left to seek fundamental reform. The social safety net, despite the best intentions of its contemporary architects and defenders, has in fact become a massive bureaucratic machine that eats both lives and property. Many people, with entrenched interests in preserving the present system, will resist this conclusion, but the average citizen is not among them. Judging from present trends in public philosophy, the general direction of reform will be away from dependence toward independence, away from the center to local communities, away from government solutions and toward private ones.

As the political culture further debates reform of the welfare system – a process which is likely to last for many years – we must also reflect on the ends we seek to achieve and the means we must choose to bring about the appropriate ends. The concept of subsidiarity must be part of this debate. People must not be allowed to be left out, forgotten by society, denied opportunity, exploited by politicians or ignored by the economic system, especially not by those who have been blessed with wealth.

[23] Rawls (1971, pp. 136–137).

But at this point, the consensus falls apart. On the ultimate ends, people agree. The dispute is on the means. Is it appropriate to deal with poverty and suffering solely through the coercive apparatus of the welfare state, the philosophy of statism and socialist democracy, or some other arrangement of government intrusion? Or is the natural order of liberty, created by free people within the overall structure of an entrepreneurial economy, exercising compassion with their communities and localities, to be preferred as the primary and normative means of help?

If people are to assist those in need, and establish an authentic social safety net that really works, they must do more than have good intentions. The central governments do not have a good historical track record in this regard, while at the same time the harm they have caused is incalculable. In fact, most of the important improvements in the lives of the least well off in society have been a result of two major forces: first, a general improvement in the standard of living resulting from free exchange in markets combined with entrepreneurial initiative, and second, from private charity exercised on a local level by people who know and understand the needs of those who are genuinely in need of help. These approaches to social assistance and the promotion of the common good gets far less attention than the alternatives. This is because this mode of social improvement is not designed by anyone in particular, nor embodied in a particular program or agency and thus tends to get overlooked. Yet the most effective remedies for human suffering are most often overlooked. Private solutions may not have the glamour of a new "jobs program" or be featured in press conferences, much less touted by politicians, but they are ultimately more effective.

7.6 Subsidiarity and Entitlements

Since the *New Deal*, the term "entitlements" has come to define the policies of the social assistance state. It is a perpetual promise by the state to provide a stream of income for those who qualify by virtue of their lowly socio-economic status. To provide this income stream in the form of welfare requires a perpetual promise to draw from the private pool of wealth, from producers, via the tax system (or the hidden tax system of debt accumulation and inflation). It should be obvious that the notion of an "entitlement" is directly contradictory to the subsidiarity.

The passage in the United States of the 1996 *Welfare Bill*, which placed some time limits on the receipt of welfare and devolved the administration of the welfare state to smaller governments, has lessened the usage of the term "entitlement" as part of the American policy vocabulary. But whether the term is used or not, there can be no question than the assumption of an entitlement mentality continues to exist. A good measure of whether the central government is truly allowing lower orders to reengage themselves in the provision of charity, and not be interfered with by the central state, is a simple one: the budget.

In 1991, Pope John II wrote of the failure of the modern welfare state in stark terms: "Malfunctions and defects in the Social Assistance State are the result of an inadequate understanding of the tasks proper to the State."[24] The Pope pointed to a practical cost of violating subsidiarity: the politicisation of society. Public agencies proliferate at the expense of smaller communities of charity and enterprise, producing what he calls a "bureaucratic way of thinking."

The costs of the welfare state have indeed, not only been economic to the extent that bureaucracy always grows at the expense of a dynamic exchange economy, but the cost is also moral, because the welfare state pursues its tasks in terms of a moral code increasingly alien from traditional Christian tenets. For example, the very concept of a welfare "entitlement" runs contrary to the scriptural understanding of aiding the poor: helping others is a moral duty that springs from spiritual commitment and is not essentially exercised through coercion or government mandates. The modern, central state has proven itself incapable of distinguishing between the deserving and the undeserving poor, and between aid that fosters independence and moral development from that which reinforces a dependency mindset and moral nihilism. The distinction between the two can only be revealed to those in need through the evangelisation function of the Church and community.

Today, those called to practice charity and to exercise concerns for others find themselves living in a society that has insufficient respect for the principle of subsidiarity. While it is true that the central government has crowded out the lower orders and has restricted opportunities for charity, that in no way relieves us of our moral obligations. The *Catechism* is without qualification when it insists that "there are many families who are at times incapable" of caring for the young, the old, the sick, the disabled, and the poor.[25]

"The abolition of private property," Aristotle writes in *The Politics*, "will mean that no man will be seen to be liberal and no man will ever do any act of liberality; for it is in the use of articles of property that liberality is practiced."[26] One of the many tragic effects of the welfare state has been to drain private capital that could have gone toward helping others invest in future prosperity. But it has had a more fundamental cost in draining what Wilhelm Roepke has called "the secret spring of a healthy society, i.e. the sense of responsibility."

> The more the state takes care of us, the less shall we feel called upon to take care of ourselves and our family, and the less we feel inclined to do so, the less we can expect help from others whose natural duty it would be to assist us when in need, the members of our family, our neighbors, our friends, or our colleagues. We have at last found in the state a secular God whom, like the lilies in the field, we may burden with all our cares, and at the same time all true charity which can only thrive on spontaneity and readiness to help…will die out.[27]

[24] *Centesimus Annus*, par. 48.

[25] *Catechism of the Catholic Church*, par. 2208.

[26] Aristotle (1976, p. 1263b7).

[27] Roepke (1992, p. 164).

7.7 Solutions in a Digital Age

It is often said that what is called the "private sector" cannot take care of the problem. It is necessary but not sufficient, some say. But it should not be forgotten just how powerful the forces of genuine charity are, especially in American society. Moreover, the subsidiarity principle does not specify that all solutions be private, only that they be as close as possible to the problem at hand. For too long, the central government has crowded out solutions that may be offered by lower orders. Once severe budgetary changes begin to remind people of their responsibilities to others, the outpouring of energy may surprise all the experts. Distant government has no monopoly on compassion; indeed, it is compassion's least able practitioner.

Being an organic part of society, a church outreach makes the individual accountable to those who are providing the aid. Close contact with the providers discourages irresponsible behaviour. This model relies on the classical view of moral tutoring which has two dimensions: we abstain from immoral behaviour because we fear its effects and we abstain because we love the good. Church-run charities hope to instill a love of good in the people they help. Yet clients may also fear being reprimanded or losing services. Fear and love are both motivators. While the latter is a preferable motive, the former works as well.

In the digital age, the opportunities for the enactment of the subsidiarity principle have become far vaster and geographically noncontiguous. Multiple platforms for giving to charity have become available online that enable charitable organisations to obtain funding at relatively low expense as compared with the past. Funding for every manner of art project, lending, borrowing, investing in project, and so much more, are available as never before. This underscores a point about the subsidiarity principle: "local" does not necessarily mean geographically limited. Local refers to the locus of decision making. Digital means make it possible to devolve decision making to the smaller unit of society while enabling that smallest unit to take advantage of maximum opportunities for learning and information acquisition. This model provides a viable means for the management of social problems without the detachment from real human beings that is typically associated with old-fashioned public policy.

7.8 Subsidiarity in Action

Marvin Olasky, in *The Tragedy of American Compassion*[28] has detailed many of the thousands of charitable organisations that thrived in the nineteenth century to deal with social problems not unlike those we confront today. The Baltimore Association for Improving the Condition of the Poor (AICP), for example, had 2,000 volunteers

[28] Olasky (1992).

who made 8,227 visits in 1891 to 4,025 families.[29] Half of these families were headed by widows who tended to receive material aid; most of the others were headed by able-bodied men who were counselled on how to break addictions from alcohol to opium, and how to get a job.

AICP promised to "aid all those whom it can physically and morally elevate, and no others." Their contributors gave of their own resources to aid people authentically, and not to simply reinforce poverty through material subsidy. The founders said that if the AICP fails in this "discrimination" and has "no higher aim than the Almshouse, why should it exist at all? Why, indeed, should those already heavily taxed for the public poor entrust funds to this charity?"[30]

AICP's rule was that relief should be a temporary state of affairs. If this rule is broken, the group wrote, "many once learning to lean on public or associated relief, not only neglect to exert the powers God has given them, but continue to call for aid long after it is right. This leads on the broad road to pauperism. Individuals or societies can hardly guard too watchfully against it."[31] The group emphasised training and improvement of the poor over material relief. Their volunteers visited homes to "guide in matters of religious observance" and to encourage and train the families to be thrifty, hardworking, and temperate.

In general, they promoted four key principles: first, poverty and pauperism, which is an "unnecessary dependence," must be distinguished; second, entitlement relief tends to pauperise because it offers disincentives for independence and discipline; third, there exists a moral obligation for those financially independent to become "personally involved with the poor"; fourth, those who are poor due to their own character flaws must show that they are willing to change the behaviour or thinking patterns that kept them impoverished. If they did not show that they were willing to improve themselves, then the volunteer must leave them for a while, return to renew the offer, and be willing to leave again if the individuals' "hearts had not changed."[32]

Robert M. Hartley, secretary of AICP for over 30 years, saw alcoholism as a large part of the poverty problem, and saw in it a much deeper collection of moral and spiritual problems. In order for a person to be raised out of poverty, he sought to "remove the causes; and these being chiefly moral – whatever subsidiary appliances may be used – they admit only moral remedies." Hartley quoted St. Paul's Letter to the Thessalonians, admonishing people to "earn the bread they eat." For most volunteers the effort would only seem worthwhile if the goals went beyond providing for material needs to include spiritual uplift as well.[33]

Today, such institutions are not as large as they were, nor do they thrive as they once did, precisely because they have been supplanted by government programs. But it is not just the private institutions which need to be recovered. It is

[29] Olasky, pp. 27–34.

[30] Olasky, p. 80.

[31] Olasky, p. 24.

[32] Olasky, pp. 27–32.

[33] Olasky, pp. 27–32.

the philosophy and the cultural assumption that the lower orders of society are responsible for assisting people in time of need, a notion more viable than ever in times of digitisation. Since the advent of the welfare state, and during its growth over the decades, we have forgotten basic knowledge from the past that was commonplace among social workers and professional charity workers.

Mary Conyngton's 1909 book *How to Help*[34] was a standard reference manual for many years. In addition to being a wonderful manual of practice, she points to a number of principles which should guide any "who contemplate undertaking any charitable work, even though his projected activity is small." The first is seriousness of purpose. "Such work means influence upon the lives of others, for good or for ill, and no one has the right to touch another's life carelessly or lightly."[35]

Another qualification is "a sympathetic imagination, which will permit the worker to share the point of view of those he is endeavouring to help." "Whoever goes among the poor with a preconceived idea of what is the cause of their trouble and what should be its cure," she tells us, "is liable to meet many disappointments."[36] In a point which could be made against Washington's bureaucracies, she says: "The poor obstinately refuse to form one class, all amenable to the same treatment." They come from every nationality. Their standards of life and behaviour differ widely among them. The solution to each situation must be specifically tailored to the individual in need.

Conyngton also mentions the need for "a sense of proportion." We should seek not perfect solutions, but "the highest practicable good attainable in each case," and that requires looking at the long run, and not just the reaching for the first available, and easiest, answer.[37]

It seems an obvious question: in what way does the federal welfare system perceive seriousness of purposes, imaginative solutions, and a sense of proportion? The answer is obvious too: it appears that the present system comes up with all the wrong answers. Yet the problem of government aid was also present when Conyngton was writing. In a section that could have been labeled "How Not to Help" she has some strong comments about public aid. "So long as an applicant can do anything for himself, or his friends can give help, it is better to refuse him public assistance, leaving private charity to piece out his insufficiencies…as… the agents of private societies" who "bring more of the personal element into their dealings." There is also the danger that the recipient of public funds will be used as "political capital," she says.[38]

Then there is the largest danger of all, one that has become most conspicuous in our day. "Many people," Conyngton writes, "are inclined to look upon public help as a right and to apply for it without hesitation, while they would regard themselves

[34] Conyngton (1909).

[35] Conyngton, pp. 26–29.

[36] Conyngton, p. 36

[37] Conyngton, p. 36.

[38] Conyngton, p. 36.

as a losing caste if they appealed to private aid."[39] That is the good thing about private charity, and the essential moral hazard associated with public charity. (She also notes cases in Brooklyn and Philadelphia when the number of poor declined after the abolition of public relief.)

The Art of Helping People Out of Trouble, a 1924 book by Karl Deschweinitz, confirms how important it is that charity always takes account of a person's self worth and attempts to preserve self respect.[40] It "is the humiliation of the man who is obliged to confess his failure to meet" his obligations "by taking as a gift the livelihood that other men are earning for themselves. It matters not whether the amount of money involved be great or small. His self respect has been invaded." When financial difficulties appear, says Deschweinitz, a person who helps should do everything possible to help without actually giving money as a gift. "Perhaps he can be aided to find more remunerative employment. Perhaps a wiser household management will fit his present resources to his needs." Only after every other path has been chosen should cash be available, but then only to "stimulate his sense of responsibility."

The fact that some today would recoil at the acknowledgement that there is a necessary link between humiliation and incentive shows the way in which highly politicised programs have reversed moral thinking on service to the poor. It is precisely the respect with which the poor are viewed that motivates higher expectations from someone who can but does not support his family. Any humiliation is caused by the circumstance not the benefactor.

Again, the federal welfare system seems to reverse these priorities, giving money first, and then fostering dependency, forgetting entirely about self respect, and then discouraging a path to independence. The point here is not simply to condemn federal welfare but to highlight the long tradition of private provision, and how much more effective it can be that the current system. Just getting government out of the way as a competitor to the genuine exercise of compassion would be a good start.

7.9 Subsidiarity and the Future of Charity

"If you take power and independence from a municipality," Alexis de Tocqueville wrote, "you may have docile subjects but you will not have citizens." He spoke of the brilliance of New England townships, but his thoughts are applicable to communities in all parts of the United States.

Communities work because the citizens have a close interest in them and share in their management; we love them because we are part of them and pour our labours into them; we invest ourselves in the community, knowing that our futures are intertwined; through them we understand basic concepts like freedom, justice, order, charity, enterprise, and social harmony; they help us generate

[39] Conyngton, p. 36.

[40] Deschweinitz (1924).

practical ideas on how to serve others and our ties to others serve as reminders of moral obligations.

Yet, can some of the functions of government welfare provision really be decentralised to such an extent? Can we afford to take the risk that it will not work? Tocqueville noted that "a very civilized society finds it hard to tolerate attempts at freedom in a local community; it is disgusted by its numerous blunders, and is apt to despair of success before the experiment is finished." We must guard against this tendency. Before we condemn local solutions as unworkable, let's be careful not to compare the likelihood of local success with an idealised model of central government programs. The socialists used to condemn the failures of existing capitalism as compared with an idealised socialism. So it is with the question of decentralisation. The relevant comparison is a federal system that has failed, and a humane, local system that, though less than perfect, will have the ability to be flexible and learn from its mistakes.

We should remind ourselves: we cannot centrally plan authentic charity any more than we can centrally plan the direction of the economy. We must trust private individuals, believing in the goodness of the American people to reach out to help others, as they would be inspired to do if the government would allow more room for the spontaneous actions of the non-government sector. There is no need to expect a dollar for dollar replacement of government dollars and private dollars. Private efforts are so effective that is not necessary.

Those people who are most generous with their time and money in the service of others are also those who tend to be most frustrated with the present system of welfare provision. Those who give are mostly married, employed, college-educated, and parents with small children, according to data from the Independent Sector and the United States Labor Department. Foundations, corporations, and individuals give as much as $300 billion each year, and households tend to donate some $1,900 each, even in difficult economic times and even with the crowding out factor of government programs.

Data from 1950 to the present shows that when government spending on welfare increases (or the public perceives that it is increasing) the percentage of personal income given to charity decreases. The post-war peak of charitable giving, 2.6 % of personal income, dates from the beginning of the Great Society. The opposite is also true; charitable donations will increase as governments cut back and the public is reminded of its moral obligations to serve others.

The issue is not how to expand the federal welfare state, or even how to make it "work better," but how to make private charity an effective alternative that can better achieve our shared goals. Even in areas of health care, individual empowerment through the private sector would appear to be the most desirable path. Yet, whatever policy routes are taken, we should focus on returning responsibility to individuals, churches, neighbourhoods, towns and cities. Every case of family tragedy, dependency, or deprivation of any sort is different, and the individuals involved have different resources, abilities, and weaknesses. A faceless bureaucracy cannot take all of these into account. Nor can it encourage moral renewal. What people need are not layers of public agencies, but other human beings who have knowledge of their real needs and a genuine commitment to help them become responsible and independent citizens. The future is with the private sector and its proven ability to help those in need.

Once the idea of the subsidiarity principle is understood, one cannot help but be impressed by how many contemporary social and spiritual difficulties could be addressed and even solved by paying it greater attention in our private lives and in public affairs. Not only does subsidiarity provide for a more workable social model than the central state in such areas as family life, welfare, education, and enterprise, it provides a perfect opportunity for the sharing of the Gospel with people in our own congregations and communities. A society that recognises subsidiarity is also a society that provides its members the greatest possible opportunity for sharing the Good News of the faith with others.

7.10 The Enterprising Community

As a final application of the subsidiarity principle, we should mention the general notion that the free enterprise economy is an institution that both requires and reinforces traditional moral concerns. Entrepreneurship is linked to the virtue of creativity. Trade, exchange, and contract are bound up with the idea of promise keeping. Private property, the foundation of the free market, represents the institutional embodiment of the commandment to respect the private ownership of what belongs to oneself and to one's neighbour. Even when the relations among traders and property owners results in large institutions like multinational corporations, the subsidiarity principle is recognised and fulfilled in institutions like individual stockholders and consumers who are the main determinants of market signals like profit and loss. Indeed, it is through large and complex economic, cultural, and social networks, based on market exchange, that the essential aim of subsidiarity can be achieved: "the establishment of true international order."

In a free enterprise system, private property provides the institutional environment whereby each person can own and control the personal space around him. By private, I am not suggesting exclusivity, but rather a demarcation that introduces predictability and stability into the common destination of goods. "Private" is to be contrasted with an institutional setting where the property owner is defined as a collective entity like the state. The purpose of property is not to acquire for oneself, but to serve others. In a liberal economy, serving others is the principal use of property and the wealth it generates.

Some people say wealth comes through using up natural resources, exploiting others, or through pure technological innovation. But this is the exception, not the rule, under free enterprise. The right of exchange itself is the major contributor to prosperity. Anytime a market exchange takes place, goods or services of a lesser value are traded for goods or services of a higher value. If people agree to this exchange voluntarily, then everyone involved in the exchange is better off. It is the great underappreciated fact of voluntary economic exchange that it allows people to trade a less desirable state of affairs for a more desirable one.

People must also have security in their property and the results of their exchanges for these institutions to contribute to the social good. When contracts are not enforced, the value of wealth in general begins to go down. A banker cannot lend money if there are not dependable ways of enforcing everyone's respective obligations. A labourer will not work for a business unless he or she knows what the terms of remuneration are beforehand. Even charity must rely on contract.

The economic system appropriate to a free and compassionate society must also reward creative liberty, or what Pope John Paul II has called the "right of economic initiative." Every person, by being created in the image and likeness of God, has within his heart and mind a capacity for thinking things anew, for renewing the space around him, and improving society. This very desire which exists within us, and which virtue requires we cultivate, is a reflection of a primary attribute of God as Creator. In economics, this creative capacity is called entrepreneurship.

These institutions have permitted vast increases in wealth over the last centuries. We have benefited so greatly that even our standards of what we call poor have changed. Imagine a family with no indoor toilet and no running water; they have to use an outhouse, or some other hole in the ground, and have to boil water from a source far away, just to get a drink or take a shower. Would this family qualify as poor? Probably. Is there a moral obligation to care for them, to provide for their well being? What if charity fails? Should the government come in to care for them, and guarantee the bare minimum standards of sanitary conditions? Yet this description applies to more than one third of American households in 1940. That was not in the nineteenth or eighteenth century, but in 1940. Only 1 % of the population is in a similar situation today. Yet it was not a massive government program administered from Washington that changed matters. It was an entrepreneurial economy.

As we rediscover the principle of subsidiarity as it applies to welfare, we need to reinforce these essential institutions, private property, free exchange, contract enforcement, and enterprise. Restrictions on the market such as the minimum wage, excessive licensure restrictions, high taxes, job-killing regulations, and the like, have effectively shut many out of markets in which they should be key participants.[41] Markets and property are among the foundations on which subsidiarity and true charity ultimately rest.

7.11 Conclusion

The concept of subsidiarity should not be ignored, but rather must be restored to the very center of serious reflection on social ethics and social structure. It has both practical and moral applications to our understanding of the role of the state, the family, the individual, the church, educational institutions, and the enterprising economy. The centralised democratic state, managing all aspects of social and economic life, though deeply entrenched in the modern social organisation, is a new

[41] Williams (1982).

institution, and it has exacted a heavy toll on the ability of the lower orders of society to solve social problems. The principle of subsidiarity, on the other hand, offers a guidepost for a new direction in the provision of social welfare and charity based on personal responsibility.[42]

References

Aristotle. 1976. *The Politics*. Trans. Hugh Tredennick. Cambridge, MA: Harvard University Press.

Benestad, J. Brian. 1990. Virtue in catholic social teaching. In *Private virtue and public policy: Catholic thought and national life*. New Brunswick: Transaction Publishers.

Bryk, Anthony, Valerie Lee, and Peter Holland. 1993. *Catholic schools and the common good*. Cambridge: Harvard University Press.

Coleman, John A. 1991. *One hundred years of Catholic social thought*. Marknoll: Orbis Books.

Conyngton, Mary. 1909. *How to help: A manual of practical charity*. New York: The MacMillan Company.

Curran, Charles E. 1985. *Directions in Catholic social ethics*. Notre Dame: University of Notre Dame Press.

Deschweinitz, Karl. 1924. *The art of helping people out of trouble*. Boston: Houghton Mifflin Co.

Hayek, F.A. 1972. The uses of knowledge in society. In *Individualism and the economic order*, 77–91. Chicago: Gateway.

Mueller, Franz H. 1984. *The church and the social question*. Washington, DC: American Enterprise Institute.

Neuhaus, Richard J. 1992. *Doing well and doing good*. New York: Doubleday.

Novak, Michael. 1982. *The spirit of democratic capitalism*. Washington, DC: American Enterprise Institute.

Olasky, Marvin. 1992. *The tragedy of American compassion*. Washington, DC: Regnery Gateway.

Rawls, John. 1971. *A theory of justice*. Cambridge: Harvard University Press.

Rodger Charles, S.J., and Drostan MacLaran. 1982. *The social teaching of Vatican II*. San Francisco: Ignatius Press.

Roepke, Wilhelm. 1992. *The social crisis of our time*. New Brunswick: Transaction Press.

Sirico, Robert. 2012. *Defending the free market: The moral case for a free economy*. Washington, DC: Regnery.

Williams, Walter. 1982. *The state against Blacks*. New York: New Press.

[42] For more on this topic and subsidiarity generally, see Sirico (2012).

Chapter 8
Subsidiarity and the German Constitution

Jürgen Bröhmer

Abstract The German Constitution (*Basic Law*) contains an explicit reference to the principle of subsidiarity only with regard to Germany's participation in the European Union. However, there are many features of the *Basic Law* which incorporate elements of the subsidiarity principle. These features extend beyond the fact that Germany is a federal state and the consequent delineation of power between the legislative powers of federal level and the German states (*Länder*), notwithstanding the fact that this is an important element of the principle which has recently led to a number of significant amendments of the *Basic Law* aimed at a recalibration of the federal power structure. The protection of lower level decision-making and personal autonomy that defines the subsidiarity principle is also visible in the administrative and judicial organisation of the Federal Republic, in the constitutional rules pertaining to local government and, not least, in the strong fundamental rights protection provided by the *Basic Law* and the procedural framework provided for effectuating this protection, the Constitutional Complaints Procedure.

Keywords Subsidiarity • European Union • Legislative powers • Administrative powers • Judiciary • Local government • Fundamental rights • Constitutional complaint

8.1 Introduction

One of the peculiarities of the Australian political debate is what appears to be a certain bias for further centralisation of an already rather centralised federal system. Whereas federalism certainly has strong proponents in Australia it often appears to

---

J. Bröhmer (✉)
School of Law, Murdoch University, 90 South Street, Murdoch, 6150 Perth, Western Australia, Australia
e-mail: j.brohmer@murdoch.edu.au

M. Evans and A. Zimmermann (eds.), *Global Perspectives on Subsidiarity*, Ius Gentium: Comparative Perspectives on Law and Justice 37, DOI 10.1007/978-94-017-8810-6_8,

be on the defensive and the Commonwealth has almost as much as "bought" whole policy areas, such as health care and education, off the states.[1]

In Europe and the United States, by contrast, the debate is markedly different. Decentralisation is the theme of the day in the European Union, or to use a more negative term, renationalisation. The United Kingdom is actively discussing taking back some powers allocated to Brussels in the European Union's foundational treaties or even taking them all back, that is, leaving the Union altogether.[2] In Germany as well, both with regard to the European Union and with regard to Germany's own political constitution, the strengthening of the role of Germany vis-à-vis the European Union and of Germany's constituent *Länder* vis-à-vis Berlin is the flavour of the day and not the other way around.

This is notwithstanding that the management of the European sovereign debt crisis appears to point in the opposite direction of an increasing trend to centralisation and communisation of important core policy fields. Fiscal policy, and policy areas referred to under the heading of creating a much tighter economic union, such as common supervision of the banking sector or tighter control of the budget and deficit processes in the member states could be cited as examples. But these phenomena can only partially distort this finding because much of what is happening in that regard is happening on an intergovernmental plane, for example, on the basis of separate treaties, and precisely not within the institutions of the European Union.

In the United States the Tea Party movement, a melting pot of views and in many ways a rainbow coalition of a special kind, has, as one of its fundamental aims, the reclaiming of powers from Washington and the revitalisation of states and local government and of government not only by the people but by the people at home.[3] In that sense the Tea Party movement is arguably the most outspoken and perhaps radical subsidiarity movement one could imagine and this particular aspect stands in sharp contrast to the disdain with which this movement appears to be met by

[1] Section 96 of the Commonwealth *Constitution* has been a particularly effective vehicle to achieve this by allowing the Commonwealth to award specific purpose grants. The German *Basic Law* prohibits this in Articles 104a and 104b and where central financing is allowed the role of the recipient *Länder* is much stronger.

[2] Cf. the British Prime Minister's speech of 23 January 2013 about his plans for a referendum on British membership in the EU. The principle of subsidiarity is not mentioned there but its importance is underlined by stipulating that "[M]y third principle [is] that power must be able to flow back to member states, not just away from them." There are many other examples in that speech, the text of which is reproduced at http://www.guardian.co.uk/politics/2013/jan/23/david-cameron-eu-speech-referendum

[3] See, for example, para. 10 of the Tea Party Movement Platform: "10. Maintain Local Independence – The strength and resilience of a grassroots movement is the ability of citizens at the local level to determine their own platforms, agendas and priorities free of an overriding central leadership. Exercising the clearly stated message of the Tea Party movement by its nature involves discourse about which policies and candidates best hold to our stated principles, and these various opinions should flourish and evolve at the local level", http://www.teaparty-platform.com/ (last accessed on 13/4/13).

many, and more so outside the United States and certainly in Germany.[4] Of course that negative image has nothing to do with the subsidiarity streak of the Tea Party but with a perceived rather right wing and radically voiced political agenda in many policy fields.

8.2 Historical Background

The principle of subsidiarity does not have an exact origin, although elements of "bottom-up" decision-making can be traced as far back as Aristotle and Thomas of Aquinas.[5] The foundation formulation of the principle of subsidiarity can be found in Pope Pius XI's encyclical *Quadragesimo Anno* of 1931.[6] The core message of the text is that of devolution. But the devolution is not one limited to governmental authorities. It is important to note that subsidiarity as proclaimed by Pope Pius XI, is not merely concerned with the organisational relationship of intra-state institutions but also with the relationship the state and individuals which will be examined later in this chapter.[7]

As a principle of state organisation subsidiarity has been strongly connected to multi-level government and it is therefore not surprising that the principle is most significant in federally structured states or state-like entities such as the European Union. Multi-level government is, however, not restricted to federally structured entities. Strong and independent local government, for example, can also be part of a unitary governmental structure based on the principle of subsidiarity. The same is true when governmental action is restricted and either delegated or otherwise moved, wholly or partially, to independent bodies as is the case in Germany for

---

[4] Polls conducted in Germany before the last United States presidential election yielded consistent support rates for President Obama of close to 90 %. See, for example, Zeit Online, 31/10/2012, http://www.zeit.de/politik/ausland/2012-10/obama-romney-umfrage-yougov (last accessed 8/5/2013): 85 % pro Obama; German Marshall Fund of the United States, Transatlantic Trends 2012, http://trends.gmfus.org/files/2012/09/TT-2012-Key-Findings-Report.pdf (last accessed 8/5/2013), p. 28: 87 %. These surveys asked for voting preferences in the race Obama-Romney. It is safe to conclude that vis-à-vis the Tea Party or a Tea Party candidate the numbers would have been even more extreme as persons affiliated with the Tea Party are regarded as less moderately conservative or more extreme than Romney was regarded as.

[5] D Fouarge, Poverty and Subsidiarity in Europe – Minimum Protection from an Economic Perspective, 2004, p. 18; Aroney (2007, 163).

[6] Text available at http://www.vatican.va/holy_father/pius_xi/encyclicals/documents/hf_p-xi_enc_19310515_quadragesimo-anno_en.html, paras 78–80 (last accessed 28/1/2013).

[7] The relationship between the original catholic formulation of subsidiarity, on the one hand, and freedom, human dignity and democracy on the other hand is also emphasized by Schambeck (2004). The standard treatise on subsidiarity in German language stems from Isensee (2001). See also Isensee (2011). From the perspective of the European Union, see the standard treatise by Calliess (1999).

public broadcasting, universities and in the welfare sector (with regard to the public insurance schemes) and for business and the professions in the various chamber organisations.[8]

8.3 Subsidiarity and the Exercise of Legislative Powers

8.3.1 Background

One major aspect of the vertical separation of power in federally structured entities such as Germany is the allocation of legislative powers. The German *Basic Law*[9] operates on the principle that all power lies with the states rather than the federal level (Article 30 GG). The federal level has only those powers that are explicitly attributed to it by the *Basic Law* (principle of enumerated powers, Articles 30, 70.1 and 83 GG).

The *Basic Law* distinguishes between exclusive legislative competences (Articles 71, 73 GG) and concurring or parallel competences (Articles 72, 74 GG). Examples of matters of exclusive federal jurisdiction, that is matters where legislative powers lie exclusively with the federal houses of parliament (*Bundestag* and *Bundesrat*), are foreign affairs and defence, citizenship, free movement and passports, currency, international trade, national cultural assets, air transport and railroads.[10] Examples for matters of concurring jurisdiction are private and commercial law (for example, the German Civil Code), criminal law including criminal procedure, the law of associations, the laws dealing with the residence of foreigners and refugees, public welfare, economic matters, labour law, research promotion, expropriation or the abuse of economic power.[11] The concurring or parallel powers are coupled with an

---

[8] See, for example, U Schliesky, Zur Zukunft der wirtschaftlichen Selbstverwaltung in Deutschland und Europa, Wirtschaft und Verwaltung (WiVerw) 2012, 27 et seq.; Stirn (2013) (with comparative views into other European countries).

[9] The German Constitution is called "Basic Law" (*Grundgesetz*, abbreviated henceforth as GG), a name chosen at inception in 1949 to underline its provisional character as the constitution of West-Germany only. It was to be replaced by a new constitution at a future reunification of Germany. However, after the reunification the *Grundgesetz* (GG) was – correctly – deemed to have so much popular support that the GG became the constitution of unified Germany without formally creating a new constitution by the unified German *pouvoir constituant*. An English-language version of the GG is available at http://www.gesetze-im-internet.de/englisch_gg/englisch_gg.html or https://www.btg-bestellservice.de/pdf/80201000.pdf (last accessed on 7/2/2013). Both versions are identical and were prepared by German and American constitutional scholars with the help of the language service of the German Parliament (*Deutscher Bundestag*). GG norms reproduced in this text are taken from this translation.

[10] For more details see Article 73 GG.

[11] For more details see Article 74 GG.

exhaustion principle, with the result that these concurring powers fall to the federal level once and in so far as the federal legislator has acted on them and passed relevant legislation. In essence, concurring powers are powers that become federal powers once the federal Parliament has acted and the federal Parliament has in fact legislated in many of the areas enumerated as concurring powers.

From a subject-matter perspective, the *Länder* of the German federation are left with legislative powers with respect to four major subject matters:

- The police power. That is, legislation in all matters that have to do with the police and its preventive function. This legislative power does not extend to the repressive police function, that is, criminal prosecution, which is part of the catalogue of concurring federal powers;
- Primary, secondary and tertiary education (schools and Universities). The federal level has retained some funding powers for capital infrastructure of universities;
- Culture and the arts. That is, all matters to do with theatres, music, or anything else that, in the broad sense of the word, falls under the heading of art and culture;
- Broadcasting and the regulation of broadcasting. That is, radio, television and all other electronic media including new technologies such as the internet.[12]

From the perspective of the number and weight of the various subject matters enumerated in Articles 73 and 74 GG one can only conclude that there is a strong bias towards the centre. That is already obvious for the matters that are exclusively attributed to the centre and even more true for matters that fall under concurrent federal legislative jurisdiction.

8.3.2 Recent Developments

The above finding, which reveals that the German legislative process is hardly governed by a strict application of the subsidiarity principle, has given rise to a number of corrective amendments of the *Basic Law*.

The first such amendment concerned the core of the legislative subsidiarity principle, as contained in Article 72.2 GG. As pointed out above, Article 72 GG concerns the concurring legislative jurisdiction of the *Bund* (that is, the federal level) attributing legislative powers of the subject areas enumerated in Article 74 GG to it but only when and insofar that the *Bund* wishes to exercise this power. To the degree that the *Bund* does not exercise these powers they remain with the *Länder*. The old

[12] Most notably in two of these areas, education and broadcasting, a quasi federal centralisation has taken place, in that many important decisions in these fields are reached by the *Länder* through compacts concluded between them and then implemented by *Länder* Parliaments. In this way the various *Länder* have in essence created a third level of federal cooperation, next to the federation itself and the individual *Länder*.

Article 72.2 GG added a subsidiarity condition to the exercise of the subject-matter legislative powers enumerated in Article 74 GG. These powers could only be exercised if there "is a need" for federal legislation of the subject-matter at issue and if

- the subject matter "cannot be effectively regulated by the legislative branches of the individual Länder"; or
- the "legislation by legislative branches of the individual Länder might impinge on the interests of other *Länder* or the country as a whole"; or
- the "realization of legal and economic unity, and especially the maintenance of uniform living conditions throughout the Federation and beyond the territory of any one *Land*, necessitates federal legislation."

However, this stipulation of the legislative subsidiarity principle in the old Article 72.2 GG remained ineffective.[13] Despite the fact that the Federal Constitutional Court (FCC)[14] consistently considered Article 72.2 GG to be a norm with justiciable, albeit discretionary, limitations, which could therefore be invoked against excessive exercise of federal legislative powers, the Court, in what might be considered an example of the application of what in the United States is known as the "political question doctrine", never interfered in practice.[15] The old version of the Article 72.2 GG required the determination of a "need" for federal legislation and stipulated that such a need could be based on the intention to maintain "uniform" living conditions. The Court consistently held that it would not interfere with the determination of such a need by the federal legislator.[16]

In 1994 this development brought about the 42nd amendment of the *Basic Law* which included, inter alia, an amendment of Article 72.2 GG. The 'uniformity of living conditions' criterion to justify centralising legislative activity in areas of concurring legislation was replaced by the lesser criterion of equivalent living conditions. The reason behind this change of language was that it will be harder to justify centralised legislation if living conditions across the various states are only required to be equivalent in the sense of comparable rather than uniform. The FCC took this up in a much discussed decision concerning the *Geriatric Care Act* in which the Court reasserted the justiciability of Article 72.2 GG and in which it explained its stricter interpretation of Article 72.2 as amended in 1994 to strengthen the subsidiarity principle in the context of concurring legislation.[17] The Court confirmed this line in subsequent decisions and held that

---

[13] BVerfGE 107, 62 at 136, http://www.servat.unibe.ch/dfr/bv106062.html, para. 292.

[14] Henceforth referred to as FCC. For general information on the FCC see http://www.bverfg.de/en/index.html

[15] For more details see Calliess (2013).

[16] BVerfGE 2, 213 at 224–5, http://www.servat.unibe.ch/dfr/bv002213.html, para. 35; see also BVerfGE 4, 115 at 127–8, http://www.servat.unibe.ch/dfr/bv004115.html, para. 50; BVerfGE 78, 249 (270), http://www.servat.unibe.ch/fallrecht/bv078249.html, para. 66.

[17] BverfGE 106, 62, http://www.servat.unibe.ch/dfr/bv106062.html (last accessed on 16/4/2013). See also Rau (2003) et seq., http://www.germanlawjournal.com/pdf/Vol04No03/PDF_Vol_04_No_03_223-236_Public_Rau.pdf (last accessed on 16/4/13).

> [...] federal legislation can be regarded as necessary for maintaining equivalent living conditions only if the living conditions in the *Länder* of the Federal Republic are either drifting apart or about to drift apart in such a way as to significantly jeopardize the federal, social framework.[18]

The FCC saw no such danger in this particular case which concerned university fees in some states. In another decision the FCC did regard federal legislation dealing with Germany's public health insurance scheme as justified by the necessity to maintain equivalent living conditions.[19]

As part of the *Federal Reform Package 1* 2006,[20] Article 72 GG was amended again to bolster the subsidiarity idea by limiting the concurring legislative powers to just 10 subject-matter areas and maintaining the higher threshold already introduced in the 1994 amendment.[21] This amendment also introduced a new Article 72.3 GG which authorises the *Länder* to deviate from federal legislation by passing superseding "variance" legislation in certain subject-matter areas, effectively creating 'opting-out' rights for the *Länder*.

However, even after these attempts to strengthen the subsidiarity principle with regard to legislative powers, the fact remains that the German federation was never one where the power-sharing is primarily achieved by allocating broad subject-matter legislative power to the lower entities, the *Länder*. The strong role of *Länder* in Germany stems from their participation in the federal legislative process through the *Bundesrat*. The *Länder* are represented institutionally, by members of their executive branches, and not merely territorially by representatives who operate independently from the political will of the entity they represent as institutionally expressed through the government and parliament of that entity. Hence the political will of the each *Land* can directly translate into the decision-making process on the federal level.[22]

8.4 Subsidiarity and the Exercise of Administrative Powers

An important subsidiarity safeguard of the German *Basic Law* is the allocation of administrative powers. Unlike in the United States, administrative powers do not follow legislative powers. In other words, the federal level might have the power to

---

[18] BVerfGE 112, 226 at 244, http://www.servat.unibe.ch/dfr/bv112226.html, para. 67 [translation by author] (last accessed on 16/4/2013). The case dealt with the question whether the federation could use a certain, no longer existing type of legislation to effectively prohibit the introduction of fees into the German University system. The FCC explained that the equivalence of living conditions could not be invoked by the federation even if the introduction of fees in some *Länder* but not in others were to lead to students moving to fee-free *Länder*, ibid., para. 76.

[19] BVerfGE 113, 167 at 198, http://www.servat.unibe.ch/dfr/bv113167.html, para. 90.

[20] 52nd amendment to the Basic Law of 28/8/2006, Federal Gazette (BGBl. I) 2034 (2006).

[21] The new Article 72.2 reads: "The Federation shall have the right to legislate on matters falling within clauses 4, 7, 11, 13, 15, 19a, 20, 22, 25 and 26 of paragraph (1) of Article 74, if and to the extent that the establishment of equivalent living conditions throughout the federal territory or the maintenance of legal or economic unity renders federal regulation necessary in the national interest."

[22] For more detail see Bröhmer (2011).

legislate in a certain subject matter but that does not include the power to create the necessary bureaucracy to execute and administer the legislation. With few exceptions, such as the foreign service,[23] all administrative powers belong to the *Länder*.[24] According to Article 84.1 GG where the *Länder* execute federal laws in their own right in accordance with Article 83 GG, they are also responsible for the establishment of the requisite authorities and for the applicable administrative procedure.

The old version of Article 84 GG allowed the federal legislator to retain some or all of the administrative powers as part of the federal legislation under the condition that the second chamber of Parliament, the *Bundesrat* (Federal Council) assented to such legislation. This provision had resulted in a large increase of so-called assent legislation, that is, legislation that required the consent of the *Bundesrat* and therefore significantly increased the influence of the several *Länder* on federal legislation. It also made policy making more difficult, especially if the political majorities in the *Länder* shift over time and the political camp of the opposition in the federal Parliament becomes the governing majority in enough *Länder* to create a majority in the *Bundesrat* (Federal Council). One disadvantageous consequence of this vertical separation of powers between the two chambers of Parliament and the strong role of the *Länder* in the *Bundesrat* is the resulting propensity for blockade politics, the rise of the – relatively faceless and small Conference Committee, a joint Committee of *Bundestag* and *Bundesrat* with the task of reaching a compromise between the two chambers, to significant practical power[25] and the inherent difficulty of determining democratic accountability for decision-making after such institutionally convoluted decision-making processes.[26]

The new version of Article 84 GG after the *Federalism Reform Package* 2006 untangled this situation. The principle remains that the *Länder* are responsible in

---

[23] Article 87.1 GG; also federal financial administration (partially, especially the customs administration); see also Art. 87b – Federal Defense Administration, Art. 87d – air transport administration; Art. 87e – rail transport administration; Art. 87f – post and telecommunications, insofar as not privatized; Art. 88 – Federal (Reserve) Bank; Art. 89 – federal waterways administration.

[24] Article 83 GG: "The *Länder* shall execute federal laws in their own right insofar as this Basic Law does not otherwise provide or permit."

[25] The legal basis for the Mediation Committee (Conference Committee) is found in Article 77.2 GG. The Committee acts on the basis of by-laws passed jointly by the two chambers, text in German available at http://www.*Bundesrat*.de/cln_330/nn_8962/DE/br-dbt/va/go/go.html. It consists of 32 members, 16 from each chamber (§ 1). Its meetings are closed to the public (§6) and any results of the mediation can only be accepted or declined by the *Bundestag* without further modification (§ 10.2). Benz (2009) illustrates the enormous de facto power of the Mediation Committee in such political constellations by pointing out that during the 14th *Bundestag* between 1998 and 2002 the Committee was called upon to mediate a compromise for 77 bills of which 65 were passed into law. The Federal Constitutional Court has consistently held that the Mediation Committee's activities must not lead to a "de-parliamentarization" and that therefore any results of the mediation in that Committee must be attributable to the *Bundestag* and that the Committee does not have a right of initiative and can only negotiate on the basis of the bill submitted to it. See BVerfG, 2 BvR 758/07 of 8.12.2009, paras. 54 et Seq. 57, http://www.bverfg.de/entscheidungen/rs20091208_2bvr075807.html (press release with English language summary at http://www.bverfg.de/pressemitteilungen/bvg10-002en.html).

[26] More broadly on the role of transparency in democratic accountability see J Bröhmer, Transparenz als Verfassungsprinzip, 2004, p. 18 et seq.

their own right for any and all administrative requirements arising from the federal legislation. However, the federal legislator is now able to provide otherwise without assent of the *Bundesrat* and in that sense the powers of the *Länder* have been diminished. In compensation for this loss of influence the *Länder* were given the right to deviate from any such federal prescription. In other words the federal level can only make an "administrative offer" in its legislation, which will stand only if there is no opposing political will that translates into deviating legislation in one or more of the *Länder*. As a result one can conclude that this reform has diminished the role of the *Länder* as a whole and the powers exercised by them jointly in the *Bundesrat*. However, at the same time the role of the *Länder* as individual entities was actually strengthened. Their power has increased because they can now individually reject federal administrative mandates even when that position could not have found a majority in the federal chamber, the *Bundesrat*.

The advantage of the new regime in Article 84 GG is that it is much easier to attribute accountability for legislative activity as the *Bundesrat* is no longer able to engage in blockade politics and the government and its majority in the *Bundestag* cannot blame any inaction on a lack of support in the *Bundesrat*.[27]

8.5 Subsidiarity and the Exercise of Judicial Powers

The principle of subsidiarity in the judicial branch has a more general scope closely linked to the federal structure of Germany. Additionally, it has a more specific aspect which has to do with the particular role of the Federal Constitutional Court and one of the specific procedures provided for in the *Basic Law* for access of citizens to that court, the so-called constitutional complaints procedure.

8.5.1 Subsidiarity in the Judicial Branch in General

Of lesser interest, but somewhat peculiar in comparison to Australia or the United States, is the fact that Germany's court system, not dissimilar to the administrative system, is not linked to the distribution of legislative powers between the federal level and the constituting entities. That is, the states do not have an independent court

[27] In the past the only means to circumvent disparate majorities in both chambers was to omit anything to do with administration from a bill and effectively leave it to the *Länder* to legislate for the administrative consequences or to propose the respective administrative part in an independent bill, which, if it fails in the second chamber would leave it to the individual *Länder* to come up with the necessary rules. This practical approach to matters was affirmed by the Federal Constitutional Court in the case concerning the constitutionality of the German Civil Union Act which wanted to end the discrimination of same sex unions but could not hope to find a majority in the *Bundesrat* where the conservatively governed *Länder* enjoyed a majority at the time. The federal bill therefore omitted everything from it which could have given rise to any rights of assent by the *Bundesrat*, especially administrative provisions speaking to the conclusion of such unions in practice. See BVerfG, 1 BvF 1/01 of 17/7/2002, http://www.bverfg.de/entscheidungen/ls20020717_1bvf000101.html

system for areas where they legislate, and the federal level does not have an independent court system for matters of federal jurisdiction. Instead, Germany's court system is a state court system on the lower levels including the first major appellate level, the superior provincial courts.[28] The highest tier and courts of last appellate resort, however, are federal courts.[29] The jurisdictional link is not entirely broken as matters of *Länder* jurisdiction will not be admissible for appeal to the respective federal Supreme Court.[30] That is especially the case in administrative law, where the appeal in law to the Federal Administrative Court is only admissible if it is based on an alleged violation of federal law.[31] Given that even federal law is administered by the *Länder*, errors based on administrative procedure and therefore governed by the respective *Länder* administrative procedure codes[32] cannot normally be appealed to the Federal Administrative Court. In other areas of the law this delineation is not as prominent as they are federal laws anyway. The jurisdiction of the criminal and civil (private) law courts headed by the Federal Court of Justice as the Supreme Court is governed mainly by the *Criminal* and *Criminal Procedure Code* respectively by the *Civil Code* and the *Civil Procedure Code*, all of which are federal statutes. Similarly, most welfare law and the law pertaining to the various public insurance schemes (health, pension, nursing, and unemployment) is also federal law.

---

[28] There are 24 Superior Provincial Courts (sometimes translated as higher regional courts). In German they are mostly referred to as *Oberlandesgerichte*, sometimes with a specific regional attribute added to the name of the seat city, for example, Pfälzisches Oberlandesgericht Zweibrücken for the court serving the palatinate district in southwestern Germany in the city of Zweibrücken. The respective court in Berlin, however, is called the "Chamber Court Berlin (*Kammergericht* Berlin).

[29] An instructive chart of the German Court system is available from the Council of Europe at http://www.coe.int/t/dghl/cooperation/cepej/profiles/CourtSystemGermany.pdf (last accessed at 23/3/2013).

[30] As can be seen from the chart referred to in fn. 26 Germany's judicial system is organized in five major subject-matter jurisdictions. Art. 95 GG stipulates: "The Federation shall establish the Federal Court of Justice [criminal and civil/private law], the Federal Administrative Court [general administrative law], the Federal Finance Court [taxation], the Federal Labour Court [labour law and industrial relations] and the Federal Social Court (social and welfare law, public health and pension insurance schemes] as supreme courts of ordinary, administrative, financial, labour and social jurisdiction." [Additions in brackets by the author]. The sixth major federal court and in many ways the most powerful of them is the Federal Constitutional Court (FCC, Articles 93 and 94 GG), which, however, is not a court of appeal in the narrow sense.

[31] Section 137.1 No. 1 of the Code for Administrative Court Procedure [Verwaltungsgerichtsordnung]. An unofficial English translation of this code as it stood at the end of 2010 is available at http://www.gesetze-im-internet.de/englisch_vwgo/englisch_vwgo.html (last accessed on 25/3/201300). The official German and latest version is available at http://www.gesetze-im-internet.de/vwgo/BJNR000170960.html (last accessed on 25/3/2013).

[32] All 16 *Länder* have their own administrative procedure codes which govern administrative decision making and administrative review of these decisions. The Federation also has its own administrative procedure code for those areas in which the administrative procedure falls within federal jurisdiction. Judicial review, as opposed to administrative review which must in principle precede any judicial review, is reserved to the (state) administrative courts and higher administrative courts and on final appeal to the Federal Administrative Court. The various administrative procedure codes are very similar or even identical.

8.5.2 *Special Delegation – Article 96.5 GG*

This provision empowers the Federal Parliament (*Bundestag*), with the assent of the Federal Chamber (*Bundesrat*) to create criminal jurisdiction for *Länder* courts for specified crimes such as genocide, crimes against humanity, war crimes, the crime of aggression and state security crimes. The idea behind this delegation of judicial power to the lower level courts is, however, not so much driven by subsidiarity considerations but by the practical consideration of creating the possibility for an appeal. If the first instance jurisdiction remained with the Federal Supreme Court there could be no appeal because there is no other court above the Federal Supreme Court. The delegation to the Superior Provincial Courts (*Oberlandesgerichte*), which are state courts, allows for an appeal to the Federal Supreme Court.[33]

8.5.3 *"Reverse Subsidiarity" – Article 99 GG*

It is interesting to note that the *Basic Law* also contains something like a "reverse subsidiarity" provision in Article 99 GG, which allows a *Land* by way of statute to allocate disputes arising under the constitution of that *Land* to the Federal Constitutional Court rather than to a court of that *Land* itself.[34] This option was used only once by the *Land* Schleswig-Holstein and only until 2008[35]; currently all *Länder* use their own constitutional courts for such disputes.

Under the second alternative of Article 99 GG, the *Länder* can also constitutionally or statutorily empower the five federal Supreme Courts to be the final courts of appeal for matters relating to legislation of the *Länder*. This provision has been used with regard to matters arising in the area of media law where the *Länder* have exclusive legislative jurisdiction and where they closely cooperate through compacts concluded among them. These treaty-like compacts contain Article 99 clauses in order to secure a unified interpretation of the compact.[36] Were it not for Article 99, only *Länder* courts could have jurisdiction to adjudicate disputes arising in this context.

---

[33] Morgenthaler in: Epping/Hillgruber, Besck'scher Online Kommentar GG, Edition 17 (1.1.2013), para. 12 (accessed on 3/4/2013).

[34] In which case the Federal Constitutional Court acts as if it were the constitutional court of the delegating *Land*, one consequence being that the FCC will in such a case only determine the compatibility of the act with the constitution of the *Land*, not with the *Basic Law*. See BVerfGE 103, 332 at 344–5, http://www.servat.unibe.ch/dfr/bv103332.html (last accessed on 3/4/2013).

[35] For the legal foundations of the new Constitutional Court of the *Land* Schleswig-Holstein see http://www.schleswig-holstein.de/LVG/DE/Rechtsgrundlagen/rechtsgrundlagen_node.html (last accessed on 3/4/2013).

[36] See, for example, § 48 of the Broadcasting Compact (Rundfunkstaatsvertrag), http://www.media-perspektiven.de/fileadmin/downloads/media_perspektiven/PDF-Dateien/2-Rundfunkstaatsvertrag.pdf (last accessed on 3/4/2013).

8.5.4 The Constitutional Complaint Procedure and Its Subsidiarity

The multi-facetted German court system is governed by relatively stringent procedural rules defining the jurisdictions of the various courts and the prerequisites for being able to bring a procedure before these courts. This is even more true for the Federal Constitutional Court (FCC). The various procedures this court can entertain are listed in Article 93 GG and are fleshed out in more detail in the statute governing the FCC's activities.[37] Arguably, the most important procedure to the FCC is the Constitutional Complaints Procedure (*Verfassungsbeschwerde*).[38]

The Constitutional Complaints Procedure allows anybody who is affected by an act of the government or a governmental agency or department, whether federal, state, municipal or independent, to challenge the constitutionality of that act.[39] Such acts could be administrative acts, court decisions or even legislation itself, if the legislation is self-executing or quasi self-executing, as for example in the case of criminal norms where having to wait for criminal prosecution to challenge the constitutionality of the underlying prescribed crime is regarded as unreasonable.

Constitutional complaints can be brought to the FCC only if regular judicial remedies have been exhausted to the last possible appeal.[40] That means that the FCC will only deal with constitutional complaints after the other 'regular' courts have rendered decisions in the matter. It is this feature that is commonly referred to as the subsidiarity of the Constitutional Complaint procedure. This subsidiarity is akin to what in public international law is known as the "local remedies rule" which requires that any action on the international plane can only be taken after all possible local remedies have been exhausted. In both cases what the principle is meant to achieve is a decision making process at the lower levels before the centralised institutions – the community of states in public international law or the FCC as the principle guardian of the German *Basic Law* – become involved.

---

[37] Federal Constitutional Court Act (Bundesverfassungsgerichtsgesetz), latest version in German available at http://www.gesetze-im-internet.de/bverfgg/BJNR002430951.html. An older and therefore not current, version in English can be found at http://www.iuscomp.org/gla/statutes/BVerfGG.htm (last accessed on 26 March 2013).

[38] The constitutional complaints procedure is by far the most popular type of procedure brought before the Court. In the year 2012 alone, 5818 constitutional complaints were brought to the court. Between September 1951 to the end of 2012, 194,005 constitutional complaints were brought to the FCC. The success rate for constitutional complaints is very small. In 2012, the FCC rendered a decision in 5327 constitutional complaints. Only 148 were successful (2.78 %). In the past decade, the success rate for constitutional complaints has always been below 3 %. Statistical data cited in this paragraph pertains to the year 2012 and is taken from the *Statistik für das Geschäftsjahr 2012*, available on the Court's website at http://www.bverfg.de/organisation/statistik_2012.html (last accessed on 3/4/2013).

[39] Article 93.1 No. 4a GG provides: "The Federal Constitutional Court shall rule: [...] 4a. on constitutional complaints, which may be filed by any person alleging that one of his basic rights or one of his rights under paragraph (4) of Article 20 or under Article 33, 38, 101, 103 or 104 has been infringed by public authority."

[40] § 90.2 BVerfGG.

There is another noteworthy aspect of this particular iteration of the subsidiarity principle that is interesting in the light of the ongoing human rights debate in Australia. The subsidiarity of the Constitutional Complaints Procedure ensures that alleged violations of the *Basic Law* must first be dealt with on the statutory level. Any and all acts of government that affect individuals must have a legal basis in statutory law. Therefore many allegedly constitutional issues can be dealt with on that statutory level, for example, by way of statutory interpretation. Only if the issue cannot be resolved in the regular courts can the matter then be brought before the FCC. That court will, in contrast to the regular courts, only apply norms of the *Basic Law* to the dispute and determine whether the statutory law as interpreted and applied by the regular courts violates constitutional norms. Whereas the FCC has no jurisdiction with regard to the application of regular statutory law, it has exclusive jurisdiction with regard to determining the unconstitutionality of acts of parliament. This stands in contrast to the United States or Australia where regular courts have the power to decide a case based on the unconstitutionality of underlying regular statutory or other law and where such a finding is subject to regular appeal. This division of judicial tasks and powers or, to formulate it more generally, a more detailed regulation of the jurisdiction of the various courts of a judicial system, including more detailed regulation of who has standing to bring what type of procedure to a particular court would go a long way in addressing the argument of opponents of bills of human rights that such human rights instruments lead to undue power concentrations in the judiciary and to judicial overreach at the expense of the democratically elected Parliament.

8.6 Subsidiarity and Fundamental Rights

The substantive fundamental rights[41] guaranteed in the *Basic Law* are themselves important pillars of the subsidiarity principle.[42] One major function of fundamental rights is to defend a sphere of individual autonomy against intrusion by the state. Under this *status negativus* (*status libertatis*) function,[43] individuals are empowered to make their own decisions and they are therefore and correspondingly entitled to be left alone by the government. That personal sphere as defined by the fundamental rights is not subject to majority rule and the fundamental rights guarantees and the limited powers of government resulting from them are therefore a quintessential subsidiarity tool.

---

[41] The term "fundamental rights" is used as a reflection of the German term "*Grundrechte*" which is the broader, more generic term for both human rights (of any human being) and rights of citizens.

[42] See also Häberle (2004).

[43] See M Stolleis, Public Law in Germany, 1800–1914, 2001, p. 350. The status concept goes back to G Jellinek, System der subjektiven öffentlichen Rechte, 1st ed. 1892, pp. 89 et seq., available at http://archive.org/stream/systemdersubjek00jellgoog#page/n9/mode/2up (2nd ed. 1905, pp. 94–114, reprinted in J Kersten (ed.), Georg Jellinek – System der subjektiven öffentlichen Rechte, 2011, after p. 52).

The personal autonomy, that is, the freedom created by fundamental rights, must not be confused with "the evil of what we have termed "individualism" in Pope Pius" subsidiarity text.[44] Pope Pius refers to individualism at the expense of others.[45] However, the structure of fundamental rights of the German *Basic Law* safeguards against this type of excessive individualism in two ways. Firstly, the *Basic Law*'s fundamental rights guarantee personal autonomy not only for individuals in the narrow sense, but also for associations of all kinds. The exercise of fundamental rights – from freedom of religion to enterprise bargaining, to freedom of expression and other rights – by associations and other organisations, is procedurally protected by the FCC's broad definition of what constitutes an association when it comes to the admissibility of a Constitutional Complaint.[46] Secondly and perhaps more importantly, the trans-individualistic nature of fundamental rights is also demonstrated by two other functions of those guarantees which complement the *status negativus* defensive function against government intrusion and which ensure that fundamental rights cannot serve as a basis for one individual to curtail the rights of others. The first of these functions is the duty to protect which arises from these guarantees, and the second one is the objective function of fundamental rights. Under the duty to protect doctrine, it is not sufficient for the government to merely abstain from interfering in rights' positions of individuals, the government must also actively protect these rights.[47] The objective function is a major vehicle for that protection because under this function fundamental rights permeate the legal order as a whole and must be taken into account when interpreting any and all other rules of law. Both these functions must be seen against the fact that fundamental rights are rights of the individual against the state (government) and are not rights against other individuals. There is, with few exceptions, no direct third party effect of these rights.[48] The duty to protect and the objective functions compensate for that lack of direct third party effect by requiring that the government must balance conflicting rights in trilateral constellations in such a manner that the broadest possible effect can be given to both or all conflicting rights involved. The constitutional scholar

[44] See supra fn. 5.

[45] The Pope specifically refers to a certain understanding of property rights in this context: "For, as one is wrecked upon, or comes close to, what is known as "individualism" by denying or minimizing the social and public character of the right of property, so by rejecting or minimizing the private and individual character of this same right, one inevitably runs into "collectivism" or at least closely approaches its tenets" (see supra fn. 5, para. 46). That the Pope refers to what one might today describe as excesses of capitalism is also confirmed by paras. 88 and 109–10.

[46] Which is not to say that the German *Basic Law* of 1949 could define what the Pope said and much less what the Pope said in 1931. However, in the context of subsidiarity it is hard to fathom that the evil the Pope saw in individualism has anything to do with the autonomous space guaranteed to individuals and groups of individuals having a protected space for their own affairs.

[47] BVerfGE 39, 1 (42 et seq.), http://www.servat.unibe.ch/dfr/bv039001.html; BVerfG, 1 BvR 357/05 of 15/2/2006, para 118, http://www.bverfg.de/entscheidungen/rs20060215_1bvr035705en.html; Cremer (2003).

[48] One notable exception is the coalition freedom in Article 9.3 GG, see infra text around fn. 48.

Konrad Hesse referred to this balancing exercise as the attempt to achieve "practical concordance".[49] In effect "practical concordance" will inherently require the limitation of the scope of one right in order to protect a competing right of another individual.[50] The "individualism" is a balanced individualism and not an egoistic one. The individual autonomy created by rights is an important means of realising subsidiarity but in such a way that the impact on the same autonomous decision-making of affected third parties are kept to a reasonable minimum and the combined scope of autonomous decision-making space is maximised.

Some fundamental rights address the principle of subsidiarity institutionally. Article 9.3 GG protects the right of trade unions and their counterpart employers' associations to "safeguard and improve working and economic provisions." This means that government only has a very limited role to play in regard to employment conditions. The so-called enterprise-bargaining autonomy ("*Tarifautonomie*") for these representative organisations of the employers and employees largely exempts a rather broad policy field from the reach of the legislator giving almost exclusive jurisdiction to the main stakeholders. The result is a very limited amount of labour law legislation in Germany and such labour law regulation, insofar as its source is not European Union legislation, constitutes a limitation of the guarantee of Article 9.3 GG and must therefore be justified and justifiable. The current debate in Germany on the introduction of a legislated minimum wage is a good example.[51] Those who regard such legislation as a justified restriction of the autonomy of the bargaining partners point to fact that such bargaining often does not take place, be it because of the structure of some industries or a lack of organisation of employees, and that therefore the intervention of the legislator is necessary to protect the weak and relieve the state from having to step in with welfare payments.[52]

Yet another subsidiarity feature has developed from the FCC's interpretation of Article 2.1 GG. Article 2.1 states: "Every person shall have the right to free

---

[49] The principle goes back to German constitutional scholar Konrad Hesse (1995); see also Schutter (2010).

[50] For example a woman's right to self-determination must be limited to protect the right to life of the fetus, who, under German constitutional law participates in the right to life guarantee, by placing some limits on abortion, which do not necessarily have to be criminally sanctioned. See for example the FCC's abortion decisions in BVerfGE 39, 1 (http://www.servat.unibe.ch/dfr/bv039001.html) and BVerfGE 88, 203 (http://www.servat.unibe.ch/dfr/bv088203.html). Likewise, free speech can be limited to protect personality rights of others against communicating defamatory lies, see for example BVerfGE 114, 339, BVerfG, 1 BvR 1696/98 of 10/25/2005, paragraphs No. 45, http://www.bverfg.de/entscheidungen/rs20051025_1bvr169698en.html. See also the Explanatory annotation and the translation of the two main abortion decisions of the FCC in Bröhmer et al. (2012).

[51] See, for example, https://www.destatis.de/EN/FactsFigures/NationalEconomyEnvironment/EarningsLabourCosts/MinimumWages/CurrentD.html; http://www.bruegel.org/nc/blog/detail/article/1036-a-review-on-germanys-minimum-wage-debate/ (last accessed on 3/4/2013).

[52] Cf. G Caspers, Mindestlohn und Tarifautonomie, in: Rieble/Junker/Giesen (eds.), Mindestlohn als politische und rechtliche Herausforderung, Tagungsband zum 7. Ludwigsburger Rechtsgespräch am, 19.11.2010 (ZAAR Schriftenreihe Band 23), pp. 147 et seq.

development of his personality in so far as he does not violate the rights of others or offend against the constitutional order." In plain language, this norm guarantees everybody the right to do what they want as long as they do not infringe on the rights of others. That is, as long as they do not break the law: what is not expressly prohibited is allowed. The FCC applies the legality principle very broadly. Any restriction on private behaviour or action instituted by law must not suffer from any legal mistake. A faulty norm cannot limit the freedom of individuals regardless of the cause of the error.[53] Article 2.1 is therefore a fall-back guarantee in that it does not have a particular substantive scope like the communication freedoms (Articles 4, 5, 8) or the guarantee of the privacy of the home (Article 13) but protects against any limitation of personal autonomy if only a legal error of any kind can be established and if no other *lex specialis* guarantee is available. For this reason Article 2.1 GG is often referred to as a subsidiary right.[54] In effect the safety net of Article 2.1 GG verifies the claim made here earlier, that fundamental rights as descriptors of the scope of personal autonomy have a quintessential subsidiarity function.

8.7 Municipal Government and Subsidiarity

8.7.1 Municipal Government vis-à-vis the Federation and Its Constituent Länder

Municipalities, namely towns, cities, districts, counties, councils or similar entities are obviously an important part of the principle of subsidiarity if these local entities retain a space of independent decision making. Germany's *Basic Law* recognises the important role municipalities play in this respect. Article 28.2 GG[55] guarantees the right of municipalities to regulate all local affairs and of self-government within the general legal framework, and to have access to an independent source of tax revenues to do so. Organisationally, municipalities are part of the *Länder* and not an independent level of government. However, this constitutionally guaranteed self-government in effect creates a quasi third level of state organisation from a subsidiarity perspective: municipalities have exclusive jurisdiction over local affairs under Article 28.2 GG. Under Article 30 GG the *Länder* have principal jurisdiction

[53] BVerfGE 6, 32 – Elfes, http://www.servat.unibe.ch/dfr/bv006032.html

[54] See for example BVerfGE 116, 202 at 221, http://www.servat.unibe.ch/dfr/bv116202.html, para. 78.

[55] Article 28.2 GG: "Municipalities must be guaranteed the right to regulate all local affairs on their own responsibility, within the limits prescribed by the laws. Within the limits of their functions designated by a law, associations of municipalities shall also have the right of self-government according to the laws. The guarantee of self-government shall extend to the bases of financial autonomy; these bases shall include the right of municipalities to a source of tax revenues based upon economic ability and the right to establish the rates at which these sources shall be taxed."

over all matters not specifically allocated by the *Basic Law* to the Federal level[56] One is inclined to think of a subsidiarity ladder – local, state and federal.[57]

The definition of what local affairs are is obviously not easy. The Federal Constitutional Court has defined local affairs as those "needs and interests that have their roots in the local community and that have a specific link to the local community."[58] The Court, however, has made it clear that this is not a sharp definition, that this concept is subject to change and that interference by state or federal legislation is to be evaluated also in the context of the potential effects the interference would have on independent municipal government.[59] Typically local affairs are grouped in those arising from the municipalities' territorial, personal, organisational and financial jurisdictions. Municipalities have the right to prescribe rules and implement them against anybody on their territory within the framework of state and federal law.[60] They have organisational jurisdiction (the right to organise and run their own administration as they see fit),[61] personal jurisdiction (to select staff who are employed by them, and not by the *Land*),[62] budget jurisdiction, (they are responsible for their own budget)[63] and planning jurisdiction, (that is, municipalities retain the power for town and area planning on their territory and thus determine their future development as a municipality).[64]

The financial aspect is of special significance as the independence of municipalities is especially under threat from burgeoning costs of existing tasks and from being the addressee of new tasks, especially in the broader welfare area, ranging from general welfare payments to the housing of refugees and asylum seekers and other

[56] See R Peffekoven/Ulrike Kirchhoff, Deutscher und Europäischer Finanzausgleich im Lichte des Subsidiaritätsprinzips, in: K Nörr/T Oppermann (eds.), Subsidiarität: Idee und Wirklichkeit – Zur Reichweite eines Prinzips in Deutschland und Europa, 1997, p. 116.

[57] The European Union, of course, is a fourth level, see infra Sect. 8.8, p. 148 et seq. and Chap. 9 by Gabriel Moens and John Trone in this book.

[58] BVerfG, 2 BvR 2374/99 of 18/5/2004, para 135, http://www.bverfg.de/entscheidungen/rs20040518_2bvr237499.html (last accessed on 5/4/2013).

[59] BVerfG, 2 BvR 2374/99 of 18/5/2004, para. 137, http://www.bverfg.de/entscheidungen/rs20040518_2bvr237499.html (last accessed on 5/4/2013). In this case the issue was the commercial use of sewage sludge and the statutory enactment of new rules for dealing with liability risks arising from the use of the sludge which had adverse impacts of municipal governments.

[60] BVerfGE 52, 95 at 118, http://www.servat.unibe.ch/dfr/bv052095.html, para 73 (last accessed on 5/4/2013).

[61] BVerfGE 91, 228 at 236, http://www.servat.unibe.ch/dfr/bv091228.html, para 25 (last accessed on 5/4/2013).

[62] BVerfGE 91, 228 at 245, http://www.servat.unibe.ch/dfr/bv091228.html, para 48; BVerfG, 2 BvR 2433/04 of 20/12/2007, para 146, http://www.bverfg.de/entscheidungen/rs20071220_2bvr243304.html (last accessed on 5/4/2013).

[63] BVerfG, 2 BvR 2433/04 of 20/12/2007, para 142, http://www.bverfg.de/entscheidungen/rs20071220_2bvr243304.html (last accessed on 5/4/2013).

[64] BVerfGE 56, 298 at 310, http://www.servat.unibe.ch/dfr/bv056298.html, para 36 (last accessed on 5/4/2013).

immigrants,[65] to the provision of childcare without necessarily being given the financial means to fulfil these tasks adequately.[66]

The difficult financial situation of many municipalities and the critically dire situation of some municipalities illustrates one major difficulty in the practical handling of the subsidiarity principle which arises at the coalface. Allocating jurisdiction to prescribe and/or jurisdiction to implement on the lowest possible level is directly connected with the allocation of the requisite financial means, or the ability to raise these means. However, the more tasks are allocated to the lower level, the less likely is it that the lower level will be able to raise the necessary money to pay for them. This is not a problem for tasks which the municipalities voluntarily undertake and for which they have to pay because in such a case jurisdiction for the task and for the necessary revenue is in the same hands. Many tasks, however, require standardisation. It cannot be left to the municipalities whether and to what extent they wish to engage with refugees or immigrants or whether and to what extent they are willing to grant welfare payments to those in need. The standardisation of these tasks is necessarily a more centralised endeavour. The administration and handling of these tasks at the lower level in keeping with the subsidiarity principle necessarily results in a disjuncture between task and costs. If the task is spelled out as an entitlement, for example, a free or almost free childcare place for every child from age 1, but the money handed over to fulfil that task is not sufficient, the entitlement still exists and the municipality must still deliver. This illustrates that subsidiarity is not as such and by itself beneficial but needs careful embedding with due regard to the overall context and with regard to potential regulatory conflicts that will then inherently arise.

The nexus between finances and delegated tasks is not new and had already in the mid-1990s led to two amendments of the *Basic Law* with the addition of the two parts of the last sentence of Article 28.2 as it currently stands,[67] in 1994[68] and 1997[69] respectively. The goal was to strengthen the financial independence of the municipalities and protect them from the removal of the main municipal tax source without supplying an adequate replacement. This is to be understood not only in regard to the allocation of financial means but also to the power to self-determine how that exclusively municipal income source will be used. These amendments

[65] There is currently a debate on the necessity of support for some communities who appear to be more affected than others by "poverty-immigrants" from eastern European nations, especially from Bulgaria and Romania, who come in on the basis of fundamental market freedoms (free movement of workers, freedom to provide services or freedom of establishment) or under the general free movement guarantee as European Union citizens. This appears to create issues of providing adequate housing and combating rental abuses by landlords and general safety, health and welfare issues. See, for example, http://www.spiegel.de/international/germany/german-cities-worried-about-high-immigration-from-romania-and-bulgaria-a-881409.html (last accessed on 5/4/2013).

[66] Statistical information on the financial situation of municipalities in Germany is available at http://www.staedtetag.de/imperia/md/content/dst/veroeffentlichungen/gemeindefinanzbericht/gfb2012_broschuere_.pdf (Report for the year 2012); see also http://www.staedtetag.de/publikationen/gfb/index.html

[67] See supra fn. 52.

[68] 42nd amendment of the Basic Law of 27/10/1994, BGBl I 3146 (1994).

[69] 44th amendment of the Basic Law of 20/10/1997, BGBl. I 2470 (1997).

must be seen in the light of a specific tax, the commercial business tax,[70] which is the major communal tax and a significant contributor to the overall revenue of municipalities, especially and more so for those who have a solid business base on their territory.[71] In the almost world-wide race to lower tax burdens in general and on business in particular to bolster employment and growth, the commercial business tax was regarded as anachronistic and stifling and there were calls for its abolishment. The amendments to the *Basic Law* sought to ensure that this could happen only if, on the income side, municipalities would gain access to a similarly potent tax over which they could autonomously dispose. To this day, the commercial business tax still exists and hence these provisions have not played a role. The dire financial situation of many municipalities, especially in those regions most heavily affected by structural changes and the loss of traditional employment with the ensuing significant rise of various welfare costs, has nonetheless persisted. An argument could be made that autonomous policy-making on the lower level in accordance with the principle of subsidiarity can only work if there is at least some financial leeway for self-determined policy decisions rather than just being able, or not even that, to implement decisions from above with no (financial) room for anything else.[72] Be that as it may, (some) municipalities are certainly an avid example for the discrepancy between theory and practice in the area of subsidiarity.

8.7.2 (Municipal) Government and Commercial Competition

The principle of subsidiarity is also legally relevant in the context of the relationship between the government and private business with a view to the question whether limitations exist for the government to enter the market place and establish businesses in

[70] Legal foundation: *Gewerbesteuergesetz* of 15 Oktober 2002 (BGBl. I S. 4167), as amended by Article 5 of the statute of 21 März 2013 (BGBl. I S. 556), http://www.gesetze-im-internet.de/gewstg/index.html. According to the written answer by the German Government to a parliamentary question only 13 of the 35 OECD states at the time (2006) had such a tax or a similar one in the sense of an independent municipal tax on businesses, *Bundestag*s-Drucksache 16/2295, 21/7/2006, p. 2, http://dipbt.*Bundestag*.de/dip21/btd/16/022/1602295.pdf (last accessed on 10/4/2012).

[71] In 2012 the *Gewerbesteuer* statistically amounted to roughly around 16 % of municipal finances: The total income realized by municipalities from this tax amounted to EUR 32.3 billion and the total revenue achieved was EUR 197.8 billion, see Federal Statistical Office, https://www.destatis.de/DE/PresseService/Presse/Pressemitteilungen/2013/03/PD13_113_71137.html (last accessed on 5/4/2013). However the income achieved by individual municipalities will greatly vary from community to community depending on their economic base and is generally lower in those areas that formerly constituted East-Germany. See the comprehensive statistics prepared by the Federal Statistical Office, Finanzen und Steuern – Realsteuervergleich – Realsteuern, kommunale Einkommen- und Umsatzsteuerbeteiligungen, Fachserie 14, Reihe 10.1, 2010 published on 17/8/2011 available at https://www.destatis.de/DE/Publikationen/Thematisch/FinanzenSteuern/Steuern/Realsteuer/Realsteuervergleich2141010107004.pdf?__blob=publicationFile (last accessed on 5/4/2014), especially at p. 35 et seq.

[72] See the decision of the Constitutional Court of Thuringia of 21/6/2005, VerfGH 28/03, www.thverfgh.thueringen.de/OVGThueringen/rechtsp.nsf/6c24af328dcfcb8cc1256ab9002dd3c7/1384da8ca88deb5dc1257028003efba5/$FILE/03-00028-U-A.pdf (in German), p. 38–9 (last accessed 10/4/2013).

direct competition to private providers. This has been especially relevant in the context of municipal governments, and the respective *Länder* statutes governing municipalities explicitly deal with this issue under the heading of subsidiarity. However, there are similar provisions to be found elsewhere. The *Federal Budget Act*, the statute that governs the parliamentary budget process, stipulates in § 65.1 No. 1 that the federation "should only" create or participate in corporations under private law if that were necessary in the pursuit of a "significant interest" of the federation and if the significant interest could not be "better or more economically" achieved otherwise.[73]

However, the Federal (or *Länder*) *Budget Acts* are dogmatically considered to be internal, organisational law which yield no subjective rights for anybody not institutionally involved in the budget process, or, to formulate it differently, these norms do not intend to protect the interests of the individual citizen or a corporation.

The various municipal government acts of the *Länder* contain similar clauses. They usually contain language to the effect that commercial activities by municipalities are allowed only under the condition that the purpose of the undertaking cannot be met equally well and economically by private businesses.[74] The effect of these provisions is controversial. Some courts have afforded these provisions the status of subjective rights, that is, rights granted to private persons as a legal bases for court action against municipal competition. Others afford these norms only an objective function in the public interest with the consequence that a private competitor cannot bring proceedings to administrative courts with the aim to stop municipal competition.[75]

It is beyond the scope of this paper to discuss the qualification of the subsidiarity norms in the various municipal government acts as containing subjective rights or not. In this context it is important to note that the application of the principle of subsidiarity in the municipal government statutes extends beyond allocating decision-making powers to a certain (lower) level of government to the delineation of power between the private and the public sphere and to the protection of private activities from government competition.

8.7.3 Local and Regional Cooperation Across Borders

In a 1993 amendment of the *Basic Law* a new Subsection 1(a) was added to Article 24 GG to facilitate regional and municipal cooperation across borders.[76] The provision

[73] Bundeshaushaltsordnung, http://www.gesetze-im-internet.de/bho/BJNR012840969.html (last accessed on 16/4/13). Similar provisions can be found in the Budget Acts of the *Länder*.

[74] For a hyperlinked list to the various municipal government acts in Germany see http://www.saarheim.de/Gesetze_Laender/go_laender.htm (last assessed on 16/4/13).

[75] For a comprehensive overview with many references to relevant court decisions and the pertinent literature see A Berger, Das kommunalrechtliche Subsidiaritätsgebot als subjektives öffentliches Recht, Die öffentliche Verwaltung (DÖV) 2010, p. 118 et seq. (see especially footnotes 15 and 16 with leads to further literature and case-law on the qualification issue).

[76] Article 24.1(a) GG states: "Insofar as the Länder are competent to exercise state powers and to perform state functions, they may, with the consent of the Federal Government, transfer sovereign powers to transborder institutions in neighbouring regions."

reflects the view that the municipalities are not a separate layer of government but are part of the *Länder*. The in-principle jurisdiction of the federal level with regard to foreign affairs is recognised by requiring the consent of the federal level to any such endeavours. However, that consent is not fully discretionary and can only be withheld if there are valid reasons to interfere with any such plans.

The provision aims to provide a legal foundation for cooperation across borders, for example in the area of municipal tasks such as waste disposal, industrial parks or public transport. If such cooperation involves the exercise of public authority vis-à-vis individuals a number of problems arise, not least how to deal with the required legal protection of these individuals. Before the addition of Article 24.1a to the *Basic Law*, only the federation itself could transfer sovereign powers to transnational institutions, such as the European Union. Now this is also possible for the *Länder* in those fields where they have prescriptive or administrative jurisdiction.[77]

The new provision cannot, however, solve all complicated legal problems of such transborder cooperation. One unsolved problem are different jurisdictional structures, or, to formulate it more fittingly for the purpose of this book, diverging approaches to subsidiarity and therefore diverging powers of municipalities on either side of the border. A municipal building authorisation in Germany has a concentrating effect such that no other authorisations will be required. If that is not the case on the other side of the border and parts of that process lie with regional or even provincial or central authorities, lower level transborder cooperation can be made impossible.[78] That notwithstanding, the concept of transborder cooperation and the joint exercise of public authority is nonetheless an interesting iteration of subsidiarity because of the transborder component and because the implementation of the will to allocate public decision-making powers according to where the necessity of decisions arises even if that requires crossing well established jurisdictional lines and the creation of new decision-making entities.[79]

---

[77] U Beyerlin, Zur Übertragung von Hoheitsrechten im Kontext dezentraler grenzüberschreitender Zusammenarbeit – Ein Beitrag zu Art. 24 Abs. 1 Grundgesetz, ZaöRV 1994, 587 ff. See also T Stein, Europäische Union: Gefahr oder Chance für den Föderalismus in Deutschland, Österreich und der Schweiz, in: VVDStRL 53 (1994), 26 ff.

[78] See the Paper of the Arbeitsgruppe "Gesetzgebungskompetenzen und Mitwirkungsrechte" der Kommission von *Bundestag* und *Bundesrat* zur Modernisierung der bundesstaatlichen Ordnung, Europa (Verbesserung der grenzüberschreitenden Zusammenarbeit, Übertragung von Hoheitsrechten, Art. 24 GG), Rechtliche Probleme nach Maßgabe der geltenden (verfassungs-) rechtlichen Rechtslage anhand konkreter Fallgestaltungen – Stellungnahme von Baden-Württemberg und Nordrhein-Westfalen, 26/4/2004 http://www.*Bundesrat*.de/nn_8364/DE/foederalismus/bundesstaatskommission/unterlagen/AU-064.pdf (last accessed on 11/4/13), which speaks about specific problems and issues of such transborder projects from Northrhine-Westfalia and the Netherlands and from Baden-Württemberg and France.

[79] C Calliess describes these transborder institutions as a complement of the traditional state to enable building "Europe from below", as opposed to the unfortunately more entrenched cliché of a Europe integrating from the top down. See Calliess (2007).

8.8 Subsidiarity and Germany's Membership in the European Union

The only explicit reference to the principle of subsidiarity in the German *Basic Law* can be found in Article 23. That article is the foundation for Germany's participation in the European Union and authorises the transfer of sovereign powers to a European Union that adheres to certain core principles and values, of which the principle of subsidiarity is one. Article 23.1 sentences 1 and 2 stipulate:

> With a view to establishing a united Europe, the Federal Republic of Germany shall participate in the development of the European Union that is committed to democratic, social and federal principles, to the rule of law, and to the principle of subsidiarity, and that guarantees a level of protection of basic rights essentially comparable to that afforded by this Basic Law. To this end the Federation may transfer sovereign powers by a law with the consent of the *Bundesrat*.

The principle of subsidiarity is thus elevated to the same level of importance as the democratic, social, federal and rule of law principle and the protection of fundamental rights and freedoms. These other principles constitute the so-called "state fundamental principles" of the German *Basic Law*, are spelled out in Articles 1 and 20, where the principle of subsidiarity is not mentioned. The special relevance of these state fundamental principles comes to the fore in Article 79.3 GG.[80] This norm prohibits amendments of the *Basic Law* by the "*pouvoir constitué*", that is, by the Parliament (*Bundestag*) and by the Federal Chamber (*Bundesrat*) that are incompatible with the core of these state fundamental principles. It follows that, for example, the reorganisation of Germany as a unitary state could not be achieved by constitutional amendment, nor could Germany in this manner become a constitutional monarchy or discard or substantively reduce its catalogue of fundamental rights in Articles 1–19 GG. The existence of these state fundamental norms makes possible such a seemingly self-contradictory notion as unconstitutional constitutional law, that is, an amendment of the *Basic Law* subsequently found unconstitutional by the FCC for violation of the state fundamental norms and therefore void.[81]

---

[80] Article 79.3 GG reads: "Amendments to this Basic Law affecting the division of the Federation into *Länder*, their participation on principle in the legislative process, or the principles laid down in Articles 1 and 20 shall be inadmissible".

[81] Cf. BVerfGE 30, 1 at 24–5, http://www.servat.unibe.ch/dfr/bv030001.html, paras 99–101. There are even those who argue that the state fundamental norms referred to in Article 79.3 GG could not even be legally overcome by a total revision of the Basic Law by the "pouvoir constituent" (the German people), a possibility addressed by the Article 146 GG. Article 146 reads: "This Basic Law, which since the achievement of the unity and freedom of Germany applies to the entire German people, shall cease to apply on the day on which a constitution freely adopted by the German people takes effect." The FCC left the question open in its decision on the *Treaty of Lisbon*. See BVerfG, 2 BvE 2/08 of 30.6.2009, marg. no. 216–7, http://www.bverfg.de/entscheidungen/es20090630_2bve000208en.html (in official English translation) with further references. See also J Bröhmer, "Containment eines Leviathans" – Anmerkungen zur Entschediung des Bundesverfassungsgerichts zum Vertrag von Lissabon, ZEuS 2009, 543 at 552 et seq.

It is noteworthy that Article 23.1 makes reference to the principle of subsidiarity and to the federalism principle. Obviously the underlying notion must have been that both are not entirely the same. Indeed, the federalism principle can be seen to incorporate more the organisational-institutional side of the relationships within multilevel government structures. The principle of subsidiarity refers more to the substantive side of actual decision making and the allocation of legislative powers in the relationship between member state and collective entity and – as prescribed in Article 5.3 *Treaty on European Union* (TEU) – allocates (legislative) competences of the European Union back to the member states when, despite the general textual allocation to the European Union in the *Treaty on the Functioning of the European Union* (TFEU), the concrete objective of a concrete legislative proposal can better be achieved at the lower level of the member states.[82]

The FCC has consistently attributed much weight to the principle of subsidiarity in its ongoing struggle to maintain its role as the court of last resort for questions of German constitutional law vis-à-vis the European Court of Justice (ECJ).[83] In its decision on the constitutionality of the *Treaty of Lisbon*, the FCC stated:

> Apart from this, it must be possible within the German jurisdiction to assert the responsibility for integration if obvious transgressions of the boundaries occur when the European Union claims competences [...] and to preserve the inviolable core content of the Basic Law's constitutional identity by means of a identity review [...]. The Federal Constitutional Court has already opened up the way of the *ultra vires* review for this, which applies where Community and Union institutions transgress the boundaries of their competences. If legal protection cannot be obtained at the Union level, the Federal Constitutional Court examines whether legal instruments of the European institutions and bodies keep within the boundaries of the sovereign powers accorded to them by way of conferral [...] whilst adhering to the principle of subsidiarity under Community and Union law [...].[84]

The passage is a caution to the ECJ that the FCC will not adhere to the supremacy of European Union law if the EU acts *ultra vires* and exceeds the competences attributed to it by the accession legislation of the German Parliament. Such attempts to assert a last resort function of the *Basic Law* and the FCC against usurpation by

---

[82] Cf. Maunz/Dürig-Scholz, GG-Kommentar, Art. 23, marg. no. 95–6. That having been said, I would still strongly agree with Halberstams assertion that "the key theoretical concept underlying a general theory of federalism is what Europeans call 'subsidiarity'." See D Halberstam, Federalism: Theory, Policy, Law, in: M Rosenfeld/A Sajó (eds.), The Oxford Handbook of Constitutional Law, 2012, p. 576 at 585.

[83] 'ECJ' is the traditional abbreviation for European Court of Justice, the court of the European Union seated in Luxembourg, see http://curia.europa.eu/jcms/jcms/j_6/. There is some confusion about the correct acronym for the Court. In this article the "old" ECJ is used. However, the official name of the institution is 'Court of Justice of the European Union' and that has given rise to the abbreviation CJEU. The institution, however, actually comprises of three courts, the Court of Justice, the General Court (formerly known as the Court of First Instance) and the Civil Service Tribunal. That in turn would point to the abbreviation 'CJ' when referring to the old ECJ. In the Background Paper: The European Union: a guide to terminology, procedures and sources, Standard Note: SN/IA/3689 (last updated 16/3/2011) the House of Commons has opted for the abbreviation CJEU, see http://www.parliament.uk/briefing-papers/SN03689.pdf (last accessed on 16/4/2013).

[84] BVerfG, 2 BvE 2/08 of 30.6.2009, marg. no. 240, http://www.bverfg.de/entscheidungen/es20090630_2bve000208en.html (last accessed on 13/4/2013). See also marg. no. 304–5.

the European Union has been almost a trademark of the FCC's jurisprudence in regard to the European Union since the notorious *Maastricht decision* in 1993.[85] However, the FCC has – fortunately – never actually acted on these threats and declared an act of the European Union invalid in Germany for violating any of the principles set out in Article 23.1 GG as determinants for German participation in the dynamic process of European integration of which the principle of subsidiarity is one. The strongest invocation of the principle of subsidiarity so far can be found in the dissenting opinion of Judge Broβ in the case concerning the constitutionality of the *German Implementation Law* for the European Arrest Warrant.[86] However, the dissent also makes it clear that it is not the European Union act that is problematic but the national implementation act which, in the dissent's view, did not give sufficient regard to the principle of subsidiarity despite the fact that the underlying European Union act had left sufficient room for taking domestic concerns into account.[87]

The coming into force of the *Treaty of Lisbon* came together with the insertion of a new Article 23.1a into the *Basic Law* to cover the procedural side of the reinforced European Union principle of subsidiarity.[88] The TEU as amended by the *Treaty of Lisbon* provides in Article 12 that "[N]ational Parliaments contribute actively to the good functioning of the Union", inter alia (Article 12(b)) "by seeing to it that the principle of subsidiarity is respected in accordance with the procedures provided for in the Protocol on the application of the principles of subsidiarity and proportionality."[89] Article 8 of the *Protocol No. 2* to the TEU[90] provides that the ECJ shall have

> jurisdiction in actions on grounds of infringement of the principle of subsidiarity by a legislative act, brought in accordance with the rules laid down in Article 263 of the Treaty on the Functioning of the European Union by Member States, or notified by them in accordance with their legal order on behalf of their national Parliament or a chamber thereof.

Article 23.1a GG picks up on this and provides in its first two sentences:

> The *Bundestag* and the *Bundesrat* shall have the right to bring an action before the Court of Justice of the European Union to challenge a legislative act of the European Union for infringing the principle of subsidiarity. The *Bundestag* is obliged to initiate such an action at the request of one fourth of its Members.

---

85 BVerfGE 189, 155, http://www.servat.unibe.ch/dfr/bv089155.html (last accessed on 13/4/2013).

86 BVerfG, 2 BvR 2236/04 of 18.7.2005, marg. no. 133 et seq., at 136–9 and 147 et seq., http://www.bverfg.de/entscheidungen/rs20050718_2bvr223604en.html

87 BVerfG, 2 BvR 2236/04 of 18.7.2005, marg. no. 152, http://www.bverfg.de/entscheidungen/rs20050718_2bvr223604en.html

88 J Kokott/M Kaspar, Ensuring Constitutional Efficacy, in: M Rosenfeld/A Sajó (eds.), The Oxford Handbook of Constitutional Law, 2012, p. 795 at 802–3.

89 Consolidated version of the Treaty on European Union, OJ C 326/1 (2012), http://eur-lex.europa.eu/LexUriServ/LexUriServ.do?uri=OJ:C:2012:326:0001:01:EN:HTML (last accessed on 3/5/2013).

90 Protocol No. 2 on the Application of the Principles of Subsidiarity and Proportionality, see above fn. 85.

What is new here is that the Parliaments themselves have a direct procedural role in defence of the subsidiarity principle.[91] That is true for both chambers and therefore allows the *Länder* to defend subsidiarity on the European Union level. The *Länder* have a strong reason to be concerned about the transfer of power to the European Union because their strong participatory role in the domestic legislative procedure is affected and that is the case even if only federal powers are at issue. The federal government might not share that concern as it will still participate in the legislative process on the European Union level.[92] Whereas in the second chamber, such subsidiarity concerns have to find a majority, that is not the case in the *Bundestag*. Under the GG's parliamentary system the executive branch of government is carried by the majority in Parliament. Hence, it is not surprising that a lack of concern of the federal government for measures taken on the European Union level, where the federal government is representing Germany in the Council of Ministers, will usually reflect a lack of concern of the majority in Parliament. The possibility of a subsidiarity complaint has therefore been construed as a minority right and only 25 % of deputies are required to obligate the *Bundestag* as an organ of state to institute proceedings before the ECJ for subsidiarity review.[93]

8.9 Conclusion

The overall result of this survey on the principle of subsidiarity is ambivalent. The principle of subsidiarity exists as an express principle of constitutional law only in Article 23.1 GG as one of the constituent principles the European Union must

[91] For more detail and a comparison of the role of the German and the Spanish Parliaments see Silvia Delgado del Saz, Die Rolle der nationalen Parlamente nach dem Vertrag von Lissabon – ein Vergleich zwischen spanischem und deutschem Recht, in: Berliner Online-Beiträge zum Europarecht, Paper No. 67, http://portal-europarecht.de/epapers (last accessed on 10/5/2013).

[92] Both chambers, the *Bundesrat* (Federal Chamber) and the *Bundestag*, are beginning to actively assert their role and have raised several formal subsidiarity complaints in accordance with Protocol No. 2. See, for example, *Bundesrat* Drucksache 193/13 of 3/5/2013, Vorschlag für eine Richtlinie des Europäischen Parlaments und des Rates zur Schaffung eines Rahmens für die maritime Raumordnung und das integrierte Küstenzonenmanagement COM(2013) 133 final, http://217.79.215.188/dip21/brd/2013/0193-13B.pdf; Drucksache 52/12, Vorschlag für eine Verordnung des Europäischen Parlaments und des Rates zum Schutz natürlicher Personen bei der Verarbeitung personenbezogener Daten und zum freien Datenverkehr (Datenschutz-Grundverordnung), 27. January 2012, http://217.79.215.188/dip21/brd/2012/0052-12B.pdf (last accessed 10/5/2013); the *Bundestag* has, for example, voiced concerns with regard to Commission proposals for a common European Sales Law, http://dipbt.*Bundestag*.de/dip21/btd/17/080/1708000.pdf (last accessed 10/5/2013).

[93] Cf. The comment of the FCC on the new Article 23.1b in its Lisbon decision, BVerfG, 2 BvE 2/08 of 30.6.2009, para. 403, http://www.bverfg.de/entscheidungen/es20090630_2bve000208en.html (last accessed on 3/5/2013).

adhere to if Germany is to participate in this Union. As such, the subsidiarity principle of the *Basic Law* points back to the subsidiarity principle enshrined in Article 5.3 TEU. It is listed in Article 23.1 together with the federalism principle without any further explanation as to what the difference might be. In any case, the principle of subsidiarity has never been directly legally relevant in the sense that any act of the European Union would have prompted the German Constitutional Court to declare that the European Union acted *ultra vires* for violating the subsidiarity principle.

Apart from the very special Article 23 GG, the principle of subsidiarity exists only indirectly if one is willing to attribute to it any and all features of the *Basic Law* that privilege decision-making on any level below the centralised federal level. In that sense the principle of subsidiarity becomes a generic term comprising of: inherent elements of federalism; describing inherent features of the functions of fundamental rights of the individual; and certain elements of special guarantees for municipal governments or certain organisational self-governing structures, from Universities or public broadcasting bodies to public social insurance schemes. One major area of practical impact of the subsidiarity principle is in the area of municipal government and the protection of private enterprise from municipal competition. Of course, the constitutional link of this aspect is somewhat weaker but can be construed through the fundamental right of freedom of commerce (Article 12) and – operating with a broad stroke – to the guarantee of municipal government in Article 28.2 GG. Strongly related to this particular aspect of subsidiarity are provisions in the *Basic Law* which reflect the privatisations of infrastructure industries in the past 25 years. Article 87e GG attributes the power to administer railways to the federal level but stipulates in Article 87e.3 that "[F]ederal railways shall be operated as enterprises under private law". Article 87f GG contains similar provisions with regard to postal services and telecommunication and provides in Article 87f.2 that such services "shall be provided as a matter of private enterprise by the firms succeeding to the special trust Deutsche Bundespost[94] and by other private providers". The state relinquished much of what previously was considered core public service provision and private enterprise took over. The state has reduced its role from that of a service provider to that of a facilitator and supervisor of service provision.[95] That is subsidiarity in its purest form. However, the principle of subsidiarity does not answer the question when it is prudent to make that shift, that is, when indeed it is better to delegate such tasks. The principle only describes the consequence but it is silent, or at least vague, as to its own conditions. It is for this reason that the principle of subsidiarity has remained legally very weak.

[94] The Federal Postal Service was the old public monopoly which exclusively ran all telecommunication activities, from telephone to broadcasting, all postal services, some banking services and public bus transport. See 41st amendment of the Basic Law on 30/8/1994, BGBl I 2245, which resulted in the addition of Article 87f and Article 143b. Art 143b.1 is the constitutional basis for this privatization. For the railways see Article 143a GG, which was inserted a year earlier in the 40th amendment (BGBl. I 2089).

[95] See P Schumacher, Subsidiaritätsprinzip und Verwaltungsrecht – eine komparative Untersuchung anhand aktueller Beispielsfelder, in: Die öffentliche Verwaltung (DÖV) 2012, 176 at 184.

And thus Pope Pius' words in the encyclical Quadragesimo Anno of 1931 come to mind again:

> [...] Just as it is gravely wrong to take from individuals what they can accomplish by their own initiative and industry and give it to the community, so also it is an injustice and at the same time a grave evil and disturbance of right order to assign to a greater and higher association what lesser and subordinate organizations can do.

It is a safe conclusion that few in Germany (or elsewhere for that matter) would like to see the days of the old monopolies again, when phones were grey and there was only one model, but it is probably equally safe to conclude that the Pope was not thinking of the privatisation of the postal services of the world.

The apparent legal weakness of the principle of subsidiarity does not render its stipulation as a legal principle over which constitutional courts, such as the FCC or – un-technically speaking – the ECJ are empowered to exercise oversight by way of judicial review meaningless even if and regardless of the fact that so far no significant legal consequences in the narrow sense have been drawn from the principle. The principle is important because it elevates the political principle behind it to a different level, legitimises the scrutiny of the levels of decision making, empowers those more critical of centralised exercise of powers and places incentives of those representing centralised power to argue more carefully.[96]

The underlying idea of subsidiarity is powerful and ever more relevant in today's globalised world. The de jure and de facto centralisation of decision making on a globalised scale, ranging from embargo resolutions of the United Nations Security Council to detailed legislation of the European Union, from G20 decisions with huge financial impacts to the global projection of political power and influence by multinational enterprises is posing the greatest governance challenges in the decades to come. The increasing need for transnational decision making of all kinds is hampered by the fact that almost all forms of democratic accountability and legitimacy have remained national. Renationalisation of decision making will lead to more governance deficits, increasing international cooperation and decision making will lead to more democratic deficits and acceptance problems. The answer to this problem will be a complex one and the principle of subsidiarity will be an important part of that answer.

---

[96] It is beyond the scope of this paper to engage with the criticism Gareth Davies expressed towards the principle because it is based mostly on the EU version of the principle. But it could be that Davies underestimates the particular political function of the principle. In the EU context it can legally only ever be applied if a power of the EU to act has already been established by linking the measure to another provision in the Treaties. Therefore the principle, if at all, only hinders the exercise of a power already existing. In that sense the worst possible outcome perceivable is the status quo ante (before the inclusion of the principle into the treaties). Any effect beyond that will largely be political, as described above, backed by the possibility of judicial review in two ways – the ECJ as the primary court for interpretation of the EU principle of subsidiarity and the FCC as "the Basic Law's Rottweiler" if the ECJ should lapse on its guarding role and all of that after the Commission as initiator of legislation, the member states in the Council and the European Parliament have failed the principle despite having had the input from national Parliaments as well. See Davies (2008).

References

Aroney, N. 2007. Subsidiarity, federalism and the best constitution: Thomas Aquinas on city, province and empire. *Law and Philosophy* 26: 161.

Benz, A. 2009. *Politik im Mehrebenensystem*, 109. Wiesbaden: VS Verlag für Sozialwissenschaften.

Bröhmer, J. 2011. The Federal element of the German Republic – Issues and developments. In *The German Constitution turns 60 – Basic law and commonwealth constitution, German and Australian perspectives*, ed. J. Bröhmer, 15 et seq. Frankfurt am Main: Peter Lang Verlag.

Bröhmer, J., C. Hill, and M. Spitzkatz. 2012. *60 years German basic law: The German Constitution and its court*, 2nd ed. 180 et seq. Malaysia: The Malaysian Current Law Journal Sdn Bhd.

Calliess, C. 1999. *Subsidiaritätsprinzip und Solidaritätsprinzip in der Europäischen Union*, 2nd ed. Baden-Baden: Nomos Verlag.

Calliess, C. 2004. Die Justitiabilität des Subsidiaritätsprinzips im deutschen Bundesstaat und der Europäischen Union – ein Vergleich [Judicial control of federal competences in Germany and the European Union – A comparison of the application of the subsidiarity principle]. In *Berliner Online-Beiträge zum Europarecht*, Paper No. 6, April 26, 2004. http://portal-europarecht.de/epapers. Last accessed on 10 May 2013.

Calliess, C. 2007. Die "Freiheit" der Kommunen als Testfall der "Subsidiarität" Europas. In *Rechtsstaat und Grundrechte – Festschrift für Detlef Merten*, ed. F. Kirchhof, H.-J. Papier, and H. Schäffer, 305 at 320. Heidelberg: C.F. Müller Verlag.

Cremer, W. 2003. *Freiheitsgrundrechte – Funktionen und Strukturen*, 228 et seq. Tübingen: Mohr Siebeck.

Davies, G. 2008. Subsidiarity as a method of policy centralization. In *The shifting allocation of authority in international law – Considering sovereignty, supremacy and subsidiarity, essays in honour of Professor Ruth Lapidoth*, ed. T. Broude and Y. Shany, 79 et seq. Oxford: Hart.

de Schutter, O. 2010. *International human rights law*, 453 et seq. Cambridge: Cambridge University Press.

Häberle, P. 2004. §7 – Wechselwirkungen zwischen deutschen und ausländischen Verfassungen. In *Handbuch der Grundrechte in Deutschland und Europa*, Band I – Entwicklung und Grundlagen, ed. Merten and Papier, Marginal No. 61–2, 340–341. Heidelberg: C.F. Müller Verlag.

Hesse, Konrad. 1995. *Grundzüge des Verfassungsrechts*, 20th ed. § 172. Heidelberg: C.F. Müller Verlag.

Isensee, J. 2001. *Subsidiaritätsprinzip und Verfassungsrecht – eine Studie über das Regulativ des Verhältnisses von Staat und Gesellschaft*, 2nd ed. Berlin: Duncker und Humblot.

Isensee, J. 2011. Die geistigen Wurzeln des Subsidiaritätsprinzips. In *Verfassung – Völkerrecht – Kulturgüterschutz, Festschrift für Wilfried Fiedler*, ed. M. Wittinger, et al., 165 et seq. Berlin: Duncker und Humblot.

Jellinek, G. 1892. *System der subjektiven öffentlichen Rechte*, 1st ed., 89 et seq. Available at http://archive.org/stream/systemdersubjek00jellgoog#page/n9/mode/2up (2nd ed. 1905, pp. 94–114, reprinted in Kersten, J (ed.). 2011. *Georg Jellinek – System der subjektiven öffentlichen Rechte*, after p. 52.). Tübingen: Mohr Verlag.

Peffekoven, R., and Ulrike Kirchhoff. 1997. Deutscher und Europäischer Finanzausgleich im Lichte des Subsidiaritätsprinzips. In *Subsidiarität: Idee und Wirklichkeit – Zur Reichweite eines Prinzips in Deutschland und Europa*, ed. K. Nörr and T. Oppermann, 116. Tübingen: Mohr Verlag.

Schambeck, H. 2004. § 8 – Grundrechte in der Lehre der katholischen Kirche. In *Handbuch der Grundrechte in Deutschland und Europa*, Band I – Entwicklung und Grundlagen, ed. Merten and Papier, Marginal No. 21–4, 358–360. Heidelberg: C. F. Müller.

Stein, T. 1994. Europäische Union: Gefahr oder Chance für den Föderalismus in Deutschland, Österreich und der Schweiz. *VVDStRL* 53: 26 ff. Berlin: Walter de Gruyter Verlag.

Stirn, I. 2013. *Lokale und regionale Selbstverwaltung in Europa – Strategien zur Bewältigung transnationaler Einflüsse auf die deutsche kommunale Selbstverwaltung*. Baden-Baden: Nomos Verlag.

Rau, M. 2003. Subsidiarity and judicial review in German Federalism: The decision of the Federal Constitutional Court in the Geriatric Nursing Act Case. *German Law Journal* 4(3): 223.

Chapter 9
Subsidiarity as Judicial and Legislative Review Principles in the European Union

Gabriël A. Moens and John Trone

Abstract The founding Treaties of the European Union make clear that subsidiarity is a judicially enforceable legal principle. However, the case law of the Court of Justice reveals that the enforcement of subsidiarity as a judicial principle has been ineffective. The Court has applied a very weak standard of review for both substantive and procedural compliance with the subsidiarity principle. By far the most significant application of the subsidiarity principle is its consideration as part of the EU legislative process. A Member State legislature may issue a reasoned opinion regarding subsidiarity aspects of a proposal. These reasoned opinions may trigger the yellow card procedure, forcing the Commission to review its proposal, or the orange card procedure, where the Parliament or Council can block the proposal. These procedures have some potential as legislative safeguards of subsidiarity: in 2013 the Commission withdrew a legislative proposal after the yellow card procedure was activated.

Keywords Judicial enforcement of subsidiarity • Legislative review of subsidiarity • Role of Member State legislatures

---

G.A. Moens (✉)
Curtin Law School, Curtin University, Kent Street, Bentley,
6102 Perth, Western Australia, Australia
e-mail: gabriel.moens@curtin.edu.au

J. Trone
Adjunct Professor, School of Law, Murdoch University, 90 South Street,
Murdoch, 6150 Perth, Western Australia, Australia
e-mail: j.trone@murdoch.edu.au

M. Evans and A. Zimmermann (eds.), *Global Perspectives on Subsidiarity*, Ius Gentium: Comparative Perspectives on Law and Justice 37, DOI 10.1007/978-94-017-8810-6_9,

9.1 Introduction

This chapter considers the failure of subsidiarity as a judicial review principle and its somewhat more successful record as a legislative review principle in the European Union (EU). Although the founding Treaties make clear that subsidiarity is a legally binding principle, the European Court of Justice has adopted an excessively deferential approach to its judicial enforcement. The *Treaty* provisions have been rendered essentially meaningless platitudes so far as judicial enforcement is concerned.

On the other hand, subsidiarity has shown more promise as a legislative principle. The parliaments of the Member States have procedural rights in the EU legislative process, though they do not have a right to veto EU legislative proposals. Under the early warning system the Member State parliaments are able to force the Commission to reconsider proposals that they consider infringe subsidiarity. The Member State parliaments have successfully used the early warning system to force reconsideration of a legislative proposal, with the Commission ultimately withdrawing the proposal.

9.2 Subsidiarity as a Judicial Review Principle

9.2.1 The Applicable Treaty Provisions

A brief history of the subsidiarity principle in the founding Treaties provides useful background to the discussion that follows as the various *Treaty* revisions are significant. The principle of subsidiarity first appeared in the Community founding treaty through the amendments introduced by the *Single European Act*, though only in relation to environmental matters and with very little detail.[1] Subsidiarity was given more prominence in the *Maastricht Treaty* when it became a general principle of EU lawmaking.[2] A Protocol elaborating upon the application of the principle of subsidiarity was added by the *Treaty of Amsterdam*[3] and amended by the *Treaty of Lisbon*.[4]

In their current versions the founding Treaties contain numerous provisions that make reference to the principle of subsidiarity. Only the more significant of these provisions need be referred to here. The preamble to the *Treaty on European Union* states that in the process of European integration "decisions are taken as closely as possible to the citizen in accordance with the principle of subsidiarity".[5]

---

[1] Art 130 R(4), Treaty establishing the European Economic Community, as amended by Art 25, Single European Act, Luxembourg, 17 February 1986, 1754 UNTS 111; OJ L 169, 29.6.1987, p. 1.

[2] Art 3b, Treaty establishing the European Community, as amended by the Treaty of European Union, Maastricht, 7 February 1992, 1757 UNTS 3; OJ C 191, 29.7.1992, p. 1. See also Title I, Art B second para, Treaty on European Union, as originally adopted.

[3] Protocol on the Application of the Principles of Subsidiarity and Proportionality, as inserted by the Treaty of Amsterdam, Amsterdam, 2 October 1997, UNTS No I: 47936; OJ C 340, 10.11.1997, p. 1 at 105.

[4] Treaty of Lisbon, Lisbon, 13 December 2007, UNTS No I: 47938; OJ C 306, 17.12.2007, p. 1.

[5] Preamble para 13, Treaty on European Union, OJ C 326, 26.10.2012, p. 13.

The *Treaty on European Union* substantively provides that the exercise of power by the EU must respect the principle of subsidiarity.[6] Subsidiarity is defined as follows: "in areas which do not fall within its exclusive competence, the Union shall act only if and insofar as the objectives of the proposed action cannot be sufficiently achieved by the Member States, either at central level or at regional and local level, but can rather, by reason of the scale or effects of the proposed action, be better achieved at Union level".[7]

The three key principles of conferral, subsidiarity and proportionality are all contained within the same Article of the *Treaty on European Union*.[8] Put briefly, the conferral principle asks "can" the EU take a proposed measure. The subsidiarity principle asks "if" the EU must defer to the Member States in relation to the proposed measure. The proportionality principle asks "how" the proposed measure may be taken.[9]

Other literature summarises conferral as concerned with the "existence" of a competence, subsidiarity with the "exercise" of a concurrent competence, and proportionality with the "intensity" of EU action.[10] The House of Commons contrasted subsidiarity and proportionality as follows: "if proportionality is looking at whether a sledgehammer can be used to crack a nut, subsidiarity is looking at whether the sledgehammer should be picked up in the first place."[11]

By the express language of the *Treaty*, the principle of subsidiarity has no application to the exercise of the exclusive powers of the Union.[12] The Court of First Instance has confirmed that subsidiarity does not restrict the use of the exclusive powers of the Union.[13] In the context of exclusive powers subsidiarity is thus "wholly irrelevant".[14] Subsidiarity restricts only the exercise of the non-exclusive powers of the Union.[15]

Until the *Lisbon Treaty* the founding Treaties did not contain a list of the exclusive competences of the Union, so the range of such competences was open to dispute.[16] Under the current version of the Treaties the EU has exclusive competence over few subject matters. These are the customs union, competition rules for the internal market, monetary policy for the Eurozone, marine biological resource conservation

[6] Art 5(1), Treaty on European Union.

[7] Art 5(3), Treaty on European Union.

[8] Art 5, Treaty on European Union.

[9] Ritzer et al. (2006, p. 737).

[10] Horsley (2012, pp. 268–269).

[11] Quoted in Conference of Parliamentary Committees for Union Affairs of Parliaments of the European Union. 2012. Eighteenth Bi-annual Report: Developments in European Union Procedures and Practices Relevant to Parliamentary Scrutiny. Brussels: COSAC Secretariat, p. 5. Available at http://www.cosac.eu

[12] Moens (2004, p. 426).

[13] *Vischim Srl v Commission* (T-420/05) [2009] ECR II-3841 at [223]. This decision was not appealed.

[14] Horsley, above n 10, p. 275.

[15] Conway (2010, p. 988).

[16] Craig (2012, p. 74). See now Art 3(1), Treaty on European Union.

and the common commercial policy.[17] The EU and the Member States share jurisdiction over a larger group of subject matters. These include the internal market, social policy, agriculture and fisheries, environment, consumer protection, transport, energy, and the area of freedom, security and justice.[18]

The Subsidiarity Protocol provides that legislative proposals must "take account of the need" for financial or administrative burdens on the Member States "to be minimised and commensurate with the objective to be achieved."[19] The *Treaty of Amsterdam* version of the *Subsidiarity Protocol* provided that subsidiarity allowed EU action to be "expanded where circumstances so require, and conversely, to be restricted or discontinued where it is no longer justified."[20] This passage no longer appears in the Lisbon version of the *Protocol*. In 2003 the Commission cited this provision when arguing that EU pre-packaging legislation was no longer required since its objectives were fulfilled by other EU Directives.[21]

The *Charter of Fundamental Rights* also briefly mentions subsidiarity. The *Charter* provides that it is "addressed to the institutions, bodies, offices and agencies of the Union with due regard for the principle of subsidiarity".[22] The Charter is legally binding upon the EU and the Member States when they implement EU law[23] and possesses the "same legal value as the Treaties".[24]

It should be noted that apart from the subsidiarity provisions, the founding Treaties themselves expressly accommodate particular national sensitivities. Some of the accompanying Protocols exempt particular Member States from various aspects of the integration programme or protect various national particularities from challenge under EU law.[25]

The Treaties also provide a framework for optional integration through enhanced cooperation between some but not all Member States.[26] The legal acts that are created under this framework bind only the Member States that are participating in this

[17] Art 3(1), Treaty on European Union.

[18] Art 4(2), Treaty on European Union.

[19] Art 5, Protocol (No 2) on the Application of the Principles of Subsidiarity and Proportionality, OJ C 326, 26.10.2012, p. 206.

[20] para 3, Protocol on the Application of the Principles of Subsidiarity and Proportionality, as adopted by the Treaty of Amsterdam, OJ C 340, 10.11.1997, pp. 105–106.

[21] Commission of the European Communities. 2003. 'Better Lawmaking 2003': Report from the Commission pursuant to Art 9 of the Protocol ... (11th Report). COM(2003)770 final, p. 20.

[22] Art 51(1), Charter of Fundamental Rights of the European Union, OJ C 326, 26.10.2012, p. 391.

[23] Art 6(1), Treaty on European Union; Art 51(1), Charter of Fundamental Rights.

[24] Art 6(1), Treaty on European Union.

[25] Protocols No 15–18, 20–22, 31–32, 34–35. See also the Protocol on the Concerns of the Irish People on the Treaty of Lisbon, Brussels, 16 May 2012, OJ L 60, 2.3.2013, p. 131.

[26] Art 20, Treaty on European Union; Art 326, Treaty on the Functioning of the European Union, OJ C 326, 26.10.2012, p. 47.

cooperation.[27] The enhanced cooperation procedure has been applied in relation to the law applicable to divorce,[28] unitary patent protection[29] and financial transaction tax.[30]

9.2.2 Actions for the Infringement of Subsidiarity

The Treaties make clear that subsidiarity is a judicially enforceable legal principle. The Subsidiarity Protocol expressly confers jurisdiction upon the Court of Justice in actions alleging infringement of the principle of subsidiarity by an EU legal act.[31] Such actions may be brought by the Member States under the rules relating to the review of the legality of EU legal acts.[32]

The national parliaments also have an indirect right to bring an infringement action under the present version of the Protocol.[33] The national parliaments do not have a direct right to bring judicial review proceedings for breach of subsidiarity, but do so through proceedings notified by the national government.[34]

In some Member States there are national legal provisions regulating the bringing of such indirect proceedings. For example, the *German Constitution* provides that both the *Bundestag* (lower house) and the *Bundesrat* (upper house) have the right to bring actions for infringement of the subsidiarity principle. The *Bundestag* is bound to bring an action if one quarter of its members pass a motion to that effect.[35] The German Constitutional Court has indicated that the purpose of this provision is to enable a minority of the lower house to assert the rights of the national parliament against the will of the majority of the house and the executive government it supports.[36]

The *French Constitution* provides that such proceedings may be instituted by either house of the legislature. Proceedings must be brought at the request of

[27] Art 20(4), Treaty on European Union.

[28] Council Regulation 1259/2010 of 20 December 2010 implementing enhanced cooperation in the area of the law applicable to divorce and legal separation, OJ L 343, 29.12.2010, p. 10.

[29] Regulation 1257/2012 of the European Parliament and of the Council of 17 December 2012 implementing enhanced cooperation in the area of the creation of unitary patent protection, OJ L 361, 31.12.2012, p. 1.

[30] Council Decision 2013/52 of 22 January 2013 authorising enhanced cooperation in the area of financial transaction tax, OJ L 22, 25.1.2013, p. 11.

[31] Art 8, Protocol No 2.

[32] See Art 263, Treaty on the Functioning of the European Union.

[33] Besselink and van Mourik (2012, p. 47).

[34] Cygan (2013, p. 169).

[35] Art 23(1a), Constitution of Germany (1949), inserted by amendment of 8 October 2008, Bundesgesetzblatt I 1926.

[36] *Treaty of Lisbon Case* [2010] 3 CMLR 276 at p. 381 (No 13); 141 ILR 554 at p. 696; BVerfGE 123, 267 at p. 431 (2009).

60 members of the lower house or 60 members of the upper house.[37] At present there are 577 members of the lower house and 348 members of the upper house.[38] The Government refers the proceedings to the Court of Justice.

In Austria either house of the federal Parliament may bring an action for breach of the principle of subsidiarity. The Chancellor notifies the Court of Justice of the action.[39] In Ireland either House of the legislature may notify the Minister of its desire that an action be brought and the Minister shall make arrangements for bringing that action.[40]

The Committee of the Regions can also challenge an EU legislative act which it considers was adopted in breach of subsidiarity.[41] There are three pre-conditions for bringing such an annulment action: the act must have been subject to mandatory consultation with the Committee, the challenged act must be a legislative act and the action must be brought within 2 months of the publication of the challenged legislation.[42] The Committee's Plenary Assembly decides whether to bring an action for infringement of the subsidiarity principle.[43]

After the Commission withdrew a proposed regulation on collective action, the Committee of the Regions issued an opinion which stated "that if the Commission had maintained its proposal … the [Committee] could have considered taking the necessary steps to lodge an ex-post appeal against it for breaching the principle of subsidiarity in terms of both the choice of legal basis and insufficient evidence of the added value of EU action in this area".[44]

9.2.3 Subsidiarity as Interpreted by the Court of Justice

The case law of the Court of Justice reveals that the enforcement of subsidiarity as a judicial principle has been strikingly ineffective. One study summarized the decisions with the observation that subsidiarity had thus far been of "little value as

---

[37] Art 88-6, Constitution of France (1958), inserted by amendment of 4 February 2008, Journal Officiel de la République Française, 5 February 2008, p. 2202.

[38] http://www.assemblee-nationale.fr/qui; http://www.senat.fr/lng/en/senators.html

[39] Art 23h, Constitution of Austria (1920), inserted by amendment of 27 July 2010, Bundesgesetzblatt I No 57/2010.

[40] s 7(4), European Union Act 2009 (Ireland).

[41] Art 8, Protocol No 2. The following provisions provide for mandatory consultation with the Committee: Arts 91, 100, 148–149, 153, 164–168, 172, 175, 177–178, 192 and 194, Treaty on the Functioning of the European Union. See Legal Service, Committee of the Regions. nd. Practical Guide on the Infringement of the Subsidiarity Principle, p. 6.

[42] Legal Service, above n 41, pp. 5, 6, 8. The time limitation is set out in Art 263, Treaty on the Functioning of the European Union.

[43] Rule 53(2), Committee of the Regions Rules of Procedure, OJ L 6, 9.1.2010, p. 14.

[44] Opinion of the Committee of the Regions on 'The posting of workers in the framework of the provision of services', OJ C 17, 19.1.2013, p. 67 at 69.

a standard of scrutiny".[45] Professor Dashwood testified before a House of Commons Committee that subsidiarity was "largely inoperable at the stage of adjudication".[46] The Council of the European Union has stated that it regards subsidiarity "essentially as a political and subjective principle".[47]

As a judicial principle subsidiarity has been a placebo rather than a panacea. The Court has never held that any EU legal act was invalid for breach of the principle of the principle of subsidiarity. The permissive standards of review applied by the Court suggest that it is likely to do so only in quite exceptional circumstances. The Court has applied a very weak standard of review for both substantive and procedural compliance with the principle.[48] The Court's examination of subsidiarity questions is also generally quite cursory. That is ironic in view of the founding *Treaty*'s requirement that the political institutions of the EU produce detailed subsidiarity justifications.

There have been relatively few subsidiarity cases in the European courts. According to one count, there were only ten subsidiarity challenges in a period of almost two decades.[49] However, if EU acts were subject to a rigorous scrutiny on subsidiarity grounds, it could reasonably be anticipated that the number of challenges would rise sharply.

There have only been a few major cases. In the *Working Time Directive* case[50] the Directive regulated rest breaks, minimum periods of daily and weekly rest, the maximum average weekly working time and the minimum amount of annual paid leave throughout the Community.[51] The Directive had been adopted under a provision of the *Treaty* which stated that the "Member States shall pay particular attention to encouraging improvements, especially in the working environment, as regards the health and safety of workers, and shall set as their objective the harmonization of conditions in this area, while maintaining the improvements made. … In order to help achieve [this] objective … the Council … shall adopt by means of directives minimum requirements for gradual implementation".[52]

The United Kingdom argued that this *Treaty* provision "should be interpreted in the light of the principle of subsidiarity, which does not allow adoption of a directive in such wide and prescriptive terms as the contested directive, given that the extent and the nature of legislative regulation of working time vary very widely between

---

45 Ritzer, above n 9, p. 760.

46 House of Commons European Scrutiny Committee. 2008. Subsidiarity, National Parliaments and the Lisbon Treaty. HC 563, Session 2007–08, p Ev 3 (evidence of Prof Alan Dashwood).

47 Committee of the Regions, Subsidiarity Annual Report. 2011 R/CdR 1188/2012, p. 31.

48 Delehanty (2010, p. 137).

49 Craig, above n 16, p. 80.

50 *United Kingdom v Council (Re Working Time Directive)* (C-84/94) [1996] ECR I-5755; [1996] 3 CMLR 671. See Moens (1997).

51 *Working Time Directive*, above n 50, [4].

52 Art 118a(1)–(2), Treaty Establishing the European Community, as revised by the Treaty of Maastricht, consolidated at OJ C 224, 31.8.1992, p. 6 at 45.

Member States."[53] The Court rejected the argument that the EC legislator had not established that the aims of the Directive would be better served at the EC level rather than at the national level. Once the European legislators had found it appropriate to improve and harmonize the level of health and safety protection within the Community, achievement of that goal justified Community-wide action.[54] The Court's decision treated subsidiarity as essentially irrelevant where the Community's purpose was harmonization.[55]

In this case the British government also emphasized that the *Treaty* provided that the Council was only empowered to adopt "minimum requirements". The government argued that four principles were relevant in determining whether the regulations adopted were such minimum requirements.[56] One of these suggested principles was that a measure would be proportionate only if it was consistent with subsidiarity. The government argued that it was therefore necessary for the Community to show that the aims of the directive would be better achieved by the EC than by the Member States.[57] The Court gave short shrift to this argument, saying that this argument was about the need for EC action, which it had already upheld.[58] The Court also construed the words "minimum requirements" as no limitation at all. Those words did not mean that EC requirements were limited "to the lowest common denominator, or even to the lowest level of protection established by the various Member States, but mea[n] that Member States are free to provide a level of protection more stringent than that resulting from Community law, high as it may be".[59]

In the *Deposit Guarantee* case[60] the German government did not argue that the challenged Directive was in breach of subsidiarity. The government's argument was that the Directive had failed to state sufficient reasons for its adoption.[61] This argument was based on a Treaty provision which required that the legislator state the reasons upon which a Directive was based.[62] The Court cited the very general reasons given in the recitals preceding the operative provisions of the Directive. The recitals showed the legislator's view that its aims would be best achieved at the Community level.[63] Another recital showed that previous Member State action had been insufficient.[64]

---

[53] *Working Time Directive*, above n 50, [46].

[54] *Working Time Directive*, above n 50, [47].

[55] Sander (2006, p. 538).

[56] *Working Time Directive*, above n 50, [50].

[57] *Working Time Directive*, above n 50, [54].

[58] *Working Time Directive*, above n 50, [55].

[59] *Working Time Directive*, above n 50, [56].

[60] *Germany v Parliament (Re Deposit Guarantee Directive)* (C-233/94) [1997] ECR I-2405; [1997] 3 CMLR 1379.

[61] *Deposit Guarantee Directive*, above n 60, [24].

[62] Art 190, Treaty Establishing the European Economic Community, as revised by the Maastricht Treaty, OC C 224, 31.8.1992, p. 6 at 67. See now Art 296, Treaty on the Functioning of the European Union.

[63] *Deposit Guarantee Directive*, above n 60, [26].

[64] *Deposit Guarantee Directive*, above n 60, [27].

The Court held that the brief reasons stated in the recitals were sufficient to satisfy the obligation to state reasons why the legislation was consistent with subsidiarity. The Court stated that it was not even necessary to expressly refer to the principle of subsidiarity.[65] The Court did not require that the reasons given be established by qualitative or quantitative indicators, but contented itself with accepting assertions in the recitals.[66]

In the *Biotechnology* case the Court held that consideration of subsidiarity was "necessarily implicit" in the recitals of the challenged Directive, which was sufficient to satisfy the obligation to state reasons. The recitals asserted that without Community action, the varied laws of the Member States relating to the protection of biotechnology were an impediment to the operation of the internal market.[67]

In the *British American Tobacco* case[68] a Directive restricted the manufacturing, marketing and sale of cigarettes. The Court considered whether the objective of the Directive could be better achieved at the Community level.[69] One objective of the Directive was to eliminate barriers to the operation of the internal market caused by differences between national laws regarding the manufacture, presentation and sale of cigarettes.[70] This objective could not be adequately achieved at the national level, given the great diversity of the previously applicable national laws.[71] This aim could thus be better achieved at the Community level.[72] The specific provisions adopted did not go beyond what was necessary to achieve this objective.[73] This case was the first occasion where the Court examined a measure on substantive rather than procedural grounds relating to subsidiarity.

In the *Personal Protective Equipment* case[74] the Court applied its *British American Tobacco* holding. The Court held that since the relevant national laws had significant divergences, they could act as a trade barrier. Given the 'scope and effects' of the harmonisation of such divergent laws, only the EC legislature was able to achieve harmonisation.[75]

[65] *Deposit Guarantee Directive*, above n 60, [28].

[66] Delehanty, above n 48, pp. 135–136; see also Evans (2012, p. 279).

[67] *Netherlands v European Parliament* (C-377/98) [2001] ECR I-7079 at [33]; [2001] 3 CMLR 49 (p. 1173).

[68] *R v Secretary of State for Health; Ex parte British American Tobacco (Investments) Ltd* (C-491/01) [2002] ECR I-11453; [2003] 1 CMLR 14 (p. 395).

[69] *British American Tobacco*, above n 68, [180].

[70] *British American Tobacco*, above n 68, [181].

[71] *British American Tobacco*, above n 68, [182].

[72] *British American Tobacco*, above n 68, [183].

[73] *British American Tobacco*, above n 68, [184]. The Court referred back to its previous discussion of this point at [122]–[141].

[74] *Commission v Germany* (C-103/01) [2003] ECR I-5369.

[75] *Commission v Germany*, above n 74, [47].

In the *Food Supplements* case[76] the Court upheld provisions of a Directive that prohibited the marketing of food supplements that did not comply with the Directive. The Court held that the aim of those provisions could better be achieved by the Community and could not be achieved by the Member States.[77] The provisions dismantled the trade barriers caused by the differing national laws relating to food supplements.[78] To rely on national laws would "perpetuate the uncoordinated development of national rules" and their consequential barriers to trade.[79]

In the *Vodafone* case[80] a Regulation concerning mobile phone roaming was challenged as violative of subsidiarity. The Regulation set a ceiling for both wholesale and retail charges and required that consumers be informed about those charges.[81] The Court observed that the EU legislature had introduced a "common approach" to facilitate the smooth operation of the internal market. Mobile phone providers would now operate within one "coherent" system of regulation.[82] Wholesale and retail charges were interdependent. Any attempt to reduce retail charges without also reducing wholesale charges would be likely to hinder the operation of the EU roaming market. The legislature considered that a "joint approach" to both wholesale and retail charges was necessary for the smooth operation of the internal market.[83] The interdependence between wholesale and retail charges meant that the EU legislature could legitimately consider that both charges needed to be regulated at the EU level.[84] The Court held that the challenged provisions were consistent with subsidiarity.[85]

In the *Airport Charges* case[86] a Directive regulated charges at some airports with fewer than five million passenger movements a year. Some airports that served larger numbers of passengers than were served by Luxembourg's main airport had been exempted from complying with the Directive, but the Directive applied to Luxembourg's airport as the main airport of its Member State. Luxembourg argued that subsidiarity was breached because the Directive applied to situations that could be regulated at a national level.[87]

The Court pointed out that an airport with less than five million passenger movements a year which was also the Member State's main airport was "assumed

[76] *R (On the Application of Alliance for Natural Health) v Secretary of State for Health* (C-154/04) [2005] ECR I-6451; [2005] 2 CMLR 61 (p. 1490).

[77] *Alliance for Natural Health*, above n 76, [107].

[78] *Alliance for Natural Health*, above n 76, [105].

[79] *Alliance for Natural Health*, above n 76, [106].

[80] *R v Secretary of State for Business, Enterprise and Regulatory Reform; Ex parte Vodafone Ltd* (C-58/08) [2010] ECR I-4999; [2010] 3 CMLR 44 (p. 1189).

[81] *Vodafone*, above n 80, [50].

[82] *Vodafone*, above n 80, [76].

[83] *Vodafone*, above n 80, [77].

[84] *Vodafone*, above n 80, [78].

[85] *Vodafone*, above n 80, [79].

[86] *Luxembourg v European Parliament* (C-176/09) [2011] ECR I-3727.

[87] *Luxembourg*, above n 86, [73].

to be in a privileged position".[88] The fact that some airports with less than five million passenger movements were exempted from compliance did not establish a breach of subsidiarity because the EU legislature had correctly taken the view that it was unnecessary to regulate those airports since they were not the main airport of their Member State.[89] The Court also held that the Luxembourg government had not argued its challenge in sufficient detail to permit the Court to determine whether Member State laws would be adequate to achieve the aim of the Directive.[90]

Several other points emerge from the cases. The Court has held that the subsidiarity principle does not apply retroactively to Community legislation adopted prior to the entry into force of the *Maastricht Treaty*.[91] It has also held that prior to the *Maastricht Treaty* subsidiarity was not a general principle of law against which the legality of Community acts must be tested.[92] The Court declined to apply the principle of subsidiarity as a restriction upon the exercise of individual rights conferred by the founding Treaties.[93]

The Legal Service of the Committee on the Regions has somewhat optimistically identified six potential grounds of subsidiarity review under the Court's case law. Legislation would be open to challenge if it did not meet various criteria for EU action:

> The situation at issue presents transnational aspects that can not be addressed satisfactorily by action at Member State level. ....
>
> Action at national level or lack of action at Union level would be contrary to the requirements of the Treaty (such as, for example, the need to strengthen social, economic or territorial cohesion) or would otherwise harm the interests of the Member States. ....
>
> For reasons related to its dimension or its effects, action at Union level would present obvious advantages over action at Member State level. ....
>
> Action at Union level is justified by the lack of national legislation to address the situation at issue. ....
>
> Action at Union level is justified taking into consideration the substantial disparity of national and/or regional legislation and the effects of that disparity on the internal market. ....
>
> Action at Union level is justified taking into account the wording of an act of secondary law that grants the Union the exclusive right to intervene, even though the policy area at issue does not fall within an area of exclusive competence.[94]

The approach of the Court of Justice has been one of excessive deference. It is a rather extreme form of judicial self-restraint that has resulted in the under-enforcement of an important guarantee of Member State autonomy. It is possible that the lack of commitment to meaningful enforcement of subsidiarity as a judicial principle may be motivated by a perception on the part of the Court that

---

[88] *Luxembourg*, above n 86, [81].

[89] *Luxembourg*, above n 86, [82].

[90] *Luxembourg*, above n 86, [80].

[91] *Kellinghusen v Amt für Land- und Wasserwirtschaft Kiel* (C-36/97) [1998] ECR I-6337 at [35].

[92] *Vereniging van Samenwerkende Prijsregelende Organisaties in de Bouwnijverheid v Commission* (T-29/92) [1995] ECR II-289 at [330]–[331], appeal dismissed (C-137/95 P) [1996] ECR I-1611.

[93] *Union royale belge des sociétés de football association ASBL v Bosman* (C-415/93) [1995] ECR I-4921 at [81]; [1996] 1 CMLR 645.

[94] *Legal Service*, above n 41, pp. 38, 41–43, 44, 51.

compliance with subsidiarity is a political judgment that should be made by the political institutions of the Union.[95]

By contrast, most constitutional courts in federal states approach federalism issues as legal rather than political questions. For example, while the United States Supreme Court has held that it does not have authority to decide political questions,[96] the Court does not treat federalism issues as political questions. The Australian High Court and Privy Council similarly considered that federalism issues were ultimately issues for judicial enforcement.[97]

In essentially leaving control of the observance of subsidiarity to the political branches, the Court of Justice's approach to this issue is reminiscent of Herbert Wechsler's famous paper that emphasised the political safeguards of federalism over judicially enforced limits.[98] In 1985 the United States Supreme Court expressly applied the Wechsler approach in a commerce power case. In the *Garcia* case by a 5-4 majority the Court held that "State sovereign interests ... are more properly protected by procedural safeguards inherent in the structure of the federal system than by judicially created limitations on federal power."[99]

However, the broader significance of the *Garcia* case was substantially eroded by the Court's subsequent decision in *New York v United States,* though the majority in that case disclaimed any necessity "to revisit the holding" in *Garcia*.[100] The Wechsler approach continued to exercise an influence upon a minority of the Justices.[101] However, the majority of the Court has preferred to craft judicially enforced limitations upon federal power such as the principle that Congress may not commandeer State legislatures or officials.[102]

Another reason for the weakness of subsidiarity as a judicial principle may lie in the limited scope of the underlying principle. Subsidiarity assumes that the Union's goals are valid and makes their achievement the paramount consideration. It asks only which level is better able to achieve those Union goals. At most the Member States will be permitted to carry out the EU's goals. The principle does not protect the right of the Member States to carry out their own goals in areas of shared competence.[103] In particular, subsidiarity "assumes the primacy of the central goal,

[95] Tridimas (2006, p. 185).

[96] *Baker v Carr* 369 US 186 at p. 217 (1962); *Nixon v United States* 506 US 224 at p. 228 (1993); *Zivotofsky v Clinton* 132S Ct 1421 at p. 1427 (2012).

[97] *R v Kirby; Ex parte Boilermakers' Society of Australia* (1956) 94 CLR 254 at pp. 267–268 (HC); (1957) 95 CLR 529 at p. 540 (PC).

[98] Wechsler (1954, p. 559).

[99] *Garcia v San Antonio Metropolitan Transit Authority* 469 US 528 at p. 552 (1985).

[100] *New York v United States* 505 US 144 at p. 160 (1992).

[101] *Seminole Tribe of Florida v Florida* 517 US 44 at p. 184 (1996) (Souter J, dissenting); Printz v United States 521 US 898 at p. 957 (1997) (Stevens J, dissenting); *Kimel v Florida Board of Regents* 528 US 62 at p. 93 (2000) (Stevens J, dissenting in part and concurring in part).

[102] *New York*, above n 100, pp. 161, 175; Printz, above n 101, p. 933; *Reno v Condon* 528 US 141 at pp. 149–150 (2000).

[103] Davies (2006, pp. 67–68).

and allows no mechanism for questioning whether or not it is desirable, in the light of other interests, to fully pursue this."[104] The goal is assumed, the only question is who is to achieve that goal.

It has been persuasively argued that to be effective subsidiarity must incorporate an element of federal proportionality since the questions of "whether" and "how" are "tied together". The Court should thus ask "*whether* the European legislator has *unnecessarily* restricted national autonomy."[105] To be an effective safeguard of subsidiarity the standard of review applied by the Court ought to prohibit disproportionate restrictions of national autonomy.[106]

There is a plausible argument that the principle of subsidiarity is applicable to the Court of Justice as an Institution of the Union in the exercise of its function of interpreting the *scope* of EU competences,[107] so it is open to the Court to have regard to subsidiarity in resolving these questions. In this respect there are glimmers of hope for the protection of Member State autonomy by the Court of Justice. Notions of subsidiarity may have influenced the Court's interpretation of a shared competence of the Union.

In interpreting the scope of EU competence in relation to the internal market,[108] the Court invoked the conferral principle in holding that this power was not to be interpreted as a "general power to regulate the internal market."[109] This holding has an echo of the decision of the United States Supreme Court that the commerce power of Congress was not to be interpreted as conferring "a general police power of the sort retained by the States."[110] While the Court expressly referred to the conferral principle rather than subsidiarity, its underlying concern might better be seen as subsidiarity since the Court was interpreting the scope of a shared competence.

It should be noted that in judicial proceedings the Member States do not speak with one voice in relation to subsidiarity. The national governments may disagree as to how the principle of subsidiarity applies to challenged legislation, so they may be on opposite sides regarding the question of its validity. The Member States have also argued against subsidiarity challenges brought by private parties.[111]

Of course it is possible for an apparently moribund principle to receive a new lease of life. In Australia Kirby J once warned that a constitutional doctrine threatened to become "a constitutional guard-dog that would bark but once".[112]

---

[104] Davies, above n 103, p. 78.

[105] Schütze (2009, p. 533).

[106] Schütze, above n 105, p. 534.

[107] Horsley, above n 10, pp. 272, 274; see also Evans, above n 66, p. 271.

[108] Arts 14, 95, Treaty establishing the European Community, as amended by the Treaty of Amsterdam. See now Arts 26, 114, Treaty on the Functioning of the European Union.

[109] *Germany v Parliament (Re the Validity of Directive 98/43 on Tobacco Advertising and Sponsorship)* (C-376/98) [2000] ECR I-8419 at [83]; [2000] 3 CMLR 1175. See Horsley, above n 10, pp. 270–271.

[110] *United States v Lopez* 514 US 549 at p. 567 (1995).

[111] Eg *British American Tobacco*, above n 68, [175]–[176]. See also Craig, above n 16, p. 81.

[112] *Baker v R* (2004) 223 CLR 513 at [54]; [2004] HCA 45.

Unlike subsidiarity, at least that dog had barked once.[113] In fact the Australian dog continues to bark, the High Court having since held that the doctrine had been infringed by several State laws.[114] By contrast, at present there seems little prospect that the Court of Justice will breathe new life into subsidiarity as a judicial principle.

9.3 Subsidiarity as a Legislative Review Principle

9.3.1 The Relevant Treaty Provisions

By far the most significant application of the subsidiarity principle is its consideration as part of the EU legislative process. This process involves both EU institutions and the parliaments of the Member States. For practical examples consideration will be given to reasoned opinions adopted by the United Kingdom Parliament and the annual reports on subsidiarity issued by the Commission.[115]

When the ill-fated European Constitution[116] was being drafted, the working group on subsidiarity expressed the view that the monitoring of the observance of the principle should be primarily preventive as part of the legislative process. The working group stated: "as the principle of subsidiarity was a principle of an essentially political nature, implementation of which involved a considerable margin of discretion for the institutions (considering whether shared objectives could 'better' be achieved at European level or at another level), monitoring of compliance with that principle should be of an essentially political nature and take place before the entry into force of the act in question."[117] The case law of the Court of Justice is certainly consistent with this approach.

Legislative control of constitutionality has been described as "directing the mouse to safeguard the cheese".[118] Fortunately, the observance of subsidiarity in practice is not safeguarded only by the questionable capacity of EU institutions to be sole judges in their own causes. The participation of the national parliaments of the Member States in the EU legislative process means that both the national and Union institutions bring their perspectives to bear in the process.

---

[113] *Kable v Director of Public Prosecutions (NSW)* (1996) 189 CLR 51.

[114] *International Finance Trust Co Ltd v New South Wales Crime Commission* (2009) 240 CLR 319; [2009] HCA 49; South Australia v Totani (2010) 242 CLR 1; [2010] HCA 39; *Wainohu v New South Wales* (2011) 243 CLR 181; [2011] HCA 24.

[115] The Commission is required to issue an annual report on the application of subsidiarity. See Art 9, Protocol No 2.

[116] Treaty Establishing a Constitution for Europe, Rome, 29 October 2004, OJ C 310, 16.12.2004, p. 1; EC 2004 No 8 (Cm 6429).

[117] European Convention. 2002. Conclusions of Working Group I on the Principle of Subsidiarity. CONV 286/02, p. 2.

[118] Barker (1991, pp. 353–354). Or "foxes guarding henhouses": Sander, above n 55, p. 546.

Consideration of subsidiarity begins at the pre-legislative stage. Respect for subsidiarity is a major responsibility of the Commission, which has the initiative in introducing legislative proposals.[119] The Commission has acknowledged that the principle "clearly establishes a presumption in favour of the Member States taking action" in areas of shared competence.[120] The Subsidiarity Protocol requires that the Commission "consult widely" before proposing legislation. In situations of "exceptional urgency" the Commission may dispense with consultation.[121]

There appears to have been a move towards greater reliance upon Directives rather than Regulations. Directives offer more scope for subsidiarity than do Regulations.[122] Directives leave the Member States with discretion as to the method to achieve a specified result, while Regulations are directly applicable in the Member States.[123]

The Commission has indicated that it considers subsidiarity at three points: in preparing roadmaps for its Work Programme, during the impact assessment process, and in the preparation of the explanatory memorandums and recitals for legislative proposals.[124] The Commission has published its guidelines regarding subsidiarity for use in preparing explanatory memorandums. These guidelines read in relevant part:

> When the subsidiarity principle applies, the proposal must meet at least one of the two conditions listed under A and B, as well as the condition listed under C. ….
>
> (a) Indicate why action by Member States would not be sufficient to achieve the objectives of the proposed action. Refer in particular to the transnational aspects that cannot be properly regulated by Member States' action.
>
> (b) Indicate why action by Member States alone would damage significantly Member States' interests.
>
> (c) Indicate why EU action will better achieve the objectives of the proposal, by referring to the scale and/or the effects of its action.
>
> 3. Indicate which qualitative indicators demonstrate that the objective can be better achieved by the Union.
> 4. Indicate which quantitative indicators demonstrate that the objective can be better achieved by the Union (Optional).
> 5. Demonstrate that the scope of the proposal is limited to what Member States cannot satisfactorily achieve and what the Union does better.[125]

---

[119] Constantin (2008, p. 160). See Art 294(2), Treaty on the Functioning of the European Union.

[120] Commission of the European Communities. 2009. Report from the Commission on Subsidiarity and Proportionality (16th Report on Better Lawmaking covering the year 2008). COM(2009) 504 final, p. 2.

[121] Art 2, Protocol No 2.

[122] Craig, above n 16, p. 75.

[123] Art 288, Treaty on the Functioning of the European Union; *Boehringer Ingelheim KG v Swingward Ltd* (C-348/04) [2007] ECR I-3391 at [58]; [2007] 2 CMLR 52 (p. 1445).

[124] European Commission. 2010. Report from the Commission on Subsidiarity and Proportionality (17th Report on Better Lawmaking covering the year 2009). COM(2010) 547 final, p. 4.

[125] Commission of the European Communities. 2007. Commission Staff Working Paper. SEC(2007) 737, p. 36.

Prior to its revision by the *Lisbon Treaty* the *Subsidiarity Protocol* elaborated upon the scope of the principle by including tests that were dubbed the necessity and EU added value tests. The relevant provision of the Protocol read as follows:

> For Community action to be justified, both aspects of the subsidiarity principle shall be met: the objectives of the proposed action cannot be sufficiently achieved by Member States' action in the framework of their national constitutional system and can therefore be better achieved by action on the part of the Community.
>
> The following guidelines should be used in examining whether the abovementioned condition is fulfilled:
>
> — the issue under consideration has transnational aspects which cannot be satisfactorily regulated by action by Member States; [the first 'necessity test']
>
> — actions by Member States alone or lack of Community action would conflict with the requirements of the Treaty (such as the need to correct distortion of competition or avoid disguised restrictions on trade or strengthen economic and social cohesion) or would otherwise significantly damage Member States' interests; [the second 'necessity test']
>
> — action at Community level would produce clear benefits by reason of its scale or effects compared with action at the level of the Member States. [the 'EU added value' test][126]

The *Lisbon Protocol* no longer incorporates the necessity and EU value added tests, but the Commission has stated that it will continue to apply those tests as part of its guidelines.[127] The national parliaments similarly continue to apply these tests. For example, the House of Commons argued that a proposal breached subsidiarity because the Commission had not demonstrated the necessity for EU action.[128]

The Commission's impact assessment guidelines set out questions which must be answered in applying the necessity and EU value added tests.[129] The guidelines state:

> 1. Does the issue being addressed have transnational aspects which cannot be dealt with satisfactorily by action by Member States? (eg reduction of CO2 emissions in the atmosphere)
> 2. Would actions by Member States alone, or the lack of Community action, conflict with the requirements of the Treaty? (eg discriminatory treatment of a stakeholder group)
> 3. Would actions by Member States alone, or the lack of Community action, significantly damage the interests of Member States? (eg action restricting the free circulation of goods)
> 4. Would action at Community level produce clear benefits compared with action at the level of Member States by reason of its scale?
> 5. Would action at Community level produce clear benefits compared with action at the level of Member States by reason of its effectiveness?[130]

---

[126] Art 5, Protocol (No 30) on the Application of the Principles of Subsidiarity and Proportionality, as adopted by the Treaty of Amsterdam, OJ C 321, 29.12.2006, p. 308.

[127] European Commission. 2010. Report from the Commission on Subsidiarity and Proportionality (17th Report on Better Lawmaking covering the year 2009). COM(2010) 547 final, p. 3; European Commission. 2011. Report from the Commission on Subsidiarity and Proportionality (18th Report on Better Lawmaking covering the year 2010). COM(2011) 344 final, p. 2.

[128] Reasoned Opinion of the House of Commons concerning a Draft Regulation on the exercise of the right to take collective action within the context of the freedom of establishment and the freedom to provide services at [14]–[17]. The House resolved to submit this opinion to the EU institutions. See House of Commons Hansard, 22 May 2012, column 1014.

[129] Impact assessments are available on the Commission website at http://ec.europa.eu/governance/impact/index_en.htm

[130] European Commission. 2009. Impact Assessment Guidelines. SEC(2009) 92, p. 22.

In its reasoned opinion on the proposed *Common European Sales Law* the House of Commons observed that it was "axiomatic" that a common sales law could be better achieved at the EU level. However, it would need to be demonstrated that the adoption of such a common regime was necessary and would produce greater benefits than if left to the Member States.[131] In several reasoned opinions the House of Lords argued that "[t]he failure of Member States to act is not in itself a reason for the Union to act."[132] The impact assessment guidelines state that since it is possible that changes of circumstances may mean that Union action is no longer necessary, subsidiarity justifications should not be based exclusively on past assessments.[133]

At the legislative stage the Commission is required to send legislative proposals to the national parliaments at the same time as it sends them to the European Parliament.[134] Legislative proposals must contain a "detailed statement" regarding subsidiarity. The reasons why the legislation would be better adopted at the EU level must be substantiated by qualitative and (where possible) quantitative indicators.[135]

The House of Commons has suggested that since the "detailed statement" is required to be contained within the legislative proposal, it should appear in the explanatory memorandum, which is translated into every official language of the Union, thereby facilitating scrutiny by the national parliaments. By contrast, the impact assessment is not translated into all of the official languages.[136]

The House of Commons has also expressed its views regarding the necessary level of detail in the statement by the Commission. The House has emphasised that subsidiarity justifications must contain "sufficient detail and clarity that an EU citizen can understand the qualitative and quantitative reasons leading to a conclusion that EU action rather than national action is justified."[137]

---

[131] Reasoned Opinion of the House of Commons: Draft Regulation on a Common European Sales Law for the European Union at [18]. The House resolved to submit this opinion to the EU institutions. See House of Commons Hansard, 7 December 2011, column 325.

[132] House of Lords European Union Committee. 2011. Subsidiarity Assessment: Distribution of Food Products to Deprived Persons. HL Paper 217, Session 2010–12, [10]. The House resolved to submit this opinion to the EU institutions. See House of Lords Hansard, 28 November 2011, column 94. The Committee had advanced the same view in its report on an earlier version of the proposal. See House of Lords European Union Committee. 2010. Subsidiarity Assessment: Distribution of Food Products to Deprived Persons. HL Paper 44, Session 2010–11, [9]. The House also resolved to submit that opinion to the EU institutions. See House of Lords Hansard, 3 November 2010, column 1693.

[133] European Commission. 2009. Impact Assessment Guidelines. SEC(2009) 92, p. 22.

[134] Art 4, Protocol No 2.

[135] Art 5, Protocol No 2.

[136] Reasoned Opinion of the House of Commons: Draft Directive of the European Parliament and of the Council on improving the gender balance among non-executive directors of companies listed on stock exchanges and related measures at [16]. The House resolved to submit this opinion to the EU institutions. See House of Commons Hansard, 7 January 2013, column 76.

[137] Reasoned Opinion of the House of Commons: Draft Directive on a common consolidated corporate tax base at [19]. A similar statement adds the words "and their elected representatives". See Reasoned Opinion of the House of Commons: Draft Regulation on a Common European Sales

The subsidiarity principle also applies to the other actors in the legislative process. An *Inter-Institutional Agreement* on subsidiarity provides that the Parliament and Council are required to justify their proposed amendments in terms of subsidiarity if the scope of Union action would be expanded.[138] The *Inter-Institutional Agreement* was adopted shortly after the *Maastricht Treaty* came into force, but has not been revised in the light of subsequent amendments to the founding Treaties.

In the Parliament responsibility for ensuring observance of subsidiarity lies with both the specific Committee that considers the proposal and the Committee on Legal Affairs.[139] In the Council that responsibility lies with the Committee of Permanent Representatives (COREPER), which is an "auxiliary body of the Council"[140] that prepares the work of the Council.[141]

EU legislative proposals have been described as a "paper tide" with which the national parliaments must now contend.[142] The enacted legislative output of EU institutions is huge. In 2012 alone there were 362 issues of the legislation series of the *Official Journal*. Of course there are even more legislative proposals than enacted legislation.

In view of this substantial addition to their normal legislative work, it is surprising that the national parliaments have only 8 weeks in which to consider and respond to EU legislative proposals.[143] This deadline is far too short. Forty national legislative chambers have to examine every submitted proposal within an 8 week period.[144]

The Committee on Constitutional Affairs of the European Parliament proposed that the Parliament resolve that there should be a "significant extension" of the 8 week deadline provided for by the Protocol.[145] The adopted version of the

---

Law for the European Union at [13]. The House resolved to submit these opinions to the EU institutions. See House of Commons Hansard, 11 May 2011, column 1304; 7 December 2011, column 325.

[138] Point II(3), Inter-Institutional Agreement between the European Parliament, the Council and the Commission on procedures for implementing the principle of subsidiarity, OJ C 329, 6.12.1993, p. 135.

[139] Rule 38a(2) and Annex VII Point XVI(2), Rules of Procedure of the European Parliament, OJ L 116, 5.5.2011, p. 1 at 23, 90; European Commission. 2011. Report from the Commission on Subsidiarity and Proportionality (18th Report on Better Lawmaking covering the year 2010). COM(2011) 344 final, p. 4. The website of the Committee on Legal Affairs is at http://www.europarl.europa.eu/committees/en/JURI/home.html

[140] *Commission v Council* (C-25/94) [1996] ECR I-1469 at [26].

[141] Art 16(7), Treaty on European Union; Art 240(1), Treaty on the Functioning of the European Union.

[142] Ritzer, above n 9, p. 758.

[143] Art 6, Protocol No 2; Art 4, Protocol (No 1) on the Role of National Parliaments in the European Union, OJ C 326, 26.10.2012, p. 203. In view of national parliamentary recesses, the month of August is not included in calculating the 8 week deadline. See Letter from the President of the Commission to Member State Parliaments, 1 December 2009, p. 4. Legislation introduced in June or July may thus be subject to up to 12 weeks scrutiny by Member State legislatures. See Danish Folketing European Affairs Committee. 2010. Report on Consideration of EU Matters by the Folketing in Relation to Subsidiarity Checks, Annex I.

[144] Korhonen (2011, p. 7).

[145] European Parliament Committee on Constitutional Affairs. 2011. Opinion on better legislation, subsidiarity and proportionality and smart regulation. 2011/2029(INI), p. 3.

resolution did not take up this suggestion.[146] The deadline was even shorter under the *Treaty of Amsterdam*: a mere 6 weeks.[147]

Within the 8 week period a national parliament or one of its chambers may issue a reasoned opinion regarding subsidiarity aspects of the proposal. The reasoned opinion may state why the legislature considers that the proposal is in breach of subsidiarity.[148] National law often regulates the procedure for the adoption of a reasoned opinion. For example, Irish law provides that each House of the legislature may submit a reasoned opinion on a proposal after passing a resolution to that effect.[149]

The reasoned opinion procedure is extensively used by the parliaments of the Member States. In 2011 national parliaments issued 64 reasoned opinions.[150] Nevertheless, the majority of Commission proposals do not produce reasoned opinions arguing that subsidiarity has been breached, so the pre-legislative process may have had some effect in reducing proposals that give rise to subsidiarity concerns.[151] Proposals that are entirely inconsistent with subsidiarity are "rare", but it is relatively common for national parliaments to identify particular aspects of proposals that infringe subsidiarity.[152] The Commission website makes available the texts of the reasoned opinions of national parliaments and its replies to those opinions.[153]

The European institutions are to "take account" of the reasoned opinions of the national legislatures.[154] It is arguable that a "mere acknowledgement by the Union institutions suffices."[155] The opinions are "merely advisory"[156] and the national parliaments must rely upon their powers of persuasion.[157] The point of the procedure is that the Commission's interpretation of subsidiarity is subject to regular challenge.[158]

Since the *Treaty of Lisbon* one third of the national legislatures are able to require the reconsideration of a proposed EU law that they believe infringes subsidiarity (the "yellow card" procedure). If the majority of national legislatures reject the

[146] European Parliament resolution of 14 September 2011 on better legislation, subsidiarity and proportionality and smart regulation, OJ C 51E, 22.2.2013, p. 87.

[147] Art 3, Protocol on the Application of the Principles of Subsidiarity and Proportionality, as inserted by the Treaty of Amsterdam.

[148] Art 6, Protocol No 2.

[149] s 7(3), European Union Act 2009 (Ireland).

[150] European Commission. 2012. Report from the Commission on Subsidiarity and Proportionality (19th Report on Better Lawmaking covering the year 2011). COM(2012) 373 final, p. 4.

[151] European Commission. 2011. Report from the Commission on Subsidiarity and Proportionality (18th Report on Better Lawmaking covering the year 2010). COM(2011) 344 final, p. 10.

[152] House of Commons European Scrutiny Committee, above n 46, [29].

[153] http://ec.europa.eu/dgs/secretariat_general/relations/relations_other/npo/index_en.htm. Reasoned opinions are also available at http://www.ipex.eu/IPEXL-WEB/search.do

[154] Art 7(1), Protocol No 2.

[155] Ritzer, above n 9, p. 753.

[156] Cooper (2006, p. 283).

[157] Cooper, above n 156, p. 293.

[158] Cooper, above n 156, p. 294.

proposed law, and the Council or the Parliament demurs to their objections, the proposed law will be blocked (the "orange card" procedure).

The yellow card procedure is based on a soccer analogy[159] while the orange card procedure is based on a traffic light analogy.[160] To continue the soccer analogy, the Protocol does not include a "red card" procedure that would give the national parliaments a power of "veto" over EU legislation.[161] The "yellow" and "orange card" procedures are often referred to as the "early warning system".[162]

In these procedures the reasoned opinions of national parliaments are treated as votes. Each national parliament has two votes, which are divided into one vote for each chamber if the legislature is bicameral.[163] In a declaration to the Final Act of the *Treaty of Lisbon*, the Belgian government stated that the two chambers of its federal Parliament and the legislatures of its Communities and Regions were all "chambers of the national parliament".[164]

If the yellow card threshold is triggered the proposal must be reviewed.[165] There are two ways in which the yellow card may be triggered. It may be triggered by a one third threshold among the national parliaments.[166] In relation to proposals concerning the "area of freedom, security and justice" the procedure may be triggered by a one quarter threshold among Member State parliaments.[167] After its review the Commission may maintain, amend or withdraw its proposal, but must provide reasons for its decision.[168]

The yellow card procedure has potential as a political tool for the protection of subsidiarity. The United Kingdom government emphasised the potential of a similar power that formed part of the ill-fated *Constitution Treaty*: "if a third of national parliaments were against any proposal, so too would their Governments be, and it would be hard to put together the qualified majority needed to pass the law in question."[169]

The orange card procedure relates to the ordinary legislative procedure.[170] This procedure is triggered by a simple majority threshold among the national parliaments. If this threshold is reached, the proposal must be reviewed. After its review the Commission may maintain, amend or withdraw its proposal. The Commission must

---

[159] Louis (2008, p. 438); Fabbrini and Granat (2013, pp. 118 n 13).

[160] Louis, above n 159, p. 438.

[161] Schütze, above n 105, p. 530; Fabbrini, above n 159, pp. 119–120, 122.

[162] See generally Kiiver (2012).

[163] Art 7(1), Protocol No 2.

[164] Declaration (No 51) by the Kingdom of Belgium on National Parliaments, OJ C 306, 17.12.2007, p. 267. See Arts 2–3, Constitution of Belgium (1994).

[165] Art 7(2), Protocol No 2.

[166] Croatia became a Member State on 1 July 2013, bringing total EU membership to 28 nations. See Treaty of Accession of Croatia, Brussels, 9 December 2011, OJ L 112, 24.4.2012, p. 10.

[167] See Art 67, Treaty on the Functioning of the European Union.

[168] Art 7(2), Protocol No 2.

[169] Foreign and Commonwealth Office. 2004. White Paper on the Treaty establishing a Constitution for Europe. Cm 6309, p. 19.

[170] See Art 294, Treaty on the Functioning of the European Union.

issue a reasoned opinion regarding subsidiarity if it decides to maintain the proposal. All of the reasoned opinions are to be submitted to the European Parliament and the Council.[171] Before the first reading of the proposal the European Parliament and the Council must consider whether the proposal breaches subsidiarity. If 55 % of the Council or a majority of the votes cast in the European Parliament take the view that the proposal is in breach of subsidiarity, the proposal may not be further considered.[172]

If either the yellow or orange card procedures was activated in relation to a proposal that was ultimately adopted by the EU institutions, it is conceivable that this might result in a more exacting scrutiny by the Court of Justice as the Court would be in possession of a more detailed legislative record than has hitherto been the case in subsidiarity-based challenges to legislation. The Court might be prompted to consider whether EU institutions had given proper consideration to the reasoned opinions.[173]

The early warning system procedure concerns only alleged breaches of subsidiarity, not alleged breaches of the principle of proportionality.[174] While reasoned opinions may be issued only in relation to alleged breaches of subsidiarity,[175] in practice reasoned opinions frequently discuss alleged breaches of proportionality as part of the broader political exchange between the Commission and the Member States.[176]

In 2008 a Member of the European Parliament told a House of Commons Committee that the early warning procedure "was not really intended to be used".[177] However, in May 2012 the yellow card threshold was reached in relation to a proposed Council Regulation on collective action.[178] Twelve national parliaments presented reasoned opinions. These 12 legislatures consisted of 7 unicameral legislatures (14 votes) and 5 legislative chambers of bicameral parliaments (5 votes).[179]

On 10 January 2013 the Commission withdrew the proposal. The Commission denied that the proposal breached the principle of subsidiarity, but acknowledged that the proposal was unlikely to be supported by the Parliament and Council.[180]

[171] Art 7(3), Protocol No 2.

[172] Art 7(3)(a)-(b), Protocol No 2.

[173] House of Commons European Scrutiny Committee, above n 46, p Ev 6 (evidence of Prof Alan Dashwood).

[174] Fabbrini, above n 159, p. 121.

[175] Cooper, above n 156, p. 293.

[176] Craig, above n 16, p. 79; Besselink, above n 33, p. 46. See generally Jančić (2012, p. 83).

[177] House of Commons European Scrutiny Committee, above n 46, [21].

[178] Proposal for a Council Regulation on the exercise of the right to take collective action within the context of the freedom of establishment and the freedom to provide services, COM (2012) 130 (Celex Number 52012PC0130). See European Parliament Committee on Legal Affairs. 2012. Report on the 18th Report on Better Legislation. A7-0251/2012, p. 5.

[179] Fabbrini, above n 159, pp. 116, 135. The yellow card threshold that applied at the time was 18 votes out of 54, based on the then 27 Member Union.

[180] Letter from the Vice-President of the Commission to the Speaker of the United Kingdom House of Commons, 12 September 2012, available at http://ec.europa.eu/dgs/secretariat_general/relations/relations_other/npo/index_en.htm

The reasoned opinions failed to establish a breach of subsidiarity since the proposal was limited to cross-border labour disputes. The opinions addressed other issues such as the legal basis of the proposal and proportionality.[181]

The regional dimension of subsidiarity requires further consideration by the Union. The founding Treaties focus upon the Union and the Member States. The Treaties contain only a few sparse passages about regional and local governments. The *Treaty's* formulation of the principle of subsidiarity adverts to regional and local governments when contrasting action at the Union and Member State levels.[182] The Subsidiarity Protocol requires that Commission pre-legislative consultations "take into account the regional and local dimension of the action envisaged."[183] The detailed statement regarding subsidiarity must consider the implications for regional legislation where relevant.[184] Regional legislatures do not participate in the early warning system.[185]

The *Subsidiarity Protocol* provides that it is for the national parliaments to consult regional legislatures "where appropriate".[186] The European Union Committee of the House of Lords has undertaken to inform the devolved legislatures about EU legislative proposals that raise subsidiarity concerns in relation to devolved matters, though not in relation to matters which are reserved for the United Kingdom government.[187]

A reasoned opinion of the House of Commons pointed out that the Welsh National Assembly considered that two draft Directives were inconsistent with the devolution scheme of the United Kingdom because they sought to impose a duty on a single national body without regard to the responsibilities of the devolved governments.[188] The Scottish Parliament also considered that the proposal would breach the principle of subsidiarity.[189]

The Committee of the Regions does not share the power of the national parliaments to give a 'yellow card' or an 'orange card'.[190] However, the Committee has taken a keen interest in subsidiarity monitoring. In 2005 the Committee issued an

---

[181] Fabbrini, above n 159, pp. 116, 136–137, 139.

[182] Art 5(3), Treaty on European Union.

[183] Art 2, Protocol No 2.

[184] Art 5, Protocol No 2.

[185] Cygan, above n 34, p. 167.

[186] Art 6, Protocol No 2.

[187] House of Lords European Union Committee. 2012. Report on 2010–12. HL Paper 13, Session 2012–13, [115].

[188] Reasoned Opinion of the House of Commons concerning a Draft Directive on procurement by entities operating in the water, energy, transport and postal services sectors and a Draft Directive on public procurement at [18], contained in European Parliament Committee on Legal Affairs Notice to Members (29/2012). The House of Commons resolved to submit this opinion to the EU institutions. See House of Commons Hansard, 6 March 2012, column 767.

[189] Reasoned Opinion, above n 188, [26]–[27].

[190] Cygan, above n 34, p. 169.

opinion that a legislative proposal was not entirely consistent with subsidiarity. The Commission subsequently withdrew the proposal.[191]

The Committee's Subsidiarity Monitoring Network informs local and regional governments of EU legislative initiatives and collects their responses for use in its advisory role in the legislative process.[192] The Committee's Rules of Procedure provide that its opinions must refer to the application of the subsidiarity principle.[193] Since 2010 the Committee has issued an annual report on the application of the subsidiarity principle.

9.4 Measures That Would Strengthen Compliance with Subsidiarity

At the judicial level the Court of Justice should adopt a more stringent test for compliance with subsidiarity. The Court could apply a federal proportionality standard,[194] deciding "*whether* the European legislator has *unnecessarily* restricted national autonomy."[195] To be an effective safeguard the standard of review applied by the Court ought to prohibit disproportionate restrictions of national autonomy.[196]

The Court should be far more exacting in its expectations for subsidiarity justifications. The Court ought to closely scrutinize the impact assessment and any reasoned opinions adopted by the national legislatures.[197] The Court should be prepared to challenge the reasoning of EU political institutions, just as it has always been willing to challenge the justifications offered by national governments when seeking to justify limitations of the fundamental freedoms under the founding Treaties.[198]

The Court could rigorously apply the necessity and EU value added tests that have been repeatedly affirmed by the Union political branches and which originate from an earlier revision of the founding Treaties.[199] The Court should assess the sufficiency of the qualitative and quantitative indicators that the EU relies upon as establishing that the objective of the legislation would be better achieved at the Union level.[200]

---

[191] Commission of the European Communities. 2006. 'Better Lawmaking 2005' Report from the Commission pursuant to Article 9 of the Protocol … (13th Report). COM(2006) 289 final, p. 8.

[192] See https://portal.cor.europa.eu/subsidiarity/Pages/default.aspx

[193] Rule 51(2), Committee of the Regions Rules of Procedure, OJ L 6, 9.1.2010, p. 14.

[194] Schütze, above n 105, p. 534.

[195] Schütze, above n 105, p. 533.

[196] Schütze, above n 105, p. 534.

[197] Craig, above n 16, p. 78; Vandenbruwaene (2012, p. 340).

[198] Eg Moens and Trone (2010, pp. 45–49).

[199] Art 5, Protocol (No 30) on the Application of the Principles of Subsidiarity and Proportionality, as adopted by the Treaty of Amsterdam.

[200] As required by Art 5, Protocol No 2.

These questions are not so subjective as to be beyond judicial expertise. Questions of fundamental rights are if anything more subjective than these questions, but the Court has successfully exercised its fundamental rights jurisdiction for several decades.[201] Furthermore, over time the practice of the European political institutions and the national parliaments will elucidate the content of these requirements, indicating understandings that would be capable of judicial application. The Court should also make clear that compliance with subsidiarity is not a political question.

If the Court does not venture so far, it could at least adopt an approach similar to the American "clear statement rule".[202] Under that rule there is a presumption against Congressional preemption of State law concerning matters of traditional State responsibility, so that such preemption will require a clear statement by Congress.[203] In an EU context such a rule could require that EU legislation demonstrate by clear and unmistakable language its intent to displace Member State law. The Court of Justice has fashioned many judicial doctrines.[204] Such a rule would be one of its more modest doctrinal innovations.

At the very least the Court ought to strengthen its procedural review. The general obligation to provide reasons for EU legislation[205] has been supplemented by the more specific and demanding obligation to provide a detailed statement regarding subsidiarity.[206] The Court of Justice has not yet considered the requirement to provide a detailed statement. When assessing whether a sufficiently detailed statement has been provided the Court should not apply the same permissive review that it has applied to the duty to provide reasons. The detailed statement requirement expressly requires much greater detail than the more general requirement to give reasons.

Several reforms should be adopted through amendment of the founding Treaties. One reform that would be likely to be adopted with relative ease would be an extension of the time available to the national parliaments to scrutinize the subsidiarity aspects of proposed legislation. An increase of the scrutiny period from 8 weeks to 12 weeks would ease the burden of the national legislatures in scrutinizing the very large body of EU legislative proposals in addition to their domestic workload. If such an amendment were not adopted, national legislatures could begin their subsidiarity monitoring when preparatory materials such as white papers are issued before a specific legislative proposal is presented, though the early warning system does not operate at that stage.[207]

---

[201] Eg *Stauder v City of Ulm* (29/69) [1969] ECR 419 at p. 425; [1970] CMLR 112 at p. 119; *Internationale Handelsgesellschaft mbH v Einfuhr-und Vorratsstelle für Getreide und Futtermittel* (11/70) [1970] ECR 1125 at [4]; [1972] CMLR 255.

[202] Schütze, above n 105, p. 534; see also Evans, above n 66, p. 272.

[203] *Gregory v Ashcroft* 501 US 452 at p. 461 (1991).

[204] Moens and Trone, above n 198, pp. 55, 59, 386–390.

[205] Art 296, Treaty on the Functioning of the European Union. See formerly Art 253, Treaty Establishing the Economic Community, as revised by the Treaty of Amsterdam; Art 190, Treaty Establishing the European Economic Community, as revised by the Maastricht Treaty.

[206] Art 5, Protocol No 2.

[207] Bermann (2008, p. 458).

The subsidiarity scrutiny process would be strengthened by the introduction of a 'red card' procedure, which would enable the national parliaments to entirely reject proposed legislation and would force the Commission to withdraw the proposal.[208] Under the present system the national parliaments may compel the Commission to review a proposal but not to abandon the proposal.[209] Given the existing thresholds for the yellow and orange cards, a red card should be triggered by a 60 % majority threshold among the national parliaments. The existing thresholds for the yellow and orange card procedures are also arguably too demanding and could be revised downwards to further invigorate the early warning mechanism.[210]

The Member States have a strong interest in securing the adoption of such amendments, so their inclusion in an amending Treaty would improve the prospects that the revision would be successfully ratified. With the expanded membership of the Union, the ratification of amending Treaties by the Member States has become a lengthy and cumbersome process.[211] Such a proposal would be unlikely to suffer the fate of the European Constitution, since it works in the direction of Member State autonomy rather than in favour of centralization in Brussels.

The regional dimension of subsidiarity has long been neglected. Regional legislatures and the Committee on the Regions do not participate in the early warning system and may not issue reasoned opinions as part of that process.[212] The Treaties should be amended so that either the Committee of the Regions or the regional legislatures themselves may participate in the yellow and orange card procedures of the early warning system. Consideration should also be given to the question of whether these bodies could be accommodated within a red card procedure.

At the political level the Commission tends to reflexively defend the compliance of its legislative proposals with subsidiarity. The Commission ought to be more prepared to amend its proposals in the light of the reasoned opinions of the national parliaments. A healthy political dialogue involves some mutual give and take.

9.5 Conclusion

The exercise of power by the European Union in areas of shared competence must respect the principle of subsidiarity. The founding Treaties make clear that subsidiarity is a judicially enforceable legal principle. However, the case law of the Court of Justice reveals that the enforcement of subsidiarity as a judicial principle has

---

[208] Delehanty, above n 48, p. 139; House of Commons European Scrutiny Committee, above n 46, [36]; Fabbrini, above n 159, pp. 119–120. The introduction of a 'red card' procedure was proposed but not adopted during the negotiations preceding the ill-fated European Constitution. See European Convention. 2003. The Early Warning Mechanism – Putting it into Practice. CONV 540/03, p. 3; Van Nuffel (2011, pp. 71–72).

[209] Cooper, above n 156, pp. 289, 293.

[210] House of Commons European Scrutiny Committee, above n 46, [23].

[211] Moens and Trone, above n 198, pp. 6–10.

[212] Cygan, above n 34, pp. 167–169.

been strikingly ineffective. The Court has applied a very weak standard of review for both substantive and procedural compliance with the subsidiarity principle. It is possible that the lack of commitment to meaningful enforcement of subsidiarity as a judicial principle may be motivated by a perception on the part of the Court that compliance with subsidiarity is a political judgment that should be made by the political institutions of the Union.

By far the most significant application of the subsidiarity principle is its consideration as part of the EU legislative process. This process involves both EU institutions and the parliaments of the Member States. A national parliament or one of its chambers may issue a reasoned opinion regarding subsidiarity aspects of a legislative proposal. These reasoned opinions may trigger the yellow card procedure, forcing the Commission to review its proposal, or the orange card procedure, where the Parliament or Council can block the proposal. These procedures have some potential as legislative protections for subsidiarity: the Commission withdrew its proposal for a Council Regulation on collective action after the yellow card procedure was activated.

References

Barker, Robert S. 1991. Taking constitutionalism seriously: Costa Rica's Sala Cuarta. *Florida Journal of International Law* 6: 349.

Bermann, George A. 2008. National parliaments and subsidiarity: An outsider's view. *European Constitutional Law Review* 4: 453.

Besselink, Leonard F.M., and Brecht van Mourik. 2012. The Parliamentary Legitimacy of the European Union: The role of the States General within the European Union. *Utrecht Law Review* 8(1): 28. Available at http://www.utrechtlawreview.org

Constantin, Simona. 2008. Rethinking subsidiarity and the balance of powers in the EU in the light of the Lisbon Treaty and beyond. *Croatian Yearbook of European Law and Policy* 4: 151.

Conway, Gerard. 2010. Conflicts of competence norms in EU law and the legal reasoning of the ECJ. *German Law Journal* 11(9): 966. Available at http://www.germanlawjournal.com

Cooper, Ian. 2006. The watchdogs of subsidiarity: National Parliaments and the logic of arguing in the EU. *Journal of Common Market Studies* 44: 281.

Craig, Paul. 2012. Subsidiarity: A political and legal analysis. *Journal of Common Market Studies* 50: 72.

Cygan, Adam. 2013. Regional governance, subsidiarity and accountability within the EU's multi-level polity. *European Public Law* 19: 161.

Davies, Gareth. 2006. Subsidiarity: The wrong idea, in the wrong place, at the wrong time. *Common Market Law Review* 43: 63.

Delehanty, Michael Marc. 2010. Subsidiarity and Seanad Éireann. *Trinity College Law Review* 13: 133.

Evans, Michelle. 2012. *The use of the principle of subsidiarity in the reformation of Australia's Federal System of Government*. PhD thesis, Curtin University School of Business Law and Taxation, Perth.

Fabbrini, Federico, and Katarzyna Granat. 2013. Yellow card, but no foul: The role of the national parliaments under the subsidiarity protocol and the Commission proposal for an EU regulation on the right to strike. *Common Market Law Review* 50: 115.

Horsley, Thomas. 2012. Subsidiarity and the European Court of Justice: Missing pieces in the subsidiarity jigsaw? *Journal of Common Market Studies* 50: 267.

Jančić, Davor. 2012. The Barroso Initiative: Window dressing or democracy boost? *Utrecht Law Review* 8: 78.
Kiiver, Philip. 2012. *The early warning system for the principle of subsidiarity: Constitutional theory and empirical reality*. London: Routledge.
Korhonen, Kaisa. 2011. *Guardians of subsidiarity: National parliaments strive to control EU decision-making*, Briefing paper 84. Helsinki: Finnish Institute of International Affairs.
Louis, Jean-Victor. 2008. National parliaments and the principle of subsidiarity – Legal options and practical limits. *European Constitutional Law Review* 4: 429.
Moens, Gabriël A. 1997. The subsidiarity principle and EC Directive 93/104. *Australian and World Affairs* 34: 51.
Moens, Gabriël A. 2004. The subsidiarity principle in European Union law and the Irish abortion issue. In *Legal culture and politics in the twenty first century*, ed. Guenther Doeker-Mach, Klaus A. Ziegert, and Klaus A. Ziegert, 424. Stuttgart: Franz Steiner.
Moens, Gabriël, and John Trone. 2010. *Commercial law of the European Union*. Dordrecht: Springer.
Ritzer, Christopher, Marc Rutloff, and Karin Linhart. 2006. How to sharpen a dull sword – The principle of subsidiarity and its control. *German Law Journal* 7(9): 733. Available at http://www.germanlawjournal.com
Sander, Florian. 2006. Subsidiarity infringements before the European Court of Justice: Futile interference with politics or a substantial step towards EU federalism? *Columbia Journal of European Law* 12: 517.
Schütze, Robert. 2009. Subsidiarity after Lisbon: Reinforcing the safeguards of federalism? *Cambridge Law Journal* 68: 525.
Tridimas, Takis. 2006. *The general principles of EU law*, 2nd ed. Oxford: Oxford University Press.
Van Nuffel, Piet. 2011. The protection of member states' regions through the subsidiarity principle. In *The role of the regions in EU governance*, ed. Carlo Panara and Alexander De Becker, 55. Berlin: Springer.
Vandenbruwaene, Werner. 2012. Multi-tiered political questions: The ECJ's mandate in enforcing subsidiarity. *Legisprudence* 6: 321.
Wechsler, Herbert. 1954. The political safeguards of federalism: The role of the states in the composition and selection of the national government. *Columbia Law Review* 54: 543.

Chapter 10
Subsidiarity and Federalism: A Case Study of the Australian Constitution and Its Interpretation

Michelle Evans

Abstract Since the landmark decision of the Australian High Court in the *Engineers* case, the Australian federation has become increasingly centralised to the extent that Australia has become less than an authentic federation. This paper evaluates whether the principle of subsidiarity, which is a fundamental characteristic of a federal system of government, could be implemented in Australia to restore legislative and financial powers to the Australian states. The chapter suggests specific constitutional and other reforms.

Keywords Australian federation • Federal balance • Subsidiarity • Government • Decentralisation • High Court • Constitutional reform

10.1 Introduction

Subsidiarity offers a means of looking at federalism in order to reveal its true foundations. There is considerable commonality and an overall compatibility between the principle of subsidiarity and federalism. Indeed, subsidiarity can be seen as a central characteristic of an authentic federal system of government, such as that envisaged by the framers of the United States and Australian Constitutions.

However subsidiarity as a central characteristic of a federal system of government can be diminished or overlooked by legislators and the Courts. Australia, for example, has seen state financial and legislative powers be incrementally taken over by the central government (known as the 'Commonwealth' or 'federal government'), through expansive legislative attempts which have been upheld by the High Court of Australia when challenged.

M. Evans (✉)
Curtin University Law School, Kent Street, Bentley, 6102 Perth, Western Australia, Australia
e-mail: michelle.evans@curtin.edu.au

M. Evans and A. Zimmermann (eds.), *Global Perspectives on Subsidiarity*, Ius Gentium: Comparative Perspectives on Law and Justice 37, DOI 10.1007/978-94-017-8810-6_10,

The message that this chapter seeks to illustrate, using Australia as a case study, is that subsidiarity is an essential characteristic of federalism that should not be ignored by the governments in which constitutional powers are reposed, or by the Courts (for example, the High Court of Australia) which police their exercise. Where federalism has been diminished in favour of centralisation, such as in the Australian federation, subsidiarity should be resurrected to inspire reforms and to encourage powers to be reposed at the level of government where they are best exercised. Most often, this will involve measures (both constitutional and otherwise) to achieve decentralisation.

This chapter will begin by defining federalism and at the same time, comparisons will be made with the principle of subsidiarity to show the compatibility of the two concepts. This chapter will then outline how the Australian *Constitution*[1] establishes a federal system of government, in which subsidiarity is evidently a fundamental characteristic, and why it is the most appropriate system of government for Australia. This chapter will continue on to explain how the Australian federal system has been distorted through expansive legislative attempts by the federal Parliament and the interpretation of the *Constitution* by the High Court. It will conclude by offering suggestions as to how the Australian federation should be reformed to restore subsidiarity as a fundamental characteristic of it. The aim is that some of these recommendations may translate to, and be of use to other federal systems of government which have become increasingly centralised.

10.2 Subsidiarity as a Federal Characteristic

A system of government can be properly defined as 'federal' if it has an entrenched constitution which divides powers between sovereign and independent central and regional governments by specifically delineating, and thereby limiting, the powers of the central government and leaving residual powers to the regional governments. This balance of power is upheld by an independent judiciary constitutionally empowered to conclusively determine the demarcation of any disputes between the two levels of government. The powers of these constitutionally entrenched institutions (including, both levels of government and the judiciary) are of a permanent nature and cannot be easily interfered with.[2]

Germane to this definition of a federal system of government is *decentralisation* and the acknowledgment that certain powers are more appropriately reposed in defined levels of government. In a federal system of government decentralisation is prescribed through the limitation of the central government's powers. At the same time there is an acknowledgment that some (albeit limited) powers are more

[1] The Australian Constitution is an act of the British Parliament, the *Commonwealth of Australia Constitution Act 1900* (UK) ('*Constitution*').

[2] For similar definitions of 'federalism', see for example, Sawer (1967, p. 1), Lijphart (1985, p. 3), cited in Elazar (1991, pp. 22–23), Irving (1999, p. xix), Aroney (2009, p. 17).

appropriately carried out at a central level with the balance of powers being reposed in regional governments. This is 'subsidiarity', and indeed, it can certainly be said that 'Federal systems across the world are generally designed according to the principle of subsidiarity, which in one form or another holds that the central government should play only a supporting role in governance, acting if and only if the constituent units of government are incapable of acting on their own.'[3]

The correlation between federalism and subsidiarity can certainly be seen in examination of the definition of subsidiarity in its many facets. The characteristics of decentralisation, and powers being carried out at their appropriate level, flows through the many facets of subsidiarity from Catholic social theory through to political theory. For example, in Catholic social theory, as espoused by Pope Pius XI in his encyclical letter *Quadragesimo Anno*, the principle of subsidiarity is premised upon empowering the individual with decision-making 'carried out as close to the citizen as is viable',[4] or at a 'grassroots level'.[5] Therefore, an institution, such as a government entity, should not intervene on an individual's behalf if the individual is capable of resolving the issue themself. If intervention is required, it is the institution closest to the individual which should do the intervening. For example, the individual's family should assist them before the state does.

The principle of subsidiarity in a political and governmental context aims to empower individual citizens and thus enhance democracy[6] through encouraging decision-making and governance at a local or community level, or in other words, closer to the source of the issue or dispute. Subsidiarity discourages centralisation unless there is 'justification of central involvement in affairs that cannot adequately be handled at the local level.'[7] Thus, as noted by Bridge, subsidiarity in a government context requires that 'decisions, whether legislative or administrative acts, should be taken at the lowest practicable political level, that is as close as possible to those who are to be affected by them.'[8] Subsidiarity, in this manner, is a characteristic of federalism because it provides for powers to be allocated where they are best exercised, and as a default, to be exercised at a lower level wherever possible. This is also noted by Bridge who states:

> Subsidiarity therefore presupposes an allocation of decision making powers within the state or other polity according to certain criteria designed to ensure that each decision is taken at the appropriate political level. The allocation of a particular decision making power to a higher or to the highest political level rather than to a lower or to the lowest political level might be made, for example, on such grounds as subject matter or effectiveness or efficiency or necessity or a combination of such grounds.[9]

---

[3] Halberstam (2009, p. 34).

[4] Hunnings (1998, s 12.0120A) cited in Montgomery (2002, p. 48).

[5] Montgomery (2002, p. 48).

[6] Longo (1999, p. 225).

[7] Halberstam, above n 3, p. 35.

[8] Bridge (1996, p. 613) cited in Bridge (1999, pp. 50–51).

[9] Ibid.

Consequently, as well as being a decentralising principle, subsidiarity allows for the centralisation of areas that are best regulated at a central level. This was something that the framers of the Australian federal system had regard to, by allocating areas pertaining to the nation as a whole, (for example, defence, external affairs, currency) or matters with an interstate, that is state border crossing element, (such as interstate or overseas trade and commerce) to the federal (that is, central) government. Although the framers did consider that some areas were best regulated at a central level, they considered that most powers should be decentralised by remaining with the states. The allocation of these powers in the *Constitution* in this manner is discussed in further detail below.

The principle of subsidiarity is now a key principle in European Union law, being incorporated into art 5(3) of the *Treaty on European Union* ('*TEU*').[10] In a similar manner to the Australian colonies prior to federation on 1 January 1901, several of the 28 Member States (as separate and independent countries) were concerned about compromising their national autonomy if they joined the European Union.[11] These concerns culminated in the inclusion of the principle of subsidiarity in art 5(3) of the *TEU*, which provides that if a matter does not fall within the exclusive competence of the Community and can be better resolved by the individual member states, the central authority (Community) should *not* intervene, so that these matters can be resolved at a member state level.[12] Again, like federalism, subsidiarity in a European Union context favours the decentralisation of power, and the exercise of power at the most appropriate level. The appropriate level for the exercise of power could very well be central, but most often it should be exercised at a regional, decentralised level.

10.3 Subsidiarity in the Australian Constitution

Although it can be said that 'subsidiarity' is a key characteristic and objective of an authentic federal system of government, the framers would not have been expressly aware of the principle of 'subsidiarity', a term coined in the twentieth century, well after the formation of the *Constitution*. However, they certainly embraced the principle's sentiment in the Australian *Constitution* under which the Australian colonies agreed to unite as states and to create a second tier of government at a

[10] *Treaty on European Union*, opened for signature 7 February 1992, [2009] OJ C 115/13 (entered into force 1 November 1993) ('*TEU*'). See also, *Protocol (No 2) on the Application of the Principles of Subsidiarity and Proportionality* [2010] OJ C 83/206 ('*Protocol*').

[11] Vause (1995, pp. 64–65).

[12] In the European Union the principle of subsidiarity has been effective as a procedural safeguard in the legislative process to guard against centralisation. However, at a judicial level, the principle has been disregarded by the European Court of Justice (ECJ), as evidenced by no directives or regulations being annulled on the basis of it. This is because the ECJ has regarded the principle as a political judgment, best left to the European Parliament and Council. These issues are discussed in more detail by Moens and Trone in Chap. 9.

federal (central) level. The federal nature of the *Constitution*, and the resultant characteristic of subsidiarity, is apparent from an examination of the structure and provisions of the *Constitution* itself. The sentiment of subsidiarity is also strong in the records of the Australian Constitutional Conventions at which the draft of the new *Constitution* was discussed and debated.[13] This was observed by Kirby J, who noted the importance of regional governments, whose consent was required to achieve federation, in his dissenting judgment in *New South Wales v Commonwealth of Australia* ('*Work Choices*'):

> It is impossible to ignore the place envisaged for the States in the *Constitution*. Reference is made to that role throughout the constitutional document. It is the people of the several states who 'agreed to unite in one indissoluble Federal Commonwealth'. Both in the covering clauses and in the text of the *Constitution* itself, the federal character of the polity thereby created is announced, and provided for, in great detail.[14]

The importance of regional governance is evident from the commentary from the Sydney session of the Australasian Federal Convention of 1891. It reveals the sentiment on the part of the founders that formulating a new *Constitution* should not result in centralisation, except where it was necessary to allocate powers at a federal level. Delegates were concerned with power being retained at a local level (that is, at a state level) as much as possible. For example, Sir Henry Parkes[15] stated:

> I think it is in the highest degree desirable that we should satisfy the mind of each of the colonies that we have no intention to cripple their powers, to invade their rights, to diminish their authority, except so far as is absolutely necessary in view of the great end to be accomplished, which, in point of fact, will not be material as diminishing the powers and privileges and rights of the existing colonies. It is therefore proposed by this first condition of mine to satisfy them that neither their territorial rights nor their powers of legislation for

---

[13] These Conventions were: The Australasian Federation Conference, held in Melbourne, from 6 February 1890 until 14 February 1890; The National Australasian Convention held in Sydney, from 2 March 1891 until 9 April 1891; The Australasian Federal Convention 1897/8. This conference was held in several sessions. The First Session was in Adelaide from 22 March 1897 until 23 April 1897. On 2 September 1897, the delegates resumed the Convention in Sydney. The Sydney session was adjourned on 24 September. The next and final session of the Convention was scheduled for 20 January 1898 in Melbourne, and went until 17 March 1898. For a discussion of the Convention Debates, see generally Quick and Garran (1901, 2002 ed) and La Nauze (1972).

[14] *New South Wales v Commonwealth of Australia* (2006) 229 CLR 1 ('*Work Choices*'), 226.

[15] Sir Henry Parkes (1815–1896) was a parliamentarian and Premier of New South Wales and has been described as the 'father of the Australian federation'. It was Parkes' idea that the colonies should unite under a Federal Council. He argued for its establishment at intercolonial conferences in 1880 and 1891, before abandoning the idea in favour of a more authentic federation of the Australian states. He was instrumental in bringing about the first Constitutional Conference in Melbourne in 1890, and the 1891 Federal Convention in Sydney and was a major participant, proposing key resolutions at both: See Williams (2003, pp. 9–17). See also La Nauze, above n 13, pp. 92–93.

> the well being of their own country will be interfered with in any way that can impair the security of those rights, and the efficiency of their legislative powers.[16]

These views were reiterated by Sir Thomas Playford (of South Australia) who said, 'we should most strictly define and limit the powers of the central government, and leave all other powers not so defined to the local legislatures.'[17] He continued on to say that it was necessary to 'lay down all such powers as are necessary for the proper conduct of the federal government, and not interfere with the slightest degree with any other power of the local legislatures.'[18] Further, Alfred Deakin[19] (of Victoria) added to Parkes' comments later in the debate by clarifying the limitation of the Federal Parliament's legislative powers to specific subjects:

> It is not a question of establishing a federal legislature, which is to have unlimited authority. The federal government is to have a strictly limited power; it is not to range at will over the whole field of legislation; it is not to legislate for all conceivable circumstances of national life. On the contrary, its legislation is to be strictly limited to certain definite subjects. The states are to retain almost all their present powers, and should be quite able to protect their own rights.[20]

When one moves from the Constitutional Convention Debates, to the resultant Constitutional document, its federal nature, and the associated characteristic of subsidiarity, is evident throughout. Firstly, the preamble announces that the *states* have agreed to federate, and have agreed to the creation of the new Commonwealth government:

> Whereas the *people of New South Wales, Victoria, South Australia, Queensland; and Tasmania*, humbly relying on the blessing of Almighty God, have *agreed to unite in one indissoluble Federal Commonwealth* under the Crown of the United Kingdom of Great Britain and Ireland, and *under the Constitution* hereby established...[21]

The assent of the states to achieve federation, and their intent not to devolve powers except when absolutely necessary, is further evident from an examination of Chapter V of the *Constitution*, 'The States'. It commences with s 106, which

---

[16] *Official Record of the Debates of the Australasian Federal Convention*, Sydney, 4 March 1891, p. 24 (Sir Henry Parkes).

[17] *Official Record of the Debates of the Australasian Federal Convention*, Sydney, 13 March 1891, p. 328 (Sir Thomas Playford).

[18] Ibid.

[19] Alfred Deakin (1856–1919) is also one of Australia's best known founding fathers. Deakin was a lawyer who also served as a member of the Victorian Parliament. He participated in all of the Constitutional Conventions, including serving on the drafting committees at both the 1891 and 1897/98 Conventions. He was the youngest delegate at the 1891 Federal Convention in Sydney. After federation he served in the federal Parliament as Australia's first Attorney-General. See generally, Norris (1981).

[20] *Official Record of the Debates of the Australasian Federal Convention*, Sydney, 5 March 1891, pp. 79–80 (Alfred Deakin).

[21] *Constitution*, Preamble. Emphasis added. Western Australia is absent because it delayed in passing an enabling Act and Referendum to approve the final draft of the Constitution Bill. However, it did so prior to Proclamation of the new Commonwealth by the Queen. Hence, Western Australia was able to be admitted as an original State of the new Federation.

provides that after federation, state constitutions will continue to have force. Section 107 states that the powers of state Parliaments shall remain, except for those that have been reallocated to the Commonwealth Parliament by the *Constitution* on federation. Section 108 in ch V further provides that state laws existing at the time of federation will continue to have force after federation, and can even be amended or repealed by a state, if they have not been made exclusive to the Commonwealth, and if the Commonwealth has not enacted the same law. It is evident from these provisions that great care was taken by the framers to make interference with state constitutions, state law-making powers, and state executive powers as minimal as possible. Section 109 provides a practical way of resolving inconsistency between a Commonwealth and state law, whereby the Commonwealth law will prevail to the extent of the inconsistency, thus contemplating the fact that broad state powers, many of which are concurrent, may result in a conflict of laws. In the words of Sawer, 'The *Constitution* was intended to preserve a wide area of governmental authority for the States …'[22]

As noted above, the framers of the *Constitution* specifically listed, and thereby limited, the powers of the Federal Parliament in s 51 which lists matters with respect to which the Federal Parliament can legislate. If it legislates on any matter not listed in s 51 or otherwise authorised by the *Constitution*, the Federal Parliament will exceed its legislative, powers and the resultant legislation will be unconstitutional. By listing, and thereby limiting, the Federal Parliament's legislative powers, the framers left the power to legislate on all other topics to the states, thus giving the states a far greater scope of legislative power, which Dicey referred to as 'indefinite'.[23] This limitation of powers was certainly part of the framers anti-centralist philosophy, and was intended to guard against centralisation.

In fact, upon reviewing the matters listed in s 51, it is evident that many concern subjects that pertain to, or affect, the nation as a whole, and are therefore best left to the Federal Parliament as a matter of consistency and practicality. In the words of Quick and Garran, these powers 'are of such a character that they could only be vested in and effectually exercised by the Federal Parliament'.[24] Subsidiarity's sentiment that powers should be carried out by the appropriate level of government was expressed by Alfred Deakin, during the *Australasian Federal Convention* held in Sydney in 1891. Deakin, in the quotation below, emphasised that 'national issues' should be regulated by the federal government, but that the balance should be left to the states:

> The argument which I have endeavoured to maintain from the beginning of this debate has been that, while there are certain state rights to be guarded, most of those rights, if not all of them, can be guarded by the division of powers between the central government and the local governments. The states will retain full powers over the greater part of the domain in which they at present enjoy those powers, and will retain them intact for all time. But in national issues, on the subject of defence, as people who desire to have their shores

[22] Sawer (1975, p. 87).

[23] Dicey (1926, p. 530).

[24] Quick and Garran, above n 13, p. 934.

> defended, and to see their resources developed by means of a customs tariff and a customs union—on these questions there are no longer state rights and state interests to be guarded in the constitution, but the people's interests are one, and they call upon us to deal with them as one.[25]

The enumerated subjects in the final draft of the *Constitution*, some of which were noted earlier in this chapter, include trade and commerce with other countries,[26] borrowing money on the public credit of the Commonwealth,[27] defence,[28] currency,[29] immigration and emigration[30] and external affairs,[31] to name a few. The listing, and therefore limiting, of the Federal Parliament's legislative powers is indicative of the framers' intention that the bulk of legislative power would remain with the states after federation. Some of these enumerated powers appear quite broad in scope, for example, 'external affairs' in s 51(xxix). However, some powers are expressly limited to ensure that the states retain sovereignty over their internal affairs. For example, the trade and commerce power in s 51(i) contains 'words of limitation', whereby the Commonwealth Parliament can only legislate about trade and commerce, 'with other countries, and among the States'. This means that the Federal Parliament cannot legislate with respect to a state's internal trade and commerce (that is, intra-state trade and commerce).[32] Further examples include, the taxation power in s 51(ii) with words of limitation 'so as not to discriminate between states or parts of states'; 'Banking, other than State Banking' in s 51(xiii); 'Insurance, other than State insurance' in s 51(xiv); and 'Conciliation and arbitration for the prevention and settlement of industrial disputes extending beyond the limits of any one State' in s 51(xxxv). Such words of limitation indicate the framers' intention to protect the sovereignty of the states from the interference of the Federal Parliament in their internal operations, and infer the sentiment that local issues are best resolved locally.

The legislative powers that the framers allocated to the Federal Parliament fall into one of two categories: exclusive and concurrent. As Quick and Garran noted, 13 of the 39 powers in s 51 were specifically created by the *Constitution* and were exclusively vested in the Federal Parliament.[33] Section 52 also gives exclusive powers to the Federal Parliament. Hence, the *Constitution* specifically provides that the states cannot legislate on these topics from the time of federation. The remaining powers,

---

[25] *Official Record of the Debates of the Australasian Federal Convention*, Sydney, 16 March 1891, 383 (Alfred Deakin).

[26] *Constitution* s 51(i).

[27] *Constitution* s 51(iv).

[28] *Constitution* s 51(vi).

[29] *Constitution* s 51(xii).

[30] *Constitution* s 51(xxvii).

[31] *Constitution* s 51(xxix).

[32] Quick and Garran, above n 13.

[33] Originally, the Federal Parliament could legislate with respect to 39 matters. This was increased to 40 in 1946 with the insertion of s 51(xxiiiA) which allowed the Federal Parliament to legislate with respect to certain social security allowances such as unemployment, pharmaceutical and medical benefits. See Quick and Garran, above n 13, p. 933.

which, prior to federation were in the domain of the state Parliaments, were 'concurrent' as at the time of federation. In other words, state legislation on these matters would continue to be valid until the Federal Parliament enacted inconsistent legislation which would trigger the operation of s 109.[34] The operation of exclusive powers, and concurrent powers that became exclusive to the Federal Parliament by virtue of the enactment of inconsistent legislation, left 'residuary legislative powers' to the states.[35] These residuary state powers are described by Quick and Garran as 'plenary'[36] and are only subject to limited restrictions.[37] The sentiment that powers are reposed by the level of government that can best exercise them is evident from the creation in the *Constitution* of two levels of government upon federation, where some areas of power originally exercised by the states were reallocated to the Commonwealth, and whereby new powers in favour of the Commonwealth were created. The significantly larger volume of legislative power left to the states evidences a de-centralist philosophy that supports regional governance in most circumstances, except where it is more appropriately carried out at a central level.

As part of their decentralist philosophy, the framers made specific provision for state representation in the Federal Parliament by creating the Senate as a 'States House' designed to safeguard against the passing of laws that were contrary to their interests. Section 7 provides that 'The Senate shall be composed of Senators for each State, directly chosen by the people of the State...' The Senate was not only designed to ensure adequate representation for the people of each state in the Federal Parliament, and to ensure the approval of central legislation by representatives of the people of each state, but was also seen as an essential requirement for the Australian federal system to function effectively in order to prevent encroachment by the Commonwealth on the powers of the states. The Senate's central role in protecting and representing state interests was described by Quick and Garran as follows:

> The Senate is one of the most conspicuous, and unquestionably the most important, of all the federal features of the *Constitution*. ... It is the chamber in which the States, considered

[34] Quick and Garran, above n 13, p. 933.

[35] Quick and Garran, above n 13, p. 935.

[36] *Union Steamship Co of Australia Pty Ltd v King* (1988) 166 CLR 1.

[37] Quick and Garran list examples from powers requiring consent by the Federal Parliament before a State may exercise that power. These include: s 91, which provides that a State may only grant an aid or bounty on the production or export of goods with the consent of Federal Parliament. Another example can be found in s 114, which provides that a State cannot raise or maintain naval or military forces, or tax property of the Commonwealth, without the consent of the Federal Parliament. See Quick and Garran, above n 13, p. 936.

Quick and Garran also note examples of where the *Constitution* restricts State powers. These include: s 51(xxxii), which, in providing that the Parliament can legislate with respect to the control of railways with respect to transport for the naval or military purposes of the Commonwealth, restricts State control of railways to that extent. Similarly, s 98 allows the Federal Parliament to make laws about State railways in connection with the trade and commerce power; s 90 restricts the power of the States with respect to taxation by making the ability to levy duties of customs and excise exclusive to the Federal Parliament; and s 92 restricts the States and Commonwealth from restricting freedom of interstate trade and movement. Quick and Garran, above n 13, p. 936.

> as separate entities, and corporate parts of the Commonwealth, are represented. They are so represented for the purpose of enabling them to maintain and protect their constitutional rights against attempted invasions, and to give them every facility for the advocacy of their peculiar and special interests, as well as for the ventilation and consideration of their grievances.[38]

Unfortunately, this sentiment has become corrupted by party politics with Senators most often voting in accordance with party policy, rather than in the interests of their States.[39] However, it is argued that the actuality of the Senate becoming less of a 'States House' in modern politics does not detract from the intention of the framers, and from the provision in the *Constitution* that the Senate should be fundamental in ensuring State approval to federal legislation and the protection of State interests against encroachment by the central government.

Further evidence of subsidiarity in the *Constitution* can be seen by the establishment of the High Court of Australia by s 71. The High Court is empowered to invalidate any law that transgresses the authority conferred on both the federal and state Parliaments by the *Constitution*. Quick and Garran describe the role of the High Court as the 'guardian' of State and Federal Constitutions[40] and of the balance of power between them. The fundamental role of the High Court in maintaining this Commonwealth-State balance of power in the Australian federation is explained by Craven:

> The positive and fundamental role of the High Court was to protect federalism. In this connection, it goes without saying that the *Constitution* itself breathes federalism, not merely implicitly, but expressly in its very terms. If one had to pick the 'great theme' of the *Constitution*, it could only be federalism, upon the broad stage of which all other concepts play their crucial but undeniably supporting roles. The critical function of the Court in relation to federalism was to maintain the Commonwealth and the States within their respective spheres, and in particular to ensure that the Commonwealth kept within the ambit of its powers and did not invade the realms of the States.[41]

The framers of the *Constitution*, by adopting a federal system of government intended to protect state power and autonomy against centralisation, necessarily embodied the principle of subsidiarity firmly in it. Central to both theories (federalism and subsidiarity) is the principle of maintaining 'states' rights' and reserving state power and autonomy over local issues wherever possible. The *Constitution* that resulted from the Constitutional Convention Debates of the 1890s limits central powers; provides for the continued existence of the states, their Constitutions and powers; and consequently, mandates a federal balance between the central and state governments. Thus subsidiarity, although not expressly mentioned in the *Constitution*, can certainly be said to be a central characteristic of it.

---

[38] Quick and Garran, above n 13, p. 414.

[39] See Sawer (1967, p. 150).

[40] Quick and Garran, above n 13, p. 725.

[41] Craven (1999, p. 221).

10.4 How Has Subsidiarity in the Australian Federation Been Disregarded?

Despite the federal origins and intentions of the framers of the *Constitution*, the Australian federal landscape has become increasingly centralised. The federal balance in Australia has been destabilised by the High Court of Australia's interpretation of the *Constitution* which has at first gradually, and in recent years exponentially, resulted in the centralisation of power that should belong to the states. Put simply, subsidiarity has been overlooked in the Australian federal system which can no longer be seen as an authentic federation.

The early High Court of Australia, led by Chief Justice Sir Samuel Griffith,[42] *did* seek to fulfill its responsibility as the protector of federalism and the states. The philosophy of the early High Court could be described as one that was mindful and respectful of subsidiarity. This is evident from decisions regarding the extent and delineation of Commonwealth and state powers after federation. As well as Griffith CJ, the other original High Court Justices (Barton and O'Connor JJ) were also involved in the drafting of the *Constitution*, and like Griffith, knew the federalist intentions behind its drafting.[43] Their interpretation of the *Constitution* sought to preserve the federal balance of power between the Commonwealth and the states as the democratically elected delegates had understood it to be when they debated the proposed provisions of the *Constitution*.[44] Their approach to constitutional interpretation became known as 'originalism' or 'intentionalism' and involved the application of two interpretive doctrines, premised upon the federal nature of the *Constitution*, namely, the state reserved powers doctrine and the doctrine of implied immunity of instrumentalities.

---

[42] Sir Samuel Griffith (1845–1920) was the first Chief Justice of the High Court of Australia. He was sworn in on 6 October 1903: see Sawer, above n 39, p. 21. Griffith had been the Premier of Queensland and had drafted the *Federal Council of Australasia Act 1885* enacted by the British Parliament to establish the Federal Council of Australasia: For background to The Federal Council of Australasia, see Quick and Garran, above n 13, pp. 109–115. Griffith also represented Queensland at the Australasian Federation Conference in 1890 and was also a delegate at the National Australasian Convention at Sydney in 1891 where he was Vice-President and also part of the drafting Committee which produced the first draft *Constitution*. See generally Quick and Garran, above n 13.

[43] Edmund Barton (1849–1920) is most famous for being Australia's first Prime Minister. When he was a New South Wales Member of Parliament, was a delegate at the National Australasian Convention in Sydney in 1891, where, with Sir Samuel Griffith, he was part of the drafting sub-Committee which formulated a first draft of the *Constitution*. Barton was also a delegate at the 1897/8 Australasian Federal Convention where he chaired the drafting Committee (of which O'Connor was also a member). Richard Edward O'Connor (1851–1912) had attended the Australasian Federal Convention of 1897/8 as a representative of New South Wales. He was a Member of the Legislative Council for 13 years. Also, O'Connor was part of Barton's first Ministry. He was one of the first senators representing New South Wales in the first Senate and was also appointed as Vice-President of the Executive Council: see generally Turner (1911).

[44] For a discussion of the founders' intentions with respect to the High Court see Craven (1995, p. 65).

The 'immunity of instrumentalities doctrine', also known as the 'implied intergovernmental immunities doctrine', was an implication developed and applied by the early High Court that was based on the federal nature of the *Constitution*. It recognised that the Commonwealth and state governments were independent entities, and consequently, could not legislate so as to interfere with the operation of each other's affairs. This meant that both the Commonwealth and states were immune from the operation of each other's legislation if that legislation impinged on the exercise of their legislative or executive powers.[45]

The High Court also implied the 'reserved powers doctrine' or 'reserved state powers doctrine', once again on the basis of the federal nature of the *Constitution*. It provided that the legislative powers of the Commonwealth prescribed by the *Constitution* should be read narrowly so as not to detract from the power of the states 'reserved' by s 107 of the *Constitution*.[46] Section 107 provides that the states will retain their powers after federation, except to the extent that they had been given exclusively to the Commonwealth, or otherwise withdrawn from the states, by the new *Constitution*.

The turning point towards centralisation was the decision in *Amalgamated Society of Engineers v Adelaide Steamship Co Ltd* ('*Engineers*')[47] in which the High Court irreparably altered the balance of power between the Commonwealth and the states by interpreting the *Constitution* literally, or in other words, as a statute of the British Parliament. In doing so, they rejected any implications based on historical context or the federal nature and structure of the *Constitution*, thus discarding the implied intergovernmental immunities and reserved powers doctrines. The result of *Engineers* was a series of subsequent High Court decisions in which Commonwealth powers continued to be interpreted expansively.[48] In the words of Geoffrey de Q Walker, the *Engineers* decision 'switched the entire enterprise of Australian federalism onto a diverging track that carried it to destinations far removed from those intended by the generation that had brought the federation into being.'[49]

The aftermath of *Engineers* saw the gradual centralisation of many of the states' financial powers, including income tax. Until World War II, Australians paid income tax to their state governments, who distributed the proceeds between both the state and the Commonwealth. However, in 1942 the Commonwealth passed several pieces of legislation, under the guise of being for defence purposes, which centralised the

---

[45] The first case to recognise Commonwealth immunity from state legislation was *D'Emden v Pedder* (1904) 1 CLR 91 and the first case to recognise state immunity from Commonwealth legislation was *Federated Amalgamated Government Railway & Tramway Service Association v New South Wales Railway Traffic Employees Association* (1906) 4 CLR 488 ('*Railway Servants*' case').

[46] See, for example, *Peterswald v Bartley* (1904) 1 CLR 497; *R and the Minister of State for the Commonwealth Administering the Customs v Barger; The Commonwealth and AW Smart, Collector of Customs v McKay* (1908) 6 CLR 41 ('*R v Barger*'); and *Huddart, Parker & Co v Moorehead* (1909) 8 CLR 330.

[47] *Amalgamated Society of Engineers v Adelaide Steamship Co Ltd* (1920) 28 CLR 129 ('*Engineers*').

[48] For example, the corporations power in *Constitution* s 51(xx).

[49] de Q Walker (2002, p. 678).

collection and distribution of income tax.[50] The centralisation of income tax withstood two High Court challenges in the *First* and *Second Uniform Tax* cases,[51] thus cementing the centralisation of income tax and ensuring the states' reliance on monetary grants from the Commonwealth. These include specific purpose grants[52] from the Commonwealth to the states where the states may accept money from the Commonwealth, subject to conditions which can impact on areas outside the normal scope of Commonwealth legislative powers, thus giving the Commonwealth considerable leverage over state policy.

A further example of the states' loss of financial autonomy occurred after the decision in *Ha v New South Wales*,[53] in which the High Court affirmed a broad interpretation of excise duties resulting in a loss of $5 billion per annum to the states because s 90 of the *Constitution* provides that only the Commonwealth can levy duties of excise. As Twomey and Withers have noted, although the states undertake 40 % of Australia's public spending, the result of *Ha* was that they are only able to raise 19 % of their own revenue, making them increasingly reliant on the Commonwealth government.[54]

The *Engineers* decision also resulted in state legislative powers being encroached upon by the Commonwealth, by acting as a precedent for expansive interpretations of powers such as the external affairs power[55] and the corporations power. For example, in the *Work Choices* decision, a majority of High Court Justices stated, using the language of the majority in *Engineers*, that it was necessary to 'construe the constitutional text … with all the generality which the words used admit'.[56] Further, following *Engineers*, these Justices also indicated their support for the supremacy of Parliament, giving Parliament the latitude to determine the limits of their own power: 'if a sufficient connection with a head of power does exist, the justice and wisdom of the law, and the degree to which the means it adopts are necessary or desirable, are matters of legislative choice'.[57] The sum of this reasoning was that the majority Justices would not limit the scope of the provision on the basis that a broad construction would 'distort the federal balance.'[58]

---

[50] *Income Tax Act 1942* (Cth), *States Grants (Income Tax Reimbursement) Act 1942* (Cth), *Income Tax (War-time Arrangements) Act 1942* (Cth) and the *Income Tax Assessment Act 1942* (Cth). For a discussion of the centralisation of income tax in the Australian Federation, see Blackshield and Williams (2006, pp. 1122–1123).

[51] *South Australia v Commonwealth* (1942) 65 CLR 373 ('*First Uniform Tax* case') and *Victoria v Commonwealth* (1957) 99 CLR 575.

[52] *Constitution* s 96.

[53] *Ha v New South Wales* (1997) 189 CLR 465 ('*Ha*').

[54] Twomey and Withers (2007, p. 36).

[55] *Constitution* s 51(xxix). For a discussion of the expansion of the external affairs power, see Zimmermann and Finlay (2010, pp. 17–19).

[56] *Work Choices* (2006) 229 CLR 1, 103.

[57] *Work Choices* (2006) 229 CLR 1, 104.

[58] *Work Choices* (2006) 229 CLR 1, 116.

This centralist interpretation by the High Court has, as a consequence of decisions such as *Engineers*, *Ha* and *Work Choices*, become cemented in Australian constitutional legal reasoning, with the likely result that future High Court challenges by the states to expansive legislative attempts by the federal Parliament will fail. Thus, it seems that subsidiarity as a characteristic of Australian federalism no longer exists, and is unlikely to be revived by the High Court.

10.5 Does Subsidiarity in the Australian Federation Matter?

It should be evident from the discussion above, that this chapter is premised upon the assumption that a decentralised, states-centred federal system of government is the best political structure for Australia, and more faithful to the structure and nature of Australia's federal system. It is contended that the advantages of federalism, in which subsidiarity is fundamental, far outweigh its disadvantages. The prolific commentary on the advantages and disadvantages of a federal system is too extensive to thoroughly traverse in this chapter. Instead, this section will briefly highlight the strengths and advantages of a decentralised federal system for Australia, where the states are responsible for regulating local issues and have sufficient financial autonomy to do so, and where the federal government exercises restraint in only regulating matters that affect the nation as a whole.

Geographically, Australia is a vast and isolated nation. It is significantly larger than, for example, the German federation which is a more homogeneous society than Australia. The Australian states have different climates, different natural resources and industries, and diverse multicultural and also indigenous populations. In short, there is environmental, economic and social diversity between the Australian states. Federalism is the best type of governance to deal with Australia's geographic remoteness and diversity because it allows local issues to be dealt with locally and more effectively because problems are able to be addressed and resolved closest to their source and impact.[59] A 'one size fits all' approach would be unable to address adequately the diversity that is Australia, nor respond quickly enough to local issues and local needs which would be subsumed as less important to national concerns.

Governance at a state level allows those who are living in that state and who are affected by, or at least close to, local issues to address them directly and more effectively as they are in a more informed position to be able to do so.[60] This local

[59] See, for example, Cramp (1913, p. 111). Cramp stated that in 'large areas' federalism is preferable because 'it is the best means of developing a new and extensive country with some interest in common with all its parts, yet with local conditions so diverse as to necessitate separate treatment'.

[60] This advantage was noted by Cramp, above n 59, p. 112 who stated that federalism allows regional governments to specifically address local issues, so citizens are represented at both a local and a central level. This representation leads to a better representation and greater involvement of the citizen in political issues.

knowledge, as well as resulting in more informed and appropriate solutions, also enhances democracy because it allows more citizens to participate directly in governance. Citizen participation in dual levels of government also guards against the totalitarianism that can arise when power is concentrated at one level, in the hands of fewer people.[61] Voters have greater 'choice and diversity' by being able to vote differently at separate state and federal elections.[62]

Federalism also allows state governments to relieve some of the burden on the central government through the division of powers between them. This allows the central government to focus on 'national business' without getting distracted by many and varied regional issues.[63] In other words, dual governance ensures the freedom of the central government to govern on and address 'bigger picture' issues that pertain to the nation as a whole, such as relations with other nations and defence, rather than becoming ensconced in day-to-day details that are, for the reasons outlined above, best addressed at a local level.

One of the major advantages of a two tiered system is the checks and balances it provides,[64] thus enhancing governmental accountability. The states can question the actions of the central government, and vice versa. This accountability is further enhanced by different political parties being in power at the different levels of government, creating more debate, dialogue, discussion and co-operation.

The main criticism of federal systems is that their dual systems of government result in duplication and therefore, inefficiency.[65] However, this duplication and the side effect of inefficiency in fact underscores one of the major benefits of federalism, being the encouragement of dialogue between governments and thus accountability, which promotes democracy and responsible government.[66] It has also been argued that this duplication and inefficiency is most often caused by the Commonwealth itself when it interferes with areas of state responsibility. This has happened in the areas of education and health.[67] A further beneficial side effect of federalism is the requirement for co-operation between the levels of

---

[61] See, for example, Cramp, above n 59, pp. 111–112 who stated that federalism promotes 'internal peace and economic progress' by uniting otherwise separate states, and in doing so: 'It remedies the narrowness of outlook of provincialism, yet avoids the possibility of a despotic central government.'

[62] Twomey and Withers, above n 54, p. 9.

[63] Cramp, above n 59, pp. 112–113.

[64] Twomey and Withers, above n 54, p. 8.

[65] Dicey, above n 23, pp. 167–168. This argument was also raised by former Prime Minister Gough Whitlam, who also argued that Australia's federal system of government is inefficient: 'It is possible to advance historical or geographical reasons for having a federal system in Australia; but it is impossible to deny that Australians pay for it dearly in delays and duplication': Whitlam (1983, 28).

[66] See, for example Craven (2004, pp. 74–75). Craven stated that 'government is not all about economy and efficiency: democracy itself is slow and messy, but we have yet to abandon it in favour of a fast, logical dictatorship. In the same way, if we have a price for the diversity, democracy and independence of the states, we can file the bill under "value"'.

[67] Craven, ibid, pp. 74–75.

government, which can lead to greater innovation and reform and also more 'checks and balances' to proposed reforms.[68]

Federalism also encourages law reform by encouraging experimentation and innovation. This was noted by Cramp who stated that 'Federalism allows of experiments in legislation and administration which could not safely be made in a large unified country'.[69] This means that a state could introduce innovative legislation, which, if it failed, would not affect other states, or the country as a whole.[70] However, if it was successful, it could result in great benefits for other states and the nation as a whole. In this sense, federalism can be said to encourage competition between states to improve services, resources and to 'attract business and residents'.[71] Research also shows that countries with federal systems of government perform better economically than those with a 'unitary' government.[72]

In conclusion, it is argued that the many advantages of a federal system of government make it the most beneficial system of government for Australia, and that it is vital to retain federalism in its authentic, decentralised sense, instead of moving toward centralisation. Hence, it is argued that subsidiarity must be restored to Australia's compromised federal system of government to ensure that these benefits are retained.

10.6 Restoring Subsidiarity to Australian Federalism

In an Australian context, several reports on reforming Australian federalism have referred to the compatibility of subsidiarity and federalism, and more specifically, subsidiarity's potential to enhance federalism. For example, Twomey and Withers recommend a reconsideration of the distribution of Commonwealth–State powers in accordance with the principle of subsidiarity. In the following passage they argue that the allocation of federal legislative powers in the *Constitution* should be revised, applying the principle of subsidiarity:

> The most commonly used principle for making such an assessment in federations today is subsidiarity. Under this principle, functions should be undertaken by the States and Territories or their local governments, unless this is not practicable. Factors that will influence the allocation of a matter to the Commonwealth or the States include whether it is a matter of national interest, such as defence, or whether national standards are required as a measure of equity, such as social security support. Other important factors include whether significant spillovers into other jurisdictions are involved, whether significant economies of scale could be achieved and whether the harmonisation of policy is needed to increase

[68] Twomey and Withers, above n 54, p. 13.

[69] Cramp, above n 59, p. 113.

[70] Ibid.

[71] Twomey and Withers, above n 54, p. 12.

[72] Twomey and Withers, above n 54, pp. 15–16.

efficiency. These factors are the core rationale for central government functions and should guide the distribution of powers. They should be respected, but not exceeded.[73]

In addition, in the *Final Report to the Council for the Australian Federation*, subsidiarity is cited as one of 'the fundamental rationales of federalism' and 'a well documented driver of effective federations'.[74] The authors' comment on the effectiveness of subsidiarity in enhancing federalism, regional governance and representative democracy:

> The principle of subsidiarity is intrinsic to the efficient and effective allocation of responsibilities in a federal system. It is a means of ensuring that decision-making remains close to citizens and enables the system to be judged for whether it remains responsive to the needs of citizens. ... State and Territory governments, being closer to their communities, are best placed to represent those communities when engaging with the national level government and in consultations over national policy frameworks. The closer the proximity of government to the community, the more authentic the notion of representative democracy becomes.[75]

Further, Aroney notes that the reports from the Productivity Commission, New South Wales Government and Business Council of Australia have referred to subsidiarity as a potentially relevant principle that may be usefully applied to the reform of the Australian federal system.[76]

The following reforms inspired by the principle of subsidiarity are suggested as a starting point to restore the federal balance of power back to the states, and to guard against future federal encroachment on state legislative powers and financial independence. In making these suggestions, it is acknowledged that any constitutional reforms at a federal level in Australia are difficult to achieve because they can only be made following a referendum process, pursuant to s 128 of the *Constitution*. Any constitutional change must be initiated in the Federal Parliament[77] and the resultant legislation proposing the constitutional reform must be put to the Australian people at a referendum. History shows us that the Australian people have a tendency to vote 'no' to any constitutional reforms with only eight proposals out of 44 having been approved by the Australian people.[78] In addition, 23 of these 44 referenda proposals asked the Australian people to approve increases in federal powers. Only 2 out of these 23 were approved by the Australian people,[79] evidencing their reluctance to expand the powers of the federal government.

---

[73] Twomey and Withers, above n 54, p. 46.

[74] Wanna et al. (2009, p. 9).

[75] Ibid.

[76] These are: Productivity Commission (2005), Warren (2006), and Business Council of Australia (2006) cited in Aroney (2011, p. 31).

[77] For a discussion of the exclusion of the states from initiating the referenda process, see Murray (2012).

[78] Moens and Trone (2007, p. 448).

[79] *Parliamentary Handbook of the Commonwealth of Australia (42nd Parliament)* cited in Zimmermann and Finlay, above n 55, pp. 55–56. Zimmermann and Finlay also argue in favour of state initiated referenda as a means of decreasing federal legislative powers (pp. 56–57).

Given that the High Court has been largely responsible for the demise of the Australian federal system through its centralist interpretation in the *Constitution*, as a starting point, it is recommended that an express statement should be inserted into the constitution to direct that it should be interpreted in the light of the federal intentions of the framers. It should include a clarification that Federal powers should be interpreted narrowly and that the *Constitution* should generally be interpreted with a view to maintaining the federal balance and without detracting from the constitutional powers of the states. With respect to the High Court, greater state involvement in the selection of new High Court Justices may seek to remind High Court Justices of the importance of the federal balance in Australia's constitutional system over any allegiance to the central government which is currently responsible for their appointment. For example, Australia could adopt the method of appointing High Court Justices suggested by Moens, where the states as well as the Commonwealth can nominate candidates, with the final appointee having to be approved by at least three state governments.[80]

In order to provide redress to the loss of state legislative and financial powers, the Commonwealth should refer some financial powers, such as the ability to levy income tax and the ability to levy duties of excise, back to the states. As well as an express statement being inserted into the Constitution to confirm that it should be interpreted as a federalist document, further safeguards also need to be implemented to guard against future expansive legislative attempts by the federal Parliament. These could include the insertion of additional words of limitation in s 51 of the Constitution wherever the legislative powers of the Federal Parliament are expressed broadly and have been interpreted expansively by the High Court. For example, the external affairs power is one of the broadest powers of the Federal Parliament, and is simply stated in the Constitution as 'external affairs' without further words of clarification or limitation. Also, reforms could be made to the Senate to achieve its intended role as a States' House. These could include Senators being chosen from the state executive governments, thus allowing the states a more direct representation in the Federal Parliament.

In addition, increased scrutiny of proposed legislation that may impact on federal balance would also help to guard against central encroachment without requiring constitutional amendment. Members of Parliament who introduce proposed legislation into Parliament could be required by Parliamentary Standing Orders to provide an explanatory statement addressing its federal implications in order to promote scrutiny and debate as to its impact on the federal balance. This proposed legislation could also be examined by Parliamentary Committees, established to scrutinise the impact of proposed legislation on the federal balance before enactment. In addition, the Council of Australian Governments (COAG) could be given an expanded role to

[80] I have omitted the territories because the focus of this paper is on state-Commonwealth relations. However, I acknowledge that the territories could also be included in this process.

guard against centralising legislative attempts by the Federal Parliament.[81] It could be re-established as an independent constitutional institution to comment on proposed legislation that may have a regional or federal impact, with its findings being tabled in the federal Parliament for further consideration and debate before enactment.

10.7 Conclusion

The framers of the Australian *Constitution* intended to create an authentic federation. This intent is evident throughout the Constitutional Convention Debates at which the Constitution was devised, and from the strongly federal nature of the *Constitution* that resulted – a *Constitution* which limits federal powers, preserves state powers and state constitutions, and ensures the continued existence of the states after federation.

However, despite these intentions, the federation that the framers created has been gradually undermined through expansive legislative attempts by the federal Parliament which have been upheld by the High Court of Australia since the seminal *Engineers* decision in 1920. *Engineers* was a turning point in Australian constitutional history because it provided a convenient precedent to justify the subsequent centralisation of legislative powers (such as workplace relations through an expansive interpretation of the corporations power in *Work Choices*) and financial powers (such as income tax in the *First* and *Second Uniform Tax* cases, and through the widening definition of 'excise' duties, culminating in the decision in *Ha*) to the detriment of the states.

The application of subsidiarity could restore a proper balance between the State and federal governments in Australia. It offers inspiration from which the authenticity of Australian federalism can be restored and safeguarded against future centralisation. Subsidiarity guards against centralisation by providing that governance should be undertaken at a local or community level, as opposed to a central level, wherever possible. Thus, the common ground between federalism and subsidiarity, in both a practical and theoretical sense, could serve as the basis for reforms to the Australian federal system, and indeed, other federations that have become centralised.

[81] COAG was established in 1992 by agreement of its members, who consist of the Prime Minister, state Premiers, Chief Ministers of the Territories and the President of the Australian Local Government Association. Its role is to promote cooperative federalism through the discussion and implementation of policy issues requiring intergovernmental cooperation, which often culminates in intergovernmental agreements.: Council of Australian Governments, *About COAG* (18 February 2010) http://www.coag.gov.au/about_coag/index.cfm. See generally, Gallop (2012).

References

Aroney, Nicholas. 2009. *The constitution of a federal commonwealth: The making and meaning of the Australian constitution*. Cambridge: Cambridge University Press.

Aroney, Nicholas. 2011. Reflections on subsidiarity: European lessons for Australia's federal balance? *Federal Law Review* 39: 31.

Blackshield, Tony, and George Williams. 2006. *Australian constitutional law and theory: Commentary and materials*, 4th ed. Sydney: Federation Press.

Bridge, John W. 1996. Subsidiarity as a principle of constitutional law. In *XIV International Congress of Comparative Law, Athens 1994, general reports*, ed. K.D. Kerameus, 613. Athens: Sakkoulas.

Bridge, John W. 1999. Constitutions, powers and the doctrine of subsidiarity. *The Bracton Law Journal* 31: 49–57.

Business Council of Australia. 2006. *Reshaping Australia's federation – A new contract for federal–state relations*. Melbourne: Business Council of Australia.

Cramp, K.R. 1913. *State and federal constitutions of Australia*. Sydney: Angus and Robertson.

Craven, Greg. 1995. *The High Court and the states*. Paper presented at the sixth conference of The Samuel Griffith Society, Townhouse Hotel, Carlton, 17–19 November 1995.

Craven, Greg. 1999. The High Court: A study in the abuse of power. *University of New South Wales Law Journal* 22(1): 216–242.

Craven, Greg. 2004. *Conversations with the constitution*. Sydney: University of New South Wales Press.

de Q Walker, Geoffrey. 2002. The seven pillars of centralism: Federalism and the Engineers' case. *The Australian Law Journal* 76: 678–715.

Dicey, A.V. 1926. *Introduction to the study of the law of the constitution*, 8th ed. London: MacMillan and Co.

Elazar, Daniel J. 1991. *Exploring federalism*. Tuscaloosa: The University of Alabama Press.

Gallop, Geoff. 2012. The COAG Reform Council: A view from the inside. In *Tomorrow's federation: Reforming Australian government*, ed. Paul Kildea, Andrew Lynch, and George Williams, 43–52. Annandale: Federation Press.

Halberstam, Daniel. 2009. Federal powers and the principle of subsidiarity. In *Global perspectives on constitutional law*, ed. Vikram David Amar and Mark V. Tushnet, 34–47. New York: Oxford University Press.

Hunnings (ed.). 1998. *Encyclopaedia of European law*. London: Sweet & Maxwell.

Irving, Helen (ed.). 1999. *The centenary companion to Australian federation*. Melbourne: Cambridge University Press.

La Nauze, J.A. 1972. *The making of the Australian constitution*. Melbourne: Melbourne University Press.

Lijphart, Arend. 1985. Non-majoritarian democracy: A comparison of federal and consociational themes. *Publius* 15(2): 3–15.

Longo, Michael. 1999. Subsidiarity and local environmental governance: A comparative and reform perspective. *University of Tasmania Law Review* 18: 225–246.

Moens, Gabriel A., and John Trone. 2007. *Lumb and Moens' the Constitution of the Commonwealth of Australia annotated*, 7th ed. Netherlands: LexisNexis Butterworths.

Montgomery, John Warwick. 2002. Subsidiarity as a jurisprudential and canonical theory. *Law and Justice: The Christian Law Review* 148: 46–53.

Murray, Sarah. 2012. State initiation of Section 128 Referenda. In *Tomorrow's federation: Reforming Australian government*, ed. Paul Kildea, Andrew Lynch, and George Williams, 332–349. Annandale: Federation Press.

Norris, R. 1981. Deakin, Alfred (1856–1919). *Australian dictionary of biography*, vol. 8 at http://adb.anu.edu.au/biography/deakin-alfred-5927

Productivity Commission. 2005. *Productive reform in a federal system*. Roundtable proceedings, Canberra, 27–28 October 2005.

Quick, John, and Robert Randolph Garran. 1901, 2002 ed. *The annotated constitution of the Australian Commonwealth*. Sydney: LexisNexis Butterworths.
Sawer, Geoffrey. 1967. *Australian federalism in the courts*. Melbourne: Melbourne University Press.
Sawer, Geoffrey. 1975. *The Australian Constitution*. Canberra: Australian Government Publishing Service.
Turner, Henry Giles. 1911. *The first decade of the Australian commonwealth: A chronicle of contemporary politics 1901–1910*. Melbourne: Heritage Publications.
Twomey, Anne, and Glen Withers. 2007. *Federalist paper 1 Australia's federal future: A report for the Council for the Australian Federation*. Melbourne: Council for the Australian Federation.
Vause, W. Gary. 1995. The subsidiarity principle in European Union law – American federalism compared. *Case Western Reserve Journal of International Law* 27: 61–82.
Wanna, John., et al. 2009. *Common cause: Strengthening Australia's Cooperative Federalism: Final report to the Council for the Australian Federation*. Adelaide: Council for the Australian Federation.
Warren, Neil. 2006. *Benchmarking Australia's intergovernmental fiscal arrangements: Final report*. Sydney: New South Wales Government.
Whitlam, E.G. 1983. The cost of federalism. In *Australian federalism: Future tense*, ed. Allan Patience and Jeffrey Scotts, 28. Melbourne: Oxford University Press.
Williams, John. 2003. The emergence of the commonwealth constitution. In *Australian constitutional landmarks*, ed. H.P. Lee and George Winterton, 1–33. Port Melbourne: Cambridge University Press.
Zimmermann, Augusto, and Lorraine Finlay. 2010. *Submission to the Select Committee on the Reform of the Australian Federation*, 19 August 2010.

Chapter 11
Subsidiarity and the Global Order

Andreas Follesdal

Abstract Subsidiarity has been proposed as an answer to the challenges of globalisation and global governance. This chapter addresses some of the strengths and weaknesses of such a principle of subsidiarity for questions of how to allocate and use authority at regional and global levels. The chapter criticises the 'state centric' versions of subsidiarity often appealed to for such global settings. In particular, there are several challenges wrought by states that fail to respect their citizens' human rights, variously interpreted. More defensible versions of subsidiarity do not provide normative legitimacy to the state centric aspects of the global order. Section 11.2 sketches some of the remarkably different conceptions of subsidiarity as a background to the usages in the European Union, the Catholic Church and as it allegedly appears in international law. The different versions drastically reduce or enlarge the scope of member unit authority. Section 11.3 considers some implications for the legitimate allocation of authority in our global order which includes many states that routinely violate their citizens' fundamental human rights. The function of the European Court of Human Rights offers a helpful contrast.

Keywords Althusius • Catholicism • Liberal Contractualism • Sovereignty • European Court of Human Rights • Global governance • International law

---

This chapter was written under the auspices of MultiRights – ERC Advanced Grant 269841– and PluriCourts – a Centre of Excellence project number 223274 funded by the Research Council of Norway. It draws on some related papers (Follesdal 2013a, b), where some of these issues are elaborated more fully

A. Follesdal (✉)
Faculty of Law, University of Oslo, St. Olavs gate 23, 0166 Oslo, Norway
e-mail: andreas.follesdal@jus.uio.no

M. Evans and A. Zimmermann (eds.), *Global Perspectives on Subsidiarity*, Ius Gentium: Comparative Perspectives on Law and Justice 37, DOI 10.1007/978-94-017-8810-6_11,

11.1 Introduction

We increasingly live in a 'globalised' world, where our decisions and institutions are interdependent on those of other actors across state and regional borders.[1] In response, we witness several attempts at governance above the state level, with varying degrees of effectiveness and legitimacy. Among the vexing problems is how to determine *which* decisions are better handled by bodies above the state, and which such bodies can be trusted to exercise such powers – ultimately in the best interest of the individuals affected.

A "principle of subsidiarity" regulates the allocation or use of authority within a political or legal order, especially where authority is dispersed between a centre and member units. The principle holds that the burden of argument lies with attempts to centralise authority. Subsidiarity has been proposed as an answer to these challenges of globalisation and global governance for at least 40 years, since Pope John XXIII's 1963 Encyclical *Peace on Earth*.[2] Further impetus for subsidiarity came from its inclusion in the 1991 *Maastricht Treaty* on European Union. Some have recommended a principle of subsidiarity as an ordering principle for international law more generally,[3] others claim that it should apply to human rights law in particular.[4] This chapter addresses some of the strengths and weaknesses of a principle of subsidiarity for questions of how to allocate and use authority at regional and global levels. In particular, there are several challenges wrought by states that fail to respect their citizens' human rights, variously interpreted. On this point the Encyclical *Peace on Earth* seems too 'state centric'. It proposes a world wide public authority such as the UN, established with the consent by *all* countries with "its fundamental objective the recognition, respect, safeguarding and promotion of the rights of the human person" (art 139). Yet such authorities above the state should only be established by consent and not constrain the state parties (art 149). In contrast, the European Court of Human Rights arguably does constrain the signatory states, through according them a 'Margin of Appreciation'. Similarly, the Rome Statute of the International Criminal Court (ICC) states a principle of 'Complementarity,' that the ICC can only exercise its jurisdiction of crimes if the State concerned is unable or unwilling to investigate or prosecute the crimes.[5]

This chapter explores subsidiarity in a global context, and criticises the 'state centric' versions of subsidiarity often appealed to for such global settings. More defensible versions of subsidiarity do not provide normative legitimacy to the state centric aspects of the global order.

To illustrate how different conceptions of subsidiarity have profoundly different implications for constitutional and institutional design, Sect. 11.2 sketches some of

---

[1] Held (1995, p. 20).

[2] John (1963, p. 140).

[3] Slaughter (2000).

[4] Carozza (2003).

[5] United Nations (1998) Preamble para 10; Art 1 and 17 1 (a).

the remarkably different conceptions of subsidiarity as a background to the usages in the European Union, the Catholic Church and as it allegedly appears in international law. Each conception rests on contested premises, with different policy tradeoffs. These different conceptions and their conflicting implications are too often overlooked. Their salient differences concern whether they *proscribe* or *prescribe* intervention by central authorities, and whether they place the authority to apply the principle of subsidiarity to the centre or with the member units. This is expanded upon below. The upshot is that the different versions drastically reduce or enlarge the scope of member unit authority. Section 11.3 considers some implications for the legitimate allocation of authority in our global order which includes many states that routinely violate their citizens' fundamental human rights. The function of the European Court of Human Rights offers a helpful contrast.

11.2 Some Theories of Subsidiarity

Alternative conceptions of subsidiarity have different implications concerning how to allocate authority. They differ as to the objectives of the various polities, the domain and roles of member units – such as states – and they allocate the authority to apply the principle of subsidiarity itself differently. Thus the choice of conception of subsidiarity matters significantly for the institutional configuration of global governance – and in particular concerning the appropriate authority of international institutions vis-à-vis states. The three accounts sketched below draw on insights from Althusius, Catholic Personalism, and recent Liberal Contractualism, respectively.[6] The latter grants the member units less authority. These accounts may regard subsidiarity as *proscribing* or *prescribing* central intervention, apply subsidiarity to the *allocation* of political powers or to their *exercise*, and *add* or *remove* issues from the sphere of political decision-making altogether. Some of these features reduce the scope of state authority, while some may protect states against intervention.

11.2.1 Liberty: Althusius

Althusius (1557–1630) is often called "the father of federalism." He developed what may be described as an embryonic theory of subsidiarity based on Orthodox Calvinism. He was "syndic" of the German city of Emden in East Friesland. One of his central political challenges was to maintain Emden's autonomy, both against its Lutheran provincial Lord and against the Catholic Emperor. He thus argued for the value of communities and associations for both instrumental and intrinsic reasons, in supporting ("subsidia") individuals' needs. Political authority, he argued, arises

[6] For further accounts see Follesdal (1998).

not on the basis of covenants among individuals, but among *associations*. This Althusian subsidiarity lends itself to a strong commitment to the immunity of local units from interference by central authorities.

This interpretation of subsidiarity takes the existing sub-units for granted, for better and worse. That is: the account offers few ways to determine which such local authorities should enjoy immunity, be it how they treat individuals or by other standards of legitimacy. Moreover, on this view the common good of the central political authorities is limited to respecting member units' immunities and to policies that are beneficial to all of them – Pareto improvements, so to speak, among the member units. This conception of subsidiarity thus only allows the central authority to undertake policies deemed by every sub-unit to be of their own interest compared to their present status quo. Coercive *redistributive* arrangements among individuals or associations, or forceful intervention into 'domestic affairs' of a member unit are deemed illegitimate.

Two weaknesses of this account are thus salient for our purposes. Firstly, it fails to deal adequately with sub units – associations or states – that lack normative legitimacy. Secondly, it does not apply to situations that require redistribution or intervention among member units, for example, according to standards of distributive justice or human rights.

11.2.2 Justice: Catholic

The Catholic tradition of subsidiarity merits detailed study. Pope Leo XIII's 1891 encyclica *Rerum Novarum* discusses a principle of subsidiarity, as part of a complex argument: The encyclical sought simultaneously to protest capitalistic exploitation of the poor, and to constrain socialism so as to protect the Catholic Church. The encyclical argued that the role of the state was to support lower social units, without subsuming them: "Whenever the general interest or any particular class suffers, or is threatened with harm, which can in no other way be met or prevented, the public authority must step in to deal with it".[7] Thus the state should protect workers against the "hardheartedness of employers and the greed of unchecked competition".[8] Pope Leo XIII further stated that "it is the province of the commonwealth to serve the common good. And the more that is done for the benefit of the working classes by the general laws of the country, the less need will there be to seek for special means to relieve them".[9]

At the same time the encyclica seeks to protect the family – and the Church: "the State must not absorb the individual or the family: both should be allowed free and untrammeled action so far as is consistent with the common good and the interest of

[7] Leo XIII (1891, para 36).

[8] ibid, para 3.

[9] ibid, para 32.

others".[10] Pius XI's 1931 encyclica *Quadragesimo Anno* developed this conception of subsidiarity further, as a defence against fascism's encroachment upon the Catholic Church.

In comparison with Althusius' version, this account holds that subsidiarity goes 'all the way down,' starting with the individual. This version of subsidiarity requires central intervention when – *but only when* – the subordinate organs cannot act alone to secure the appropriate objectives: "every social activity ought of its very nature to furnish help to the members of the body social, and never destroy and absorb them. The supreme authority of the State ought, therefore, to let subordinate groups handle matters and concerns of lesser importance, which would otherwise dissipate its efforts greatly".[11] The function of the state is thus to serve the common interests of individuals, and intervene in other bodies only to further individuals' autonomy as necessary.

Member units do not enjoy veto rights – nor do they have the authority to interpret and apply the subsidiarity principle: this is sometimes best left to the central body. For instance, this view allows and may require transfers among member units, including individuals, when required for the 'common good' – as defined by the authorities. Intervention into member units is legitimate and required when the public good is threatened, such as when a particular class suffers.[12] It would also seem consistent with this conception of subsidiarity to permit or even require international intervention when a state violates its standards of legitimacy: the state must comply with natural and divine law to serve the common interest.[13] But this is contested, for example, in the encyclical *Pacem in Terris*.

Some weaknesses of this conception merit mention. Assessment of member units, as well as the proscription and prescription of central action must draw on a normative conception of the social order and its objectives. The Catholic version includes conceptions of the human good as a particular mode of human flourishing. This may either be specified on the basis of a 'thick' conception of the good life, or – not necessarily – based on an explicitly theological conception, as willed by God. Some such normative accounts are contested and difficult to combine with respect for other reasonable conceptions of the good life. This account cannot easily settle disagreement on such matters. Consider the 'social function' of families, or labour unions. Which constellations should count as families, whether labour cleavages should be embedded, and with what responsibilities, are contested.

11.2.3 A Liberal Contractualist Case for Subsidiarity

Finally, consider a brief sketch of subsidiarity compatible with Liberal Contractualism of the kind associated with John Rawls (1971, 1999), T.M. Scanlon (1998) or Brian

[10] ibid, para 33.

[11] Pius XI (1931, paras 79–80).

[12] Leo (1890, paras 36, 37); Pius XI (1931, para 78).

[13] John XXIII (1961, para 20); Leo (1891); John (1963, para 77).

Barry (1989). This position acknowledges a – limited – role for subsidiarity, for reasons tied both to the interests of members of the sub unit and the interests of other members of the larger legal and political order. To accommodate the pluralism among citizens concerning their conception of the good life, the set of interests is limited. Individuals are firstly acknowledged as having an interest in controlling the social institutions that shape values, goals, options and expectations. Such political influence is justified by reference to four important interests. Political power firstly helps protects our interest that the institutions remain *responsive to our best interests* – as we see it. Secondly, such influence, for example, in the form of universal suffrage, helps us *avoid domination* by others. Thirdly, such democratic control helps individuals *maintain legitimate expectations*, by letting all participate in regulating institutional change. Those similarly affected are more likely to comprehend the need and room for change. Thus when individuals share circumstances, beliefs or values, they have a claim to influence institutional change, so as to reduce domination and the breaking of legitimate expectations. Insofar as this holds true of members of sub-units, there is a case for subsidiarity: central authorities should seek to support member units' democratic and informed decision making, and should respect their immunity against influence – as long as the decisions respect the best interests of its members and avoids local domination, for example, by respecting human rights. A fourth interest that may support subsidiarity concerns its role in character formation. Public arguments about subsidiarity may facilitate the socialisation of individuals into the requisite sense of justice and concern for the common good, on such matters as the legitimate status of sub-units, the proper common goal, and the likely effects of sub-unit and centre-unit action.

There are further reasons for subsidiarity stemming from the interests of those in the rest of a legal order. They have a legitimate interest to avoid political power over issues that do not affect them. Such authority would require them to spend resources to determine alternatives and their consequences on affected parties, without any effect on themselves. They may reasonably want to spend such resources on their own other interests, and on those in need. One implication of such accounts is support for granting democratic states a 'Margin of Appreciation' as the European Court of Human Rights does. That is: in determining whether a state complies with its human rights obligations, this margin allows different laws and policies – within a range – to accommodate different natural and social circumstances and in acknowledgment that domestic courts may be better informed about likely effects and alternatives.[14]

There are several weaknesses of this conception of subsidiarity, especially considered as a defence of a state-centric global order. It only provides a limited role and weight for this principle of subsidiarity. Its defence of immunity is limited when vital interests or human rights are at stake, or when the common good includes egalitarian or distributive or redistributive norms. One example is stated in the German Grundgesetz: the federal level is responsible for "the maintenance of legal or economic unity, especially the maintenance of uniformity of living conditions beyond the territory of any one land".[15] Moreover, this account does not single out states as

[14] Letsas (2006).

[15] Grundgesetz für die Bundesrepublik (1949, Art 72.2.3).

the only relevant sub-units. A further challenge to such contractualist accounts is disagreement about the conception of the person that justifies the substantive interests that ground the various arguments. A further weakness of such liberal contractualist arguments is that they *underdetermine* subsidiarity. *Other* rules for the exercise of political power could serve the same interests. The case for subsidiarity must also be filled out by theories of institutional design in order to identify suitable institutional reforms. Whether sub-units should enjoy veto, votes or only voice is a matter of the likely effects when it comes to protecting human rights and other vital interests, on character formation, and on the likely effects on institutions' likelihood to remain sufficiently responsive to the best interests of citizens.

One result of these brief sketches is that the earlier Althusian account of subsidiarity seems to offer the strongest defence of a state centric global order which respects the immunity of such states from outside intervention. However, this account seems less defensible, due to its fundamental lack of standards of legitimacy for states. The two later versions seem somewhat better justified. They can address the challenges wrought by states that fail to respect their citizens' human rights, variously interpreted. However, it is not clear that they will support non-intervention into such states.

11.3 Conflicting Conclusions

I now consider some of the issues where these different conceptions of subsidiarity yield surprisingly different recommendations. These differences stem from several features: whether the account of subsidiarity places the authority to apply the principle of subsidiarity itself either centrally or with the member units and whether they *proscribe* or *prescribe* intervention by the centre. Consider two main issues: who should have the authority to apply the principle, and which objectives guide the application of subsidiarity: Pareto improvements, human rights, or redistribution across member units? We conclude by illustrating the dilemmas for the European Court of Human Rights, which grants states a 'Margin of Appreciation' justified by subsidiarity.

11.3.1 Who Should Have the Authority to Apply the Principle of Subsidiarity?

A central contentious issue is who should be authorised to use the principle of subsidiarity to allocate authority or when making policies? Conceptions that favour centralisation may place these issues with the central authorities, for example, with central legislatures, or with a regional or international court. Other more state centric conceptions may place the assessment of subsidiarity with the member units. There are two main ways to do so: by granting them veto powers. This practice is known from international law among states, and from confederal arrangements.

Alternatively, the authority can be placed with a body composed of member unit representatives of some sort.

Consider arguments for placing the authority to apply subsidiarity with the member units, typical of the Althusian tradition, and central to international treaties. Local authorities are indeed often better equipped to make decisions that maximise local preference satisfaction. This is especially so when local tastes, preferences or religious beliefs, geographical resources or specific risks are clustered within one area. When such subsets have the requisite authority, this allows them to act on those preferences to increase efficiency.[16] But which such 'local public' goods and hence sub units should be established remains largely a matter of local preferences and circumstances.

Alternative ways to grant member units control is to allow them to check central decisions, or to include them in central decision making. The former is illustrated by the EU's Lisbon Treaty. It allows a certain number of national parliaments to appeal EU draft legislative acts that these parliaments believe violate subsidiarity.[17] The latter form of control may include a common judicial body that consists of apex court judges from the member units.[18] Other examples may be a second legislative chamber typical of 'interlocking' federations.

There are potential drawbacks with either allocating authority over subsidiarity decisions with the member units or with the centre. Member units may use their veto to bargain for unfair shares of joint benefits, or ignore externalities of their own decisions.[19] Placing authority with central bodies creates risks of undue centralisation well known from federal arrangements – at the risk of their long term stability.[20] A central challenge is to create institutions that prevents undue centralisation, protects minorities against undue majority rule – and at the same time remaining sufficiently flexible to change the allocation of competences in the face of changing social circumstances and new risks.[21]

11.3.2 Objectives: Pareto Improvement, Human Rights or Just Redistribution?

Some of the most striking differences in impact of subsidiarity arise in political orders with different objectives. Here again the three different accounts have drastically different implications.

One concerns how to identify, assess and address externalities – that is, costs wrought outside the borders of one unit. What counts as costs is in part a matter of

[16] Oates (1972).

[17] Cooper (2006); Follesdal (2006).

[18] see Resnik et al. (2008, p. 767).

[19] Dahl (2001, pp. 147–489).

[20] Follesdal (2007); McKay (2004).

[21] Filippov et al. (2004).

which objectives are recognised as legitimate for the local and central legal orders. Consider cases where one unit creates *competition* by maintaining attractive regulations, for example, lower tax rates and corresponding lower redistributive services to the distraught. Other units may regard such competition as a race to the bottom, insofar as businesses exit and thereby limit taxation opportunities. For these units this may count as a negative externality. But the unit that lowers its tax rate may disagree – for example, if domestic redistribution is not part of its objectives. Whether central action is required is thus in part in the eyes of the beholder. It depends on whether the objectives of the member units include solidarity or other forms of redistribution. A further example of an externality is the plight of those who have nothing to offer on the market. Consider the needs of those who are dependent on public support. Few if any member units will compete to attract them, since there is no gain to be had. They will in practice be immobile, and be more destitute due to their home unit's reduced tax ability. If their plight counts, such competition will render their situation worse. Such challenges are clear for the Catholic conception of subsidiarity which draws on distributive conceptions of the objectives of society. Thomas Aquinas held in *Summa theologiae*,[22] that "Man should not consider his material possessions as his own, but as common to all, so as to share them without hesitation when others are in need."

This premise, cited in *Rerum Novarum*,[23] is used in a subsidiarity argument to support central redistribution by the state and other bodies, to secure the needs of the poor. The Catholic conception explicitly requires constraints on market exchanges, insisting on the need for public intervention in favour of workers who "have no resources of their own to fall back upon and must chiefly depend upon the assistance of the State".[24]

The upshot is that it seems necessary to allow international bodies to impose certain norms on states, even contrary to their will, insofar as the global order must satisfy some distributive objectives, – or at least when globalised markets impose extra burdens on some states. Examples include Germany's federal constitution, as mentioned above, which requires central action when necessary to ensure uniformity of living conditions across the member units, by tax transfers if necessary. Another example is the Treaty of Lisbon in the European Union, which includes among its many objectives "economic, social and territorial *cohesion, and solidarity* among Member States".[25]

A second challenge to all these conceptions of subsidiarity concerns the protection of human rights within the member units. This is often regarded as a model case for central action, for instance insofar as the authorities of the larger order are unlikely to abuse such permissions. Cases in point in the United States include the abolition of slavery and the end of segregation. Yet althusian arguments seem unable to address such concerns, since they tend to proscribe intervention by the

[22] II–II, q. 66.

[23] (22).

[24] Leo (1891, para 37).

[25] *Treaty of Lisbon* 2007, Art 3.

centre. Indeed, it may be relevant to note that the South African practice of *apartheid* and separation into "homelands" were defended precisely by this Althusian tradition of subsidiarity, of "sovereignty in one's social circle".[26]

The Catholic conception of subsidiarity is better able to allow or even require interventions in member units for the sake of individuals' interests – including protection of human rights. However, the comprehensive conception of the good found in that particular conception stands in some conflict with several central human rights laid out in treaties or among political philosophers. Examples include freedom of religion extended to non-Catholic faiths, or women's rights in the workplace, rights of lesbians and homosexuals and rights concerning divorce.

But this preparedness to intervene for human rights stands in tension with the encyclica *Pacem in Terris,* which insists that international governance institutions must be based upon "the consent of all nations".[27] Why is this presumption for state consent a necessary requirement for legal obligations of states? It is surely open to normative questioning, especially with regard to states whose normative credentials are dubious.

States are recognised as sovereign largely in virtue of satisfying certain aspects of statehood as we know it, specified by international law – that is, by states themselves – concerning population, territory and autonomy. The normative grounds for holding *these* criteria to be exhaustive of legitimate members of the community of states are absent. Why should all states thus identified enjoy such sovereign immunity? Insofar as it is states that *de facto* control territories and populations, effective and sustainable compliance –that is, problem solving – may require states' consent. State consent still seems insufficient to determine that the authority of an international institution is legitimate. The lack of consent by dictatorships and other normatively worrisome states does not appear to detract from the international institution's normative legitimacy. This lack of 'normative quality control' of states is flawed in the same way as Althusian subsidiarity: Public international law is unable to specify further requirements for which states *should* receive such standing. The state centric versions of subsidiarity – and *Pacem in Terris* – seem at a loss to defend this general presumption, except as a precaution to prevent unjustified interventions.

Several authors have argued that state consent has become less central in international law more generally.[28] I submit that more plausible conceptions of subsidiarity, such as the Catholic or Liberal Contractualist, may welcome this trend – *if* the substantive contents of contemporary international law satisfy the appropriate normative standards.

[26] Kuyper (1880); de Klerk (1975, pp. 255–260).

[27] John (1963, p. 138).

[28] Kumm (2009).

11.3.3 On the European Court of Human Rights' Margin of Appreciation

An example that illustrates several of these conflicts among conceptions of subsidiarity is the European Court of Human Rights (ECtHR), which adjudicates the European Convention on Human Rights.[29] Who should interpret treaties, and how? More state centric conceptions of subsidiarity may grant states much such authority. The risk of tyranny from the centre, and other Althusian claims that local needs are better identified and secured by local authorities, may support a state centric position. Catholic and Liberal Contractualist accounts may question precisely why international institutions should aim to promote the interests of states instead of the interests of individuals. They may be more favourable toward stronger human rights protections against citizens' own government. From this perspective the challenge is not how to defend this challenge to state sovereignty, but rather: how to set up reliable international human rights authorities that are themselves not likely to be abused. Thus the Catholic and Liberal Contractualist theories will agree with Althusian conception about these real risks of abuse of central authority – but the former insist that other risks are also paramount.

One illustration of how to balance respect for self determination and the risks of abuse by state governments is the practice of the European Court of Human Rights to accord the states a 'margin of appreciation' when it comes to determining compliance with the ECHR. This example is particularly relevant since several authors note that this practice is no longer limited to the ECtHR, but is also found in the International Court of Justice. Some argue that it should be adopted for international law more generally.[30] This practice grants states the final authority to determine whether certain policies are in compliance with the ECHR – thus expressing the centrality of states.[31] Again, the Althusian and confederal conceptions of subsidiarity will support an expansive margin of appreciation, while the Catholic and Liberal Contractualist accounts will be more concerned to *also* recognise the need to constrain the margin.

In support of the latter view, it makes little sense to insist that subsidiarity requires as few human rights as possible should be adjudicated by the ECtHR, since the objective of the convention and its court is precisely "the maintenance and further realisation of human rights and fundamental freedoms" – by means of the ECtHR. A similar comment can be made with regard to who should demarcate permissible local mores in terms of human rights. In particular, what should be done when there is *doubt* about whether rights have been violated: should the final judgment be with the member unit, that is, the state, or with the ECtHR, which may possibly grant the national judiciary a margin of appreciation – and if so, why? The Margin of Appreciation is a way to respect domestic democratic processes by the ECtHR judges. One reason is epistemic: these judges are "neither equipped to make detailed

---

[29] Council of Europe (1950).

[30] Shany (2005).

[31] Bernhardt (1994).

investigations inside the States nor are they competent to evaluate all the political and social conditions on the national level".[32] But how broad should that margin be? For instance, the ECtHR leaves for Italian courts to permit crucifixes,[33] but it overruled Norwegian courts to prohibit some religious instruction in Norwegian Schools.[34] How are we to make sense of this, if at all?

The various accounts will all agree that the rampant value pluralism and variations in natural and social conditions across states globally does counsel a certain leeway concerning how states should best respect and promote various objectives – including human rights. The room for discretion is especially important with several partly conflicting objectives, ranging from conflicts among human rights to conflicts between human rights and other important objectives. The different theories of subsidiarity will disagree more with regard to how and where to draw the limits of such a margin, partly due to different assessments of risks. Liberal Contractualist reasons for *constraining* the margin include firstly, to ensure the objectives of the treaties – in the case of human rights treaties: the protection and promotion of individuals' human rights against state inaction or worse. The less state centric conceptions of subsidiarity will be concerned to constrain such variations, in order to also secure other vital interests of individuals in addition to their right to self determination. One of the central challenges at the global level is indeed the broad range in domestic values and cultures – also concerning human rights. The appropriate response to all violators of treaties whose defence is simply that the treaty is counter to their own values is hardly leniency.[35]

An implication may be that such margins of appreciation should be broader for democracies – for example, within in the European Union – than for non-democratic states. The assessment of the democratic quality of any given state is no easy task, however – and underscores the risk of according courts and other treaty bodies too much discretion. A second reason to constrain the margin of appreciation is precisely to reduce the risk of domination by the courts and treaty bodies. Flexibility in interpretation and adjudication by these bodies can be abused. A third reason to maintain a narrow margin is to protect the courts and treaty bodies against confrontations with powerful states.[36] There is a real risk that the powerful do as they will, and the weak do as they must. Thus the ECtHR may find itself the weak party when confronting a powerful signatory such as the European Union. The risks of abuse of power may be even greater in the global sphere, with weaker treaty bodies.

The upshot is that whilst state-centric conceptions of subsidiarity are likely to favour granting states a broad margin of discretion, those conceptions more favoured

[32] Bernhardt (1994, p. 309).

[33] *Lautsi and others v Italy [GC]* ECHR 2011, Docket 30814/06.

[34] *Folgero and others v. Norway*, ECHR 2007 Docket 15472/02.

[35] Beitz (2009).

[36] Macdonald (1993, p. 123).

by Catholic and Liberal Contractualist accounts are more sceptical – while agreeing that the risk of granting treaty bodies authority is real and merit institutional responses.

11.4 Conclusion

This chapter has sketched some implications of applying a principle of subsidiarity to the global order. In particular, three traditions have been elaborated, to see how they may help address the important questions of which authority should be placed with bodies above the state. I have suggested that the present 'state centric' global order is difficult to combine with plausible conceptions of sovereignty. To illustrate this, we have seen that Pope John XXIII's encyclical *Pacem in Terris*, its many strengths notwithstanding, seems to restrict the legitimate authority of such regional and global bodies unduly. To require that they must be based on the consent of all states seem incompatible with a plausible commitment underlying several conceptions of subsidiarity: that political authority must be justified in terms of the effects on individuals' best interests, as units of ultimate moral concern in the global order.

References

Barry, B. 1989. *Theories of justice*. Berkeley: University of California Press.

Beitz, C.R. 2009. *The idea of human rights*. Oxford: Oxford University Press.

Bernhardt, R. 1994. Human rights and judicial review: The European Court of Human Rights. In D.M. Beatty (Red.) *Human rights and judicial review: A comparative perspective*, s. 297–319. Dordrecht: Martinus Nijhoff.

Carozza, P.G. 2003. Subsidiarity as a structural principle of international human rights law. *American Journal of International Law* 97(38): 38–79.

Cooper, I. 2006. The watchdogs of subsidiarity: National Parliaments and the logic of arguing in the EU. *Journal of Common Market Studies* 44(2): 281–304.

Council of Europe. 1950. *Convention for the protection of human rights and fundamental freedoms*. Rome.

Dahl, R.A. 2001. *How democratic is the American constitution?* New Haven: Yale University Press.

de Klerk, W.A. 1975. *The Puritans in Africa*. London: R. Collins/Penguin.

Filippov, M., P.C. Ordeshook, and O. Shvetsova. 2004. *Designing federalism: A theory of self-sustainable federal institutions*. Cambridge: Cambridge University Press.

Follesdal, Andreas. 1998. Subsidiarity. *Journal of Political Philosophy* 6: 231–259.

Follesdal, A. 2006. Subsidiarity, democracy and human rights in the Constitutional Treaty for Europe. *Journal of Social Philosophy* 37: 61–80.

Follesdal, A. 2007. Toward self-sustaining stability? How the Constitutional Treaty would enhance forms of institutional and national balance. *Regional and Federal Studies* 17(3): 353–374.

Follesdal, A. 2013a. Competing conceptions of subsidiarity. In *Nomos*. New York: New York University Press.

Follesdal, A. 2013b. Subsidiarity as a constitutional principle in international law. *Global Constitutionalism* 2(1): 37–62.

Grundgesetz Für Die Bundesrepublik, Deutschland. 1949. *Bundesgesetzblatt (BGBl) Teil III, Gliederungsnummer 100-1*.

Held, D. 1995. *Democracy and the global order*. Cambridge: Polity Press.

John XXIII. 1961. Mater et Magistra. http://www.vatican.va/holy_father/john_xxiii/encyclicals/documents/hf_j-xxiii_enc_15051961_mater_en.html

John XXIII. 1963. Pacem in Terris. In *The Papal encyclicals 1958–1981*. Raleigh: McGrath.

Kumm, M. 2009. The cosmopolitan turn in constitutionalism: On the relationship between constitutionalism in and beyond the state. In J.L. Dunoff and J.P. Trachtman (Red.), *Ruling the world? Constitutionalism, international law, and global governance*, s. 257–324. Cambridge: Cambridge University Press.

Kuyper, A. 1880. *Souvereiniteit in eigen kring: rede ter inwijding van de vrije Universiteit den 20sten October 1880*. Amsterdam: J.H. Kruyt.

Leo XII. 1890. Sapiente Christianae. In J.F. Cronin (Red.), *Catholic social principles: The social teaching of the Catholic Church applied to American economic life*. Milwaukee: Bruce.

Leo XII. 1891. Rerum Novarum. In *The Papal encyclicals 1903–1939*. Raleigh: McGrath Publishing Company. Available at http://www.vatican.va/holy_father/leo_xiii/encyclicals/documents/hf_l-xiii_enc_15051891_rerum-novarum_en.html

Leo XIII. 1891. Rerum Novarum. http://www.vatican.va/holy_father/leo_xiii/encyclicals/documents/hf_l-xiii_enc_15051891_rerum-novarum_en.html

Letsas, G. 2006. Two concepts of the margin of appreciation. *Oxford Journal of Legal Studies* 26(4): 705–732.

Macdonald, R.S.J. 1993. The margin of appreciation. In R.S.J. Macdonald and F. Matcher (Red.), *The European system for the protection of human rights*. New York: Springer.

McKay, D. 2004. The EU as a self-sustaining federation: Specifying the constitutional conditions. In *Political theory and the European constitution*, ed. L. Dobson and A. Follesdal, s. 23–39. London: Routledge.

Oates, W. 1972. *Fiscal federalism*. New York: Harcourt Brace Jovanovich.

Pius XI. 1931. Quadragesimo Anno. http://www.vatican.va/holy_father/pius_xi/encyclicals/documents/hf_p-xi_enc_19310515_quadragesimo-anno_en.html

Rawls, J. 1971. *A theory of justice*. Cambridge, MA: Harvard University Press.

Rawls, J. 1999. *The law of peoples*. Cambridge, MA: Harvard University Press.

Resnik, J., J. Civin, and J. Frueh. 2008. Ratifying Kyoto at the local level: Sovereigntism, federalism, and translocal organizations of government actors (TOGAs). *Arizona Law Review* 50(3): 709–786.

Scanlon, T.M. 1998. *What we owe to each other*. Cambridge, MA: Harvard University Press.

Shany, Y. 2005. Toward a general margin of appreciation doctrine in international law? *European Journal of International Law* 16(5): 907–940.

Slaughter, A.-M. 2000. A liberal theory of international law. *American Society of International Law Proceedings* 94: 240.

Treaty of Lisbon. 2007. Treaty of Lisbon amending the Treaty of European Union and the Treaty establishing the European Community (adopted 13 December 2007, in force 1 December 2009) [2007] Official Journal of the European Union C306/1. *Official Journal of the European Union C306/1*(C 306 of 17 December 2007).

United Nations. 1998. *Rome Statute of the International Criminal Court (Entered into Force 2002)*, A/Conf.183/9.

Editors' Conclusion: Future Directions for Subsidiarity

Subsidiarity is primarily a de-centralising principle, which aims to empower the individual by ensuring that decisions are made, and problems are resolved, closest to where they arise. In turn, decision-making and action taken by those directly affected allows for problems to be resolved more quickly, and more accurately than if a higher-level decision maker who is distanced from the problem, were to become involved.

This book has provided an overview of the development of the principle of subsidiarity, from ancient times in the philosophical writings of Aristotle and Aquinas, as discussed by Aroney in Chap. 2, through to its more practical operation in the European Union as a procedural, political and legal principle, as discussed by Gabriel Moens and John Trone in Chap. 9. The principle's subsequent development as a political philosophy capable of informing scholarship on a range of issues such as individual autonomy, democracy, the welfare state, federalism, globalisation and human rights was also explored. It has not been possible, in this one volume, to discuss every possible aspect and application of the principle of subsidiarity. However, we hope that this book has illustrated the key aspects and applications of this diverse principle in order to encourage a wider consideration of the principle in scholarship across a diverse range of discourses including philosophy, theology, politics and law.

On this note, although the principle of subsidiarity has its basis firmly in Western philosophical, theological and legal traditions, in a similar manner to Weinberger's discussion of sphere sovereignty and subsidiarity in Chap. 4, or Chaplin's discussion of sphere sovereignty and social pluralism in Chap. 5, further scholarship on subsidiarity may extend to drawing parallels with other religions such as Judaism. Parallels between the principle of subsidiarity and the decentralist characteristics of non-Western philosophies and religions, such as Buddhism or Hinduism could also be explored.

Besides its enunciation in Catholic social teaching, as discussed by Brennan in Chap. 3, we should not overlook the many opportunities for further scholarship on subsidiarity to occur within other Western traditions, such as an exploration of the

M. Evans and A. Zimmermann (eds.), *Global Perspectives on Subsidiarity*, Ius Gentium: Comparative Perspectives on Law and Justice 37, DOI 10.1007/978-94-017-8810-6,

relationship between subsidiarity and other key concepts in Catholic social thought such as solidarity, the common good, dignity of the person and the governance of the Church itself; and the presence of the principle in the works of philosophers such as John Stuart Mill, and in political philosophies such as deliberative democracy.

In Chaps. 6 and 7 respectively, Zimmermann and Sirico applied the principle of subsidiarity to draw attention to the disempowerment and disillusionment of the individual in the welfare state. When government power increases, personal freedom must decrease, because an excess of government power diminishes choice and opportunity for people to excel. Arguably, if a nation embraces subsidiarity, the power of its government must be limited enough so that it does not take too much freedom from the people. Conversely, 'powerful' governments that make more and more decisions for the people eventually destroy personal freedom and all the incentives for individual action and economic growth.

In this sense, future scholarship on subsidiarity could also extend into other areas of economics such as taxation, and the rights of property owners. After all, the ability to live in freedom, to make free choices and be responsible for them, is an essential component of subsidiarity as a decentralising principle. As such, the opposite of subsidiarity is analogous to an organic society in which a central government regulates and controls all aspects of life, thus hindering personal freedom and, as such, economic prosperity.

Chapters 8, 9, and 10 discussed subsidiarity as a decentralising principle in a political, governmental and constitutional context. For example, the operation and effectiveness of the principle of subsidiarity in the European Union was discussed in Chap. 9 by Moens and Trone. In Chap. 8, Brohmer discussed the principle's operation in the context of the German Constitution (*Basic Law*), and the unwritten characteristics of subsidiarity that are evident from an examination of the administrative and judicial functioning of the German Federal Republic. In Chap. 10, Evans argued that the principle could be used to reform the Australian federal system of government, which has become increasingly centralised despite the framers intention to maintain state powers and autonomy wherever possible.

Given that the world is becoming a much smaller place due to advances in travel, communication and increased international cooperation, Follesdal discussed the intricacies of the principle's application in the context of globalisation, global governance and international human rights. As noted above, whilst we have been able to touch on issues such as human rights, there is much room for further scholarship on subsidiarity in the context of human rights, as well as in areas such as deliberative democracy.

In addition to this book's focus on subsidiarity in a public context, subsidiarity also has a potential application in the private sphere, for example, in corporate and University governance. Both Corporations and Universities have centralised systems of governance, often with very limited decision making abilities being devolved to lower level management and individual employees. Similarly, subsidiarity also has relevance in the areas of employer-employee relations, human resources, marketing and business management, and in the running of other institutions such as not-for-profit organisations and trade unions.

In short, the principle of subsidiarity is somewhat of a chameleon due to its ability to adapt to, and to inform scholarship across many disciplines and in social, religious, philosophical and legal contexts. We hope that this book will contribute to an increased contemplation of this often neglected, but highly useful, important and relevant principle, and to the development of subsidiarity scholarship in areas that have yet to be explored.